Manic Street
Preachers

For James, Nicky, Richey and Sean

Manic Street Preachers:

Album by Album

Edited by Marc Burrows

Foreword by The Anchoress

WHITE
OWL

First published in Great Britain in 2021 by
White Owl
An imprint of
Pen & Sword Books Ltd
Yorkshire – Philadelphia

ISBN 978 1 39901 621 6

A CIP catalogue record for this book is
available from the British Library.

Typeset by Mac Style
Printed and bound by CPI Group (UK) Ltd, Croydon, CR0 4YY

Pen & Sword Books Limited incorporates the imprints of Atlas,
Archaeology, Aviation, Discovery, Family History, Fiction, History,
Maritime, Military, Military Classics, Politics, Select, Transport,
True Crime, Air World, Frontline Publishing, Leo Cooper, Remember
When, Seaforth Publishing, The Praetorian Press, Wharncliffe
Local History, Wharncliffe Transport, Wharncliffe True Crime
and White Owl.

For a complete list of Pen & Sword titles please contact

PEN & SWORD BOOKS LIMITED
47 Church Street, Barnsley, South Yorkshire, S70 2AS, England
E-mail: enquiries@pen-and-sword.co.uk
Website: www.pen-and-sword.co.uk

Or

PEN AND SWORD BOOKS
1950 Lawrence Rd, Havertown, PA 19083, USA
E-mail: Uspen-and-sword@casematepublishers.com
Website: www.penandswordbooks.com

Contents

Acknowledgments

A huge thank you to everyone who has contributed to this book – Rhian, Laura K, Emma, Phoenix, Andrzej, Dom, Adam, Mayer, Erica, Tracey, Claire, Laura W, Lindsay and Emily – some of whom I've known for many years, and some of whom I can't wait to meet. It has been, for all of us, a huge labour of love, I think.

I am delighted and indebted to Catherine, whom I'm proud to call a friend, for her beautiful foreword. I hope she knows that every time I see her, resplendent in leopard print, taking the mic for 'Little Baby Nothing' or 'Dylan & Caitlin' I am always so proud I could burst ... but not as proud as I was when I first hit play on *The Art of Losing*. Spot your cameo in the *Rewind The Film* essay.

I am hugely indebted to Gillian at Hall or Nothing for making sure this book stays current for at least a few more years, and for all her help.

I am indebted to Jonathan Wright at Pen & Sword/White Owl for taking a chance on an idea that's traditionally out of the company's comfort zone, and for being so supportive and patient, and to Lori, Aileen and Laura for all of their hard work. Special thanks goes to newly-minted Manics fan, the delightful Melanie Clegg for her sharp proofing eye and occasionally exasperated comments.

Finally, a huge thank you and all the love to my wonderful Nicoletta Wylde, who was absolutely right, as usual.

Foreword

Manic Street Preachers are the band that changed my whole world: as a reader, as a consumer of culture, and as a small-town girl plotting a big escape to the world they sketched out in the epigraphs for their albums. They've left an indelible mark not only on my mind but also on the course my whole life has taken as a musician and writer.

'Faster' was the first Manics song I ever heard. I can still remember how it just completely stopped me in my tracks with its litany of literary name-dropping. There was no hope for me after that. Being of Welsh blood, horribly precocious, and a council estate girl with aspirations for something beyond the life I was born into, I decided at the age of 12 that they were my compass through it all. I set about a project of self-reinvention and self improvement where I would write down every book and author that they had referenced in old interviews I would scour the internet for. Then I'd go to the local public library with 'The List' and order Andrea Dworkin's *Mercy* or Brett Easton Ellis' *American Psycho*, accumulating piles of books and scribbled notes as I slowly educated myself into a new future of possibilities.

Libraries gave us power indeed...

So goes the opening lines of what John Harris has called 'British rock music's last masterpiece'. But the opening gambit of 'A Design For Life' is so much more than a great epigraph. It's something of a manifesto, not only for the band themselves but for the army of listeners and fans who have found their own 'power' inside the pages of the books opened only because they were directed there by a certain Welsh rock band. Nicky Wire has spoken about the origins of the now infamous opening lines: 'I think it's at Pill library, over the door it just says "knowledge is power..." At the time I was reading a lot of George Orwell and my wife was working in the libraries of Newport... and it was just a question of putting the two together.' It certainly sums up the impact of the band on my own life – the first in my family to go to university – a path I certainly would not have even thought I could have chosen were it not for the literary signposts of the Manics.

Here is a band who have acted as surrogate teachers for generations of impressionable young minds, hungry to escape into the pages of books and the worlds of possibility sketched out in the lyrics of a band daring enough to litanize Plath, Pinter, Miller and Mailer into one single song chorus. Who were these mysterious names dropped amidst a squall of abrasive, angular guitar? I know I won't be the only one who began their handwritten reading list after hearing James Dean Bradfield rattle off what seemed like an instruction to go seek and read these mysterious names I knew nothing about.

As the collection of essays that follows stands testament to, not only have the Manics consistently produced albums of depth and complexity, but they also continue to inspire a devotion and intellectual curiosity in their fans that is unique in the pantheon of modern rock music. While many bands can lay claim to a devoted and fanatical audience, few can boast of having educated a notable percentage of music fans, both politically and literarily speaking.

For me though, what's particularly interesting is the relationship the Manics have with their female fans. It disrupts much of what we think we know about music fandom. As a young girl, being a fan of a band can be as much a process of sexual awakening – a cathexis of all the pent-up frustrations of pre-adolescence projected onto the idealised Other. The history of the 'boy band' post-Beatles is also the history of generations of young heterosexual women's sexual identities being forged in the fire of imagined trysts and bedroom walls plastered with first crushes. And then we have the Manics. The band who wrote 'Little Baby Nothing' - a song that almost perfectly inhabits the female psyche and imagines how it feels to be nothing more than an object of vacant desire.

While there was certainly some element of the 'non-threatening male' in Nicky and Richey's androgynous looks and kohl-rimmed eyes, as a Manics 'groupie' (and I use the term very loosely here) you were more likely to end up with a PhD than an STD. This was a band that encouraged you to devour books and films and suck in culture; to open your mind, not your legs. They were a band that glamorized the idea of being intelligent – a notion that can be endlessly empowering for a young girl looking for a way to be valued in a world that seems only concerned with the value of appearances. As the working class kid who'd been taught that education is your only route to social mobility, and as that kid who'd been relentlessly bullied for being 'smart', this was a revelation to me. You could be well-read *and* wear fake leopard print. You could have intellectual aspirations *and* be glamorous. The two were not mutually exclusive. Wow, I thought. This changes *everything*.

I think it was Nicky Wire who once said that he thought they were the only band who had inspired more fans to go out and get a PhD than to form a band. I myself managed to combine both goals and, shortly after finishing my own PhD on the American epic poets at University College London, I recorded my debut album as The Anchoress and found myself being invited to support the Manics in 2016 at the Eden Project – the first of many times that we would also duet together onstage.

While I have gone on to both record and tour extensively with the band, I have never stopped being a fan - not only of their powerful, impactful music, but also of the ethos and ideals that they espouse and live by. The music industry can be a hostile and unwelcoming place for a woman from a working class background, sadly still the domain of the white, upper middle class male, so to have been taken under the wing of a band who practice what they preach (excuse the pun) certainly proves contrary the old adage that you should never meet your idols, let alone go on to collaborate with them.

Beyond music and beyond traditional notions of fandom, the Manic Street Preachers that I hear time and time again has steered the course of people's lives and been the catalyst for so many novels, satellite town escapes, and minds opened to a world of possibility. And this is what music should do, isn't it? If we are to think of its loftiest ambitions, beyond soundtracking key moments in our lives and making the mundanity of it all that little easier to bear...

Catherine Anne Davies (aka The Anchoress)

Introduction

Manics fans aren't like the fans of other bands. Sure, just like any fandoms there's the dress-code (eyeliner, leopard print, maybe some military chic if you're feeling adventurous), the encyclopedic trivia ('let's all go to Blackwood and find where The Dorothy cafe was! Maybe we'll meet Flicker!'), the playlists ('Songs About Cities', 'Complete Damaged Goods/Heavenly era', 'Nicky Wire Sings!',) and memes (INTENSELY INTENSE!). That's a given. Manics fans have more though. We have lists of artwork and poetry. We have superbly referenced quotations and an approved canon of background reading. We have films to see and plays to read … and you better do your homework. Miller, Mailer, Plath *and* Pinter. 'We've never inspired anyone really, band-wise,' Nicky told me – completely wrongly, as it turns out – during an interview for *Drowned In Sound* back in 2014, 'but we've inspired lots of journalists and academia and people doing PhDs on RS Thomas.'[1] That last point is undoubtedly true. Manics fans, possibly above all else, like to *write*. Sometimes what they're writing is their phone number on someone's arm in eyeliner. Sometimes it's the lyrics to 'Yes' on the back of their GCSE maths paper,[2] sometimes it's really, *really*, terrible poetry on an online forum devoted to teenage depression. Many of us, though, have taken it further. We have become Manics fans *professionally*.

The Manic Street Preachers, it's fair to say, punch above their weight in the music press for the simple reason that 'music journalist' is one of those professions that attracts Manics fans. Rub away at a *Guardian* reviewer of a certain age and you will find a 'THIS IS YESTERDAY' tattoo eight times out of ten. As a breed we are genetically predisposed to be interested in the Manic Street Preachers and pitch them to our also-Manics-fan editors. Not that the coverage is undeserved; in fact it's easy to get so caught up in the mythology, history, politics, romance and sheer *context* around the band that

---

1. This is the quote Catherine is referencing in her brilliant foreword, by the way. I'm not sure she realised that it was from one of my interviews. Or possibly Nicky just said it a lot. He does that.
2. I actually did this.

you overlook *how genuinely great they are*. In thirty years they have rarely delivered an album that didn't deserve its deep dives. Still, there are lots of great bands ... not all of them get 3,000 words in *The Guardian* for every new album. Not many of them are still having books written about them. Ocean Colour Scene sold as many records in the late 90s as the Manics did, and are still plugging away. When did *they* last get the lead review in the *Sunday Times*? The Stereophonics probably still out-sell MSP, but you'll struggle to find a lengthy thinkpiece on their latest reissue on *Pitchfork*. Being popular isn't the same as people really, truly, caring. With the Manics people *care*. Deeply. Occasionally, obsessively. They inspire imagination en-masse in a way few of their contemporaries did, and almost none of that generation still do. A new Manics record is still an event that generates column inches and reappraisals and, well, books, partly because they inspired so many into careers in writing. Obviously if the band turned in any old tosh, that enthusiasm would quickly fade. Fortunately, they never do. You can write an essay on every Manics album, from *Generation Terrorists* (1992) to *Resistance Is Futile* (2018) and whatever comes next. So ... we have.

There are 14 essays in this collection; one devoted to each Manic Street Preachers record – and a bonus one about b-sides – covering 35 years of the band's history; each written by someone who has been inspired by the band and taken that inspiration into their professional and personal life. We've tried not to constrain the writers here. Some of these essays are traditional music criticism, some are social histories, and some are personal reflections, all from a range of fans from different backgrounds and with different experiences. Rhian Jones' piece on *Generation Terrorists* sets the tone nicely. Rhian has written extensively about the band in the past, notably in her contribution to the brilliant *Triptych*, which forensically examines 1994's *The Holy Bible*. She's also a historian, with an expert knowledge of protest movements and left-wing politics (her 2015 book *Petticoat Heroes*, about the cross-dressing would-be revolutionaries of 19th century Wales, is about as Manic Street Preachers as history can possibly get). Here she sets the Manics' debut into its contemporary context, looking at the impact of class and culture (and alienation, boredom and despair) on *Generation Terrorists* ... and *Generation Terrorists*' impact on class and culture. It's this book in microcosm. Elsewhere we have true deep dives into the music and biography of the band, as with Andrzej Lukowski's thoroughly entertaining deconstruction of *Know Your Enemy* (2001), or Adam Scott Glasspool's case for the defence of *Lifeblood* (2004). Dom Gourlay, a man who was there to witness Nicky Wire belting a security guard with a bass at Reading 1992, is the perfect person to write an overview of Manics b-sides, including the ones *Lipstick Traces* (2003) neglected. I loved Mayer Nissim's wade through the chaotic, triumphant days of *Send Away The Tigers* (2007) especially as, for me, it rehabilitated an album I've often been dismissive about and made me examine it all over again. The best music writing does that.

Elsewhere we have essays rooted in more personal experiences. Laura Kelly finds the centre of the venn diagram between teenage outsiderdom and the Manics' probably unique ability to mix feminism and cock rock, and sets it against the backdrop of early-90s Belfast and the Troubles in her piece on *Gold Against The Soul* (1993). I think Emma O'Brien's look at *The Holy Bible* and Phoenix Andrew's memories of *Everything Must Go* (1996) work beautifully as a pair (as do those albums, defining one another in opposition), documenting the fan culture of the early on-line era, and the maddening, exhilarating experience of clinging on for dear life as a band with such specific personal resonance is embraced by just-about-everybody; and that's before we get into what those two essays are able to say about personal trauma, sexual identity and gender. Erica Viola, meanwhile, is that rarest of creatures, the American Manics Fan, a peculiar breed doomed, in the band's commercial heyday at least, to manifest their fandom by trawling record shops for imports and hoping desperately against all hope that one day, just maybe, the Manics will once more cross the water and embrace them. Her piece on *Journal For Plague Lovers* (2009) also includes the single most brilliantly Manics-fan sentence in this whole book. I can't recommend Tracey Wise's memories of *Postcards From A Young Man* (2010) highly enough, a beautiful examination of how a new record from your favourite band can soundtrack the emotional peaks and valleys of your life, and how the music and the trauma can imprint upon one another. I'm proud to have been able to include it.

I'm also proud of the pieces that use the Manics to reflect back the themes and the times in which each record was made. I wrote about how *This Is My Truth, Tell Me Yours* (1998) is the quintessential record of the late-Britpop era, capturing a uniquely pre-millennial, death-of-a-party exhausted alienation. Claire Biddles has written a fascinating, inciteful dive into how *Futurology* (2014) links the band's Welshness with their occasionally-naive feminism, while Laura K Williams looks at *Resistance Is Futile* (2018) in the context of the post-Brexit Britain of Jeremy Corbyn and Theresa May, a time of fake news and divided households.

Sticking out like a sore thumb is the short story I have written for *Rewind The Film* (2013). A quick note on that – originally I was going to write a more traditional piece of music critique for that record; then the writer due to cover *This Is My Truth, Tell Me Yours* dropped out at the last minute (for very good reasons) and I realised I'd have to write that one as well. I knew exactly what I wanted to say about *This Is My Truth*, but didn't want to write two similar pieces, so changed tack for *Rewind The Film*, exploring that album's themes of aging, nostalgia, and exhausted regret through fiction instead. As someone who has that aforementioned 'This Is Yesterday' tattoo, it felt appropriate to write about being lost in the past. There's some thematic autobiography in there, but the story itself came out of my head. I hope you can indulge me.

The Timeline
Each essay in this book is bridged by a fairly detailed, month-by-month timeline of the band's activities. I always knew I'd need linking material of some kind between the essays, if only to give the context and 'bigger picture' of the band's story, especially for readers less intimately familiar with the Manics narrative. Originally this was going to be a few short points to put the essays in perspective. However, once I started I inevitably found myself drawn into the detail and enjoying the research. Before I knew it, I was basically writing a full biography in bullet points. I think it was worth the effort. The timeline was pieced together from several sources, notably Simon Price's *Everything (A Book About Manic Street Preachers)*, Martin Powers's *Nailed To History: The Story of Manic Street Preachers*, Paula Shutkever's *Manic Street Preachers: A Design For Living*, Kevin Cummins' *Assassinated Beauty* and Nicky Wire's own *The Death Of The Polaroid*, as well as the BBC's 1998 *Close Up* documentary, the excellent *No Manifesto* (2018) and Kieran Evens' Manics films, especially *Culture, Alienation, Boredom and Despair* (2013), *Escape From History* (2017) and *Truth And Memory* (2018), with all of those cross-referenced against one-another and contemporary press to iron out the (surprisingly common) discrepancies. On top of that, there was the news archive on *manics.co.uk* and *NME.com*, Nicky and Sean's Twitter and Instagram accounts and, most helpfully of all, the *Forever Delayed* website, which has handily archived pretty much every piece of press the Manics have ever had. Considering a pandemic has kept libraries closed, that has been an absolute godsend.

I've tried to include every major event, and many minor ones in the band's history, though obviously I had to draw the line somewhere. For example, the Manics' first appearance on *Top of the Tops* is worth mentioning because in that era landing a spot on the show was a huge deal. However, the band recorded a *TOTP* appearance for nearly every single they released until the show went off air in 2006 – I've only mentioned the ones where something interesting happened. Similarly, I've only listed individual tour dates, in-stores or TV/radio appearances if they tell us something interesting about the band at that stage of their career.

There's a few points where I've indulged myself a bit, and hopefully I've been able to keep what could have been a fairly dry list of dates and releases interesting. I've also included details of every official Manics release from 'Suicide Alley' in 1988 to the re-recording of 'Spectators of Suicide' in 2020 (at the time of writing, the most recent Manics output), but haven't gone into specifics about remix discs, Japanese bonus tracks or full tracklistings for reissues unless I felt they were important to the story of the band. *Let the facts tell the story* was the golden rule. I found tracking the ebb and flow of the band's popularity, attitudes and profile genuinely fascinating. If you're as much of a Manics nerd as I am (and surely *someone* must be), hopefully you'll get something out of it.

So here we are. Libraries give us power, after all, and what is a library if not a collection of stories, essays and biographies? So go ahead, dive in, let it charge you up. And when you're done, it'll be time to start writing.

Inevitably,

Stay Beautiful

Marc Burrows, May 2021

Part One

1985–1992

1985

- In Blackwood, South Wales, Fifteen-year-old James Dean Bradfield and his school friend, Nick Jones, start writing songs together. Bradfield's cousin, Sean Moore, who shares a bedroom with him, soon joins on drums improvised from a biscuit tin. They make their first demos in the autumn of that year (by which point Sean has managed to get a real drum kit), influenced by *NME*-style jangle-pop and The Smiths.

1986

- A documentary celebrating the tenth anniversary of punk becomes a year-zero moment for the trio, who quickly start to fold The Clash and Sex Pistols into their style.
- The band names themselves 'Manic Street Preachers' after an insult shouted at Bradfield while busking in Cardiff.
- At some point this year another school friend, Miles 'Flicker' Woodward, joins the band on bass.

February 5
- The Manics play their first show, at the Railway Hotel, Crumlin. The setlist includes three covers (The Jesus and Mary Chain's 'Just Like Honey', The Undertones' 'Teenage Kicks' and the Sex Pistols' 'God Save The Queen') and four Manics originals, including early versions of 'Spectators of Suicide' and 'Suicide Alley', and lasts just over ten minutes. The band will play at least five more gigs in and around South Wales before the end of the year.

September
- Richey Edwards, a close friend of Jones, Bradfield and Moore, leaves Blackwood to attend Swansea University. He will stay constantly involved with his friend's band, however, driving them around when he can and helping out with writing.

October 4
- The third Manic Street Preachers show takes place at Blackwood's Little Theatre, opening for a local goth band, Funeral In Berlin. The 200-strong audience includes a faction of boozed-up rugby lads, who promptly kick off when James lifts his shirt to reveal the words 'I Am Sex' written across his chest. A minor riot ensues, beer glasses are thrown and much of the gear, including a piano belonging to the venue, is wrecked. The police are called. The Manics won't play a full show in Blackwood again until 2011.

1987

- Another Blackwood teenager, Jennifer Watkins-Isnardi, becomes the band's lead singer. According to her memoir *In The Beginning*, a version of 'Motorcycle Emptiness' was already part of the band's set. The now-five-piece briefly re-name themselves 'Betty Blue'. Watkins-Isnardi's tenure with the band lasts until the summer.

1988

- Early 1988, punk-purist Woodward quits, claiming the band's music is becoming too commercial and that being in the Manics is contributing to his drinking problem. Nick, now calling himself 'Nicky Wire' switches to bass and the Manic Street Preachers become a three-piece.

May
- The Manics and their friends, having formed a sort-of art collective called 'The Blue Generation' which they describe as 'a definite body of ideas and people', write a press release and send it to *Impact*, a Cardiff listings magazine, to promote an upcoming gig. It lists the Blue Generation's names as 'Seany Dee, Jamie Kat, Nicky Wire and Richie Vee' and challenges the reader to 'dig it kats or buy a body bag' and promises they will 'protude our tight arses and heroic bulges on deep blue nights'.

June
- The trio use money borrowed from James' dad to pay for a day's studio time at South Bank, Cwmfelinfach to make their first professional recordings. They track Bradfield/Moore/Wire originals 'Suicide Alley' and 'Tenessee (I Get Low)'. James play's Nicky's bass parts in order to save time. Inspired by DIY punk, the trio decide to self-release the fruits of their efforts, with 'Suicide Alley' as the A-side, on the completely fictional 'SBS' records (it's given the catalogue number SBS002 to imply the label has other releases). 300 self-funded 7″ singles are pressed. The band glue the sleeves themselves. The cover photo is taken by Richey Edwards, who also writes a press release and acts as the band's driver. They will send it out to journalists and venues throughout the rest of the year.

June 2
- Manic Street Preachers play at Brahms and Lizt, Newport. It is one of their only shows in 1988, partly due to Nicky's A-levels and university plans.

September
- Nicky Wire leaves Blackwood to study at Portsmouth Polytechnic, he later transfers to Swansea University to be closer to his home and to Richey.

1989

January
- Mark Brennan of the fanzine *Beat The Street* gives 'Suicide Alley' a rave write up, and is impressed enough to include both A and B sides on a punk rock compilation, *Underground Rockers Volume 2*, released on Link Records.

March (approx)
- *NME* journalist Steven Wells awards 'Suicide Alley' 'Single of the Week'. Somewhere around this point Jello Biafra from Dead Kennedys orders a copy via postal order.

Spring (approx)
- The band play TJs in Newport. They wear tight white jeans on stage for the first time, adopting a punky look based on the Clash's early image, notably at odds with the music scene of the 1980s.
- The other Manics talk Richey Edwards into officially joining the band on second guitar, despite him having no experience on the instrument. He debuts during the encore at a show at Swansea University to play 'Sorrow 16'; it is the first time the core members of the Manic Street Preachers perform together publically. Richey smashes his newly acquired guitar at the end of the song.

August 20
- The Manics make their London debut at the Horse and Groom, Great Portland Street. By now they are wearing t-shirts spray painted with slogans like 'SUICIDE BEAT' and 'NEW ART RIOT'. *Melody Maker* writer, (as well as St Etienne member and future pop-historian) Bob Stanley is in attendance. They open with a new song, 'New Art Riot', and finish with 'Suicide Alley'. The band sufficiently impresses promoter Kevin Pearce, who books them three more times that year. One of the shows is caught by Ian Ballard, the founder of London indie label Damaged Goods Records.

1990

March
- Bob Stanley becomes the first person to independently release a Manics song when he includes 'UK Channel Boredom', recorded at Sound Bank Studios, as a flexi disc with his fanzine, *Hopelessly Devoted*.
- Ian Ballard agrees to release the band's debut EP on Damaged Goods and pays for a two-day recording session at Workshop Studios, Redditch, with producer/engineer Robin Wynn Evans. The band put down 'New Art Riot' and four other songs.
- The Manics play support slots with Mega City Four and The Levellers. Nicky misses his graduation ceremony at Swansea University (he received a 2:1 in politics) due to the dates.

June 22
- *New Art Riot* (Damaged Goods)
  Tracklist:
  A1) 'New Art Riot'
  A2) 'Strip It Down'
  B1) 'Last Exit Yesterday'
  B2) 'Teenage 20/20'
  Format:
  12″ vinyl, 1,000 pressed

June
- *Melody Maker* awards 'New Art Riot' Single of the Week

Summer
- *NME*'s Steve Lamaq recommends that the band approach the Stone Roses' manager Philip Hall, the founder of the management and PR company Hall Or Nothing. Hall and his brother Martin attend a rehearsal in Gwent.

August
- The band play a sparsely-attended show at the Rock Garden, Covent Garden, London. In the tiny audience is Philip Hall as well as Heavenly Records' Jeff Barrett and Martin Kelly. The Manics are offered a deal with Heavenly on the spot. The next day, Hall or Nothing management agree to take on the band as clients.
- Edwards, Wire, Bradfield and Moore move to London, bunking with Philip Hall and his wife, Terri, in their small Shepherds Bush home. The band start to realise that Edwards', who puts himself to sleep with vodka every night, has a drinking problem. Edwards also commits minor but still alarming acts of self-harm in front of their hosts.

October 25
- Heavenly funds the band's longest recording session yet: four days at London's Power Plant. The sessions are assisted by a young engineer called Dave Eringa. Ten songs are recorded, including 'You Love Us', 'Motown Junk', 'Sorrow 16', 'We Her Majesty's Prisoners', 'Spectators of Suicide' and 'Star Lover'.

October 27
- Journalist Paul Moody reviews a Manics show for *Sounds* magazine, in which he paints them as a 'breathless' punk pastiche. His review ends with 'This is Wales's revenge for traitors like The Alarm who fattened up punk for the US market ... this lot are still anorexic.'

November
- The Manics hit the road supporting Heavenly label-mates Flowered Up, playing their first shows in Manchester, Scotland and their first international show in Paris.

December
- The band self-fund studio time to record two songs, a new version of 'New Art Riot' and an early demo of 'Repeat', and give the recordings to Bob Stanley to release, as a thank you for his support.

1991

January 5
- *NME* runs its first proper feature with the band, written by Steven Wells who says he is 'in hate with a poxy Welsh rock band'. The interview is conducted outside Buckingham Palace.

January 11
- Manic Street Preachers play their first show of the year at Royal Holloway College, Egham. Hall persuades several record label A&R men to attend, including representatives from Def Jam, EMI, Sony and WEA.

January 21
- *Motown Junk* (Heavenly)
  Tracklist:
  1. 'Motown Junk'
  2. 'Sorrow 16'
  3. 'We Her Majesty's Prisoners'

Formats:
CD, 12″ vinyl, 7″ vinyl
- The Manics make their television debut on BBC Two's *SnubTV*, featuring an interview and footage from a show in London the previous year

January 28
- 'Motown Junk' charts at number 92

February 1
- Manic Street Preachers begin their first UK headline tour, kicking off at the Adelphi in Hull. Wire develops a thyroid cyst on his neck after the second night, and the next four gigs are cancelled (the band put out a statement blaming boredom, and 'a diet of chips and coke' as the root cause). The tour resumes in Oxford on February 8, and ends on Feb 18 in Nottingham. More dates follow in March and April, including two headline shows at London's Marquee club. The band will be on the road or in the studio for much of 1991.

April 7
- Bob Stanley interviews the band for the *Melody Maker*, the most substantial music press feature dedicated to the Manics so far.

May 7
- *You Love Us* (Heavenly)
  Tracklist:
  1. 'You Love Us'
  2. 'Spectators Of Suicide'
  3. 'Starlover'
  4. 'Strip It Down (live)'
  Formats:
  CD, 12″ vinyl
  Notes:
  The ascending strings that intro 'You Love Us' are sampled from Polish producer Krzysztof Penderecki's *Threnody To The Victims of Hiroshima*. The outro is built round the drum part from Iggy Pop's 'Lust For Life'.

May 11
- The Manics feature on the cover of the *NME* for the first time. The cover shot, by photographer Kevin Cummins, features a glammed up Nicky Wire and Richey Edwards, who give each other lovebites for the

shoot. Wire has 'CULTURE SLUT' written on his bare chest in lipstick. Edwards attempts to scratch 'HIV' into his chest with a razor, using a mirror, but unfortunately (or perhaps fortunately), does it backwards by mistake.

May 15
- Manic Street Preachers play Norwich Arts Centre. After the show, *NME*'s Steve Lamacq asks if the band's fiery rhetoric is genuine. Richey Edwards uses a razor blade to scratch the words '4 REAL' into his forearm. He is then rushed to hospital, where he receives 17 stitches; though not before the *NME*'s photographer, Ed Stirs, had taken a lurid shot of the wound. The next day *NME* staffers, including a shaken Lamacq, debate whether to run the photos – a recording of that conversation will later be used as the b-side to the charity single 'Theme From *M*A*S*H* (Suicide Is Painless)' under the name 'Sleeping With the *NME*'. A picture of Edwards, staring passively into the camera while displaying his wounds is eventually printed in black and white in the paper's news section. The Manics' next show is cancelled due to Richey's injury. The incident passes into Manics folklore, though few at the time realise the extent to which Edward's self-injury will go. Richey will later call the *NME* office to apologise for any upset he might have caused. The '4Real Incident' will dog the band for the rest of their career.

May 21
- Bradfield, Edwards, Wire and Moore sign a 10-album deal with Columbia Records/Sony, following something of a bidding war. Their advance is £250,000. The band gift £6,000 to Heavenly Records to cover any losses the label has incurred.
- Wire and Edwards, the band's 'ministers for propaganda', begin saying in interviews that the Manics have a grand plan: to release a double-album, sell 16 million copies, headline Wembley stadium, bring about a cultural socialist revolution, bring down the monarchy, set fire to themselves on *Top of the Pops* and then split up; all within a year. They frequently tell journalists that their two favourite bands are Guns N' Roses and Public Enemy.

June
- Recording session for the Manics' debut releases on Sony, at Manor Studios, Oxfordshire, with producer Steve Brown. They track several songs for the A and B sides of their first major label singles.

July
- Feminine Is Beautiful (Caff)
  Tracklist:
  A. 'Repeat After Me'
  B. 'New Art Riot'
  Formats:
  7″ picture disc, 500 copies sold by mail-order only. These are different recordings of the songs than those found on *New Art Riot* or *Generation Terrorists*.
  Notes:
  These are the tracks recorded for Bob Stanley in December 1990 and released via his Caff label by mail order only.

July 29
- **Stay Beautiful** (Sony/Columbia)
  Tracklist:
  1. 'Stay Beautiful'
  2. 'R.P. McMurphey'
  3. 'Soul Contamination'
  Formats
  CD, 12″, 7″ (latter omits 'Soul Contamination')
  Notes: When producer Steve Brown first met the band he was reported to have said 'we'll be fine as long as you don't have "why don't you just fuck off" in the middle of a song', which of course was the original chorus to 'Stay Beautiful'. The expletive was replaced with a guitar sting. The song became a perennial live favourite as the audience screamed out the missing words.

August 4
- Manic Street Preachers make their UK Top 40 chart debut, when 'Stay Beautiful' is a new entry at number 40. It drops out after a week.

August
- The first of many, many British Manics fanzines, *Last Exit*, is published by Jacqui Blake and Carrie Askew. The duo would later form the band Shampoo. They sell their first copies at an MSP show in Fulham on August 13.
- Mid August the band enter Black Barn Studios, Ripley with Steve Brown to record their debut album. Recording will continue for the rest of the year at a cost of £500,000 (which is double their advance from Sony). They opt to use a drum machine, programmed by Steve Brown and Sean, rather

than live drums. Richey does not play on the record, but does assemble the artwork and packaging.

September 4
- The Manics play London's Marquee club, the set is broadcast live on BBC Radio One, and is filmed for BBC Two's *Def II TV* show.

October 28
- *Love's Sweet Exile/Repeat* (Sony/Columbia)
  Tracklist:
  1. 'Love's Sweet Exile'
  2. 'Repeat (UK)'
  3. 'Democracy Coma' - *CD and 12" only*
  4. 'Stay Beautiful (live)' - *12" only*
  Formats
  Double A-side 7", CD, 12"

November 3
- 'Love's Sweet Exile'/'Repeat' enters the chart at 29. It will peak at 26, the following week.

December
- The Manics appear in both the 'Brightest Hope' *and* 'Worst band' categories in both *NME* and *Melody Maker*'s end-of-year readers polls.
- Damaged Goods re-release the *New Art Riot EP* on CD and vinyl, which gets to number one in the indie charts.

1992

January 16
- *You Love Us* (Sony/Columbia)
  Tracklisting:
  1. 'You Love Us'
  2. 'A Vision of Dead Desire'
  3. 'We Her Majesty's Prisoners' - *CD and 7" only*
  4. 'It's So Easy (live)' - *CD and 12" only*
  Formats:
  Double A-side 7", CD, 12"
  Notes:
  A different, much beefier recording of the song than that put out by Heavenly the previous year, with the original 'Lust For Life' ending

replaced with a Guns N' Roses-style rock-out. The dramatic ascending-strings sample at the start of the song is also absent.

January 30
- Debut appearance on *Top of the Pops* performing 'You Love Us'.
- The *Generation Terrorists* UK and Ireland tour begins at Leicester University. It will run through to March 14.

February 2
- 'You Love Us' goes to Number 16 in the UK charts, giving the band their first Top-20 hit.

February 10
- **Generation Terrorists** (Sony/Columbia)
  Tracklist:
  1. 'Slash N' Burn'
  2. 'Natwest-Barclays-Midlands-Lloyds'
  3. 'Born To End'
  4. 'Motorcycle Emptiness'
  5. 'You Love Us'
  6. 'Love's Sweet Exile'
  7. 'Little Baby Nothing'
  8. 'Repeat (Stars and Stripes)'
  9. 'Tennessee'
  10. 'Another Invented Disease'
  11. 'Stay Beautiful'
  12. 'So Dead'
  13. 'Repeat (UK)'
  14. 'Spectators Of Suice'
  15. 'Damn Dog'
  16. 'Crucifix Kiss'
  17. 'Methadone Pretty'
  18. 'Condemned To Rock N'Roll'
  Formats:
  Double 12" album, CD, Cassette
  Notes:
  - Though not *really* the double-album the band had promised (the CD is kept to just one disc), the 18-tracks do cover two vinyl records, so on a pure technicality they succeeded.
  - The original album version of 'Little Baby Nothing' features a sample from *A Streetcar Named Desire* removed from the single edit ('7" version') and all subsequent pressings of the record for copyright reasons.
  - 'Damn Dog' is the only track on the record to feature live drums.

Generation Terrorists

By Rhian E Jones

'You have to go big if you don't want to go home'

The Manic Street Preachers were nothing if not ambitious. Given their starting point, they had to be. Like many young working-class bands from small towns, they had to set their sights high on stardom and have a strategy for how to get there. This explains much of what drove their early direction and explains both the love and the hate that they attracted, not least in the case of their debut album. The first line of *Generation Terrorists'* penultimate track 'Methadone Pretty' tips its hat to Marx's description of 'that revolutionary daring which flings at the adversary the defiant words: *I am nothing but I must be everything'*. The album itself may not have fulfilled the band's stated intention to change the world, but it remains an outstanding document of absurd and admirable ambition.

Generation Terrorists, and its surrounding project of a band's bid for fame, was one of the most ambitious of its era. The band's intention was to become their own myth, to live out a predetermined rock n' roll fairytale: to shoot straight to the top rather than adhering to the ethos of ploddingly working one's way up and paying one's dues, from there to change the world and then, their work here done, to spectacularly and romantically implode. Their actions and expectations were fuelled by a very un-working-class sense of deserving entitlement and a very recognisably working-class desperation to escape their small-town lives in South Wales' Blackwood. To achieve this goal they manufactured themselves, and manipulated both their champions and their critics, sending out DIY propaganda from the Valleys in the shape of demos and letters that were precision-targeted to catch the London industry's attention.

The Manics' early vaulting ambition discarded any care for critical credibility in favour of pursuing their idiosyncratic version of 'cool'. They wanted not flattering obscurity, but instant global fame – or thought they did. They quickly realised the context into which they had emerged made this unlikely, and that they could emulate their idols – an arrestingly eclectic pantheon featuring the Clash, Public Enemy, Guns n' Roses and McCarthy

– in look and sound but not necessarily – McCarthy aside – in record sales. Retrospectively recognising the flaws of *Generation Terrorists*, Richey Edwards admitted: 'The world had changed, perhaps more than we realised. People didn't care about such things anymore. It wasn't like 1977, when you could make a statement and get taken seriously'.

Where 1977 in the UK had social and political crisis that fed into the musical ferment of punk, 1992 had post-Cold War complacency and a musical context where 'working-class' bands were meant to be down-dressed, lumpen and unspectacular. The Manics, by contrast, were earnest and obvious in an age of irony and subtlety. A mutually beneficial relationship of mutual antagonism developed between a music press who saw themselves as arbiters of indie credibility and a band who rejected the very concept of it, expressing their devotion to rock's full-frontal vulgarity, taking greater pleasure in getting to the top of the UK rock charts than the indie, and dubbing the contemporary music scene 'cultural Chernobyl'. Press attitudes were often patronising when not openly hostile or mocking: Simon Price noted in his 1998 biography *Everything (A Book About Manic Street Preachers)*, that the press were happy to give the band coverage in proportion to the provocation they produced – 'but dare to take them seriously and you would be laughed out of town'.

For ambition to succeed, it needs both talent and belief. The Manics' story could not have successfully unfolded without the band's belief in themselves, and the belief of others in them. Key figures in the music press and record industry – their first manager Phillip Hall, publicist Caffy St Luce, early press cheerleaders like Simon Price – were instrumental in bringing the band to a place where they could attract wider critical attention and a small but quickly devoted fan following. By the point of *Generation Terrorists'* release, the band's ambition had gained them a media profile that far outstripped their record sales. This press and industry attention had triggered an energetic bidding war for their first album, eventually won by Sony, which took the band from the small indie label Heavenly to the huge Columbia Records for a ten-album deal worth £250,000.

When the music press, predictably, took the opportunity to accuse the band of selling out by signing to a major label, Richey offered Public Enemy, also on Columbia, as a subversive precedent. James Dean Bradfield responded pragmatically in *RAW* magazine that 'we could never reach as many people as we wanted unless it was on a major. We were willing prostitutes'. This somewhat blithe and banal link between celebrity and sex work was a preoccupation of the young Manics – like their fondness for the word 'sluts' as self-descriptor – and would be more soberly reflected on a few years later in *The Holy Bible*'s 'Yes'. For now, the band's self-conscious sensationalism and self-exploitation was also on show when, a few months before the recording of *Generation Terrorists*, Richey attempted to prove his 'punk' authenticity to a sceptical *NME* journalist by cutting the phrase 4-REAL into his forearm. Incidents like this vividly demonstrated that the concept of 'authenticity' was relatively useless to a band whose class status meant they had to be luridly cartoonish in order to be noticed at all. If there was a darker side to this provocation and courting of outrage – masochism or nihilism – it was more usually embarked on with humour and defiant glee.

* * *

All of this made *Generation Terrorists* a perfectly preposterous record. A militantly sincere, kamikaze, this-is-it last stand of a first album. Meant to take eight weeks to record at Surrey's Black Barn Studios, the recording period ended up stretching to 23 weeks from August to December 1991. This perhaps further reflected the band's concern that the album had to be all or nothing, that they would be allowed no second chances to forge their weapon to destroy rock n roll. Rather than being sleekly honed to deadly perfection, however, the album, produced by Steve Brown and clocking in at 18 tracks and 73:11 minutes, proved more of an overloaded siege weapon in its scattergun approach.

Released in February 1992, *Generation Terrorists* sold three hundred thousand copies but failed to dent the top ten of the UK album chart. Ironically enough, the album's slick rock stylings, although built on the Manics' love for Sunset Strip glam metal, completely missed its mark when aimed at the US in The Year That Grunge Broke. In the more supportive – or at least attentive – UK press, it received a better critical response: *NME's* Barbara Ellen rounded off her review with '10 out of 10 and stuff the marking system', acknowledging that this was an album that could not be judged purely on musical terms but by everything that surrounded and drove it.

The Manics' first three records form their 'Richey trilogy', and although they otherwise have little in common, they serve to document the band's rapid stylistic and musical development. *Generation Terrorists*, almost overwhelmingly earnest but with a leavening thread of humour and exhilaration throughout, is different from the more downbeat and po-faced follow-up, *Gold Against the Soul*, while their third album, *The Holy Bible*, is widely acknowledged to be in a more mature and accomplished class of its own. The eclectic influences blended and spread across the debut album mean that if *The Holy Bible* was, in Bradfield's words, 'a series of essays', then *Generation Terrorists* was an essay in itself, albeit an overlong and overly ambitious one handed in late with a hopeful grin.

Nonetheless, many aspects that would be retraced, expanded or sharpened in the band's later career are already evident on their debut. *Generation Terrorists'* emphasis on the disaffection bred in the midst of Western wealth and cultural complacency, and the intertwining of this political alienation and personal angst, would both later be perfected on *The Holy Bible*. This pessimistic and fatalistic worldview was given little representation in mainstream culture and politics in the 1990s and is frequently absent from retrospectives of the decade. But *Generation Terrorists* approaches it in a more playful way than *The Holy Bible* would – and this is perhaps a function of it being the sound of a much younger and less beleaguered band. Although its creators were well into their twenties at the time of the album's release, *Generation Terrorists* – from its very title onwards – expresses a kind of militant teenage angst, a seething half-articulate contempt for the circumstances in which its creators find themselves alive.

Edwards' and Wire's collaborative work on the band's lyrics produced a peculiar shorthand, a lyrical vernacular unique to the early Manics. Although sometimes so impressionistic as to be impenetrable, at other times their lyrics attain a striking clarity and precision – a cross between tabloid headlines and spray-painted Situationist slogans. *Generation Terrorists* is stuffed with lines and images so exact, or so arrestingly absurd, that I can recall them word-perfect decades later. A line like 'Born to End's *'Europe freed by McDonald's and Levis'*, which incisively interrogates the triumphalism of the post-Cold War West, prefigures some of the band's later, more carefully considered capitalist critique, but it loses nothing by the impatient condensing of its argument. The wrecking-ball swing at multinational finance in 'Natwest Barclays Midlands Lloyds' – the absolutism of comparing prosperity to Pol Pot sounding slightly comical at the time – now sounds astoundingly far-sighted in a post-crash era. Many of the songs slam impressions and concepts together without stopping to explain, but the listener is trusted to decode them. Some of the album's recurrent imagery and themes – makeup and spray paint, the allure of self-destruction, neon signs against grey devastation, lollipops mixed with narcotics – constitute lyrical pictures worth a thousand words of explanatory commentary. Sloganeering asides like *'Repression says depravity's cute'* might have dissolved on critical examination, but are meant to be enjoyed long before they are examined.

Although it attempts to deal with Big Issues – exploitation, addiction, inequality, epidemics, economic and environmental disasters – *Generation*

Terrorists has the band raging against a world they have barely experienced, while *The Holy Bible* has them having experienced too much of that world. Compared with *The Holy Bible*, too, the album's politics can sound glib, often naively referencing the radical rhetoric of the past. Musically, it can make listeners cringe with its cheese, its bombast, its wildly squealing and wheedling guitars. Conversely, a handful of songs with more appealingly aggressive early versions – notably 'You Love Us' – had their edges filed down by production techniques that sounded dated almost on arrival. The cover art too was a deliberate 80s throwback (the record company proposed, and the band vetoed, much sillier cover art: a Cruise missile emerging from red velvet stage curtains with "Generation Terrorists" lipsticked on the tip). Musically, aesthetically and politically, the album sees the band trying to fit into a particular history, attempting to update the politics of 1968 and the punk of 1977, but in a context which had largely forgotten both. Their context made their content absurd because it was so out of place. But what's more punk than that?

'Slash 'n' Burn', the opening track and fourth single, signals the album's excitable and agitated intent with its urgent, insistent riff scribbled over a metronome backbeat, Bradfield's performative drawl launched into the chorus on a firework display of guitar. Alongside the showy slabs of glam metal fretwork, there are more subtle US influences displayed on the album, from its Public Enemy-inspired sampling – extending beyond the Bomb Squad's pedestrian remix of 'Repeat (Stars and Stripes)' – to the introduction of 'Love's Sweet Exile' and 'Crucifix Kiss' with interjections of spoken-word poetry from Wire's elder brother, Patrick Jones. The young Manics had spent many afternoons at Blackwood's Café Dorothy, gathering near the jukebox to write their early songs and feeling 'like we were members of the Beat Generation,' recreating the coffee-shop culture of decades earlier in which poetry played a central role.

This commitment to consciously retro references also infuses 'Motorcycle Emptiness', an instantly anthemic standout track which tends to get a grudging nod of approval even from the band's harshest detractors. Released in June 1992 as the album's fifth single, the song had begun life in Richey and Nicky's student days, and was heavily influenced by the S E Hinton novel *Rumble Fish*, an iconic study in vintage ennui. On *Generation Terrorists*, the song is an appropriately extravagant six minutes long and, although it comes barely a quarter of the way through the track list, feels like the album's centrepiece and centre of gravity. It is musically assured, a yearning, aching and oddly romantic confection of smoothly ascending guitars and a machined backwash of buoyant drums, and its cinematic conjuring of spiritual desolation in the heart of material plenty encapsulates many of the album's central themes. The song's critical reception and commercial success – reaching only no.17 but staying in the Top Forty for a month, becoming their biggest-selling single to date – marked a general switch in attitudes to the band. Critics began to cut them some slack and audiences simmered down from hostility to muted admiration and occasionally to frenzied adoration. An appearance two months later at that summer's Reading Festival was also well-received despite – or perhaps because of – the band continuing their customary audience-baiting.

The album's sheer amount of bulk and ballast can weigh it down in places, like the mechanically muscular 'Love's Sweet Exile' or the mournful 'Spectators of Suicide', but there are other points at which it soars: the eerily atmospheric piano outro of 'Natwest…', the understated punchiness of 'Methadone Pretty' or the casually melodic 'So Dead', the bitter bombast of 'Crucifix Kiss', or the virtuoso guitar work that anchors 'Condemned to Rock n Roll'. 'Little Baby Nothing', the album's final single, released in November 1992, is a sophisticated standout, and a precursor of the band's later and more intricate exploration of the intersection of sexual and economic exploitation. The enlisting of former porn actress Traci Lords, though she was the band's second choice after Kylie Minogue (that overreaching ambition again!), was a more fitting and inspired collaboration. Lord's sugary but spiky vocals pierce the song's shell of E-Street keyboards and crooning, leavening its forgivable sense of male-feminist melodrama. The song builds to a perversely uplifting crescendo, ending with a line – *'Culture, Alienation, Boredom and Despair'* – that had been the album's working title and has since provided the band with an enduring mission statement.

If 'Motorcycle Emptiness' is acknowledged as the album's crown jewel, songs like 'Stay Beautiful' and 'You Love Us' sparkle just as brightly as statements of intent and self-fulfilling prophecies – seeing the band to some extent writing their own theme tunes. 'Stay Beautiful' was the album's first single, released in July 1991. Reaching number 40 in its second week, it gave the band their first hit, albeit an underachieving one. On the album it provides a frantic, jerky shot of alienated adrenaline, smearing itself in the same glamour it savages, its fizzing and dizzying rush unwinding into the pay-off line of *'anxiety is freedom'*, another line that might have been the motto of *the Generation Terrorist*-era Manics. (Indeed, the song had initially appeared, in a more raw incarnation, on their 1990 demo *Bored Teenagers* under the title 'Generation Terrorists'.) 'You Love Us', released in January 1992 as the third single, was a rerecording, and the album version is missing the sampling and shout-along coda of its early single version on the Heavenly label. Nonetheless, its effervescent spiral of guitars is enjoyably unsubtle, as is its Guns 'N' Roses indebted fadeout, and its convulsive chorus is a gleefully defiant raising of two fingers in the face of a hostile universe. Despite the sometimes questionable musical quagmire that surrounds them, both of these songs lace the album with enough cocky and vitriolic vitality that when the record is over, you're left lying dazed in glitter-strewn wreckage, feeling desperate to start your own band.

*   *   *

Where did all of this come from? *Generation Terrorists* is a melting-pot of the influences that shaped the Manics, and accordingly messy and incoherent. But these influences also demonstrate the ambitious intellectual and cultural curiosity in which the band was rooted. In this, they were a product of their background in working-class South Wales, a place with a long tradition both of broadening one's horizons through self-education and of brightening up one's depressing surroundings through music, dressing-up, and the particular combination of the two.

The musical history of Wales extends beyond harpists and male voice choirs, or even Tom Jones and Shirley Bassey. The young Manics had grown up in an 80s Valleys awash with love for UK punk and US glam, and bands like the Clash and Guns 'N' Roses influenced the Manics' aesthetic as much as they did their world-conquering ambitions. So did the tragic transatlantic glamour of James Dean, Marilyn Monroe and Sylvia Plath. Reading widely and consuming avidly throughout their teenage years, the band added to these reference points an awareness of a longer history of outsider art, politics and counter-culture, bringing in cult movements from the Beats to the Situationists and activists from Marx to Malcolm X. On *Generation Terrorists*, all of these musical and subcultural legacies are thrown at the wall with an endearing if chaotic energy. The album's sleevenotes, art and lyrics showcase a dazzling range of references which, besides highlighting working-class literacy and political awareness, functioned for any curious listener as a portal to a cultural, artistic and political past and present far beyond what most bands offered their fans.

The Manics' blend of escapist glam plus radical aesthetics – Situationism crossed with Adrian Street – was a fundamental component of their early years. Their style was deliberately provocative, ludicrous and defiant as a means of self-defence, and as a frantic attempt to evade the world of 'rubble and shit; with which they had grown up. Wire described 'dressing up' to *Gay Times* in 1991 as 'the ultimate escape... if you're hopelessly depressed like I was.' This particular aesthetic was worlds apart from their early-90s peers and lent the band an undeniably retro and arguably unique sex appeal, whether Richey and Nicky's glam androgyny or James Dean Bradfield, who confessed his very name had 'lumbered [him] with a sort of iconoclastic eroticism'. The Manics' early fanbase was significantly female, with many of their followers discovering personal or professional empowerment through their association with the band. Their first British fanzine, *Last Exit*, was put together by Carrie Askew and Jacqui Blake, a co-dependent duo from the London suburbs who went on to find cult fame of their own as the band Shampoo. In the later 90s, the band also inspired the provincial punk-pop perfection of Kenickie.

I was no exception to the band's peculiar allure. Between the ages of twelve and eighteen, I was a Manics fan to the exclusion of being anything else. I painted my bedroom wall black and stuck up an obsessive collage of 1950s film stars, lipstick kiss-prints, Clash lyrics and quotes from Ginsberg, Lenin, and Sylvia Plath. My pencil case and school folder read 'culture – alienation – boredom – despair'. I ran off to follow tours in my ratty fake-fur coat, glitter and feather boa. I sent off for fanzines through the post from all corners of the country and beyond, in an early prototype of later online fandom. I wrote an awful lot of bad poetry. I spent a year getting weird looks in second-hand bookshops in my search for a copy of *Lipstick Traces*. I joined the Socialist Labour Party. I drank neat vodka. I stencilled my shirts with slogans and lyrics. I wrote in to *Melody Maker* to complain about a bad review. I was That Sort Of Manics Fan.

Growing up in a post-industrial small town, part of why I connected so strongly with the Manics was down to how well they managed to express that sense of being nihilistic and resentful simply because of how at a loss you were to find any function you could satisfactorily or meaningfully fulfil. Every teenager feels like this, to the point of cliché, but in post-industrial communities, that stage of listless boredom, short-termism, and lack of any real faith in the future almost seems to have become a way of life. Although both Richey and Nicky had been offered previous chances at ways out of the Valleys – via a grammar-school scholarship and football, respectively – the band's ultimate escape route demonstrates that it can be easier to transcend as part of a more secure collective, bearing the shared weight of responsibility and representation more easily than an individual can.

This explains both the intensity of their Last Gang in Town stylings and the immense appeal it had for a fanbase consisting initially largely of lonely and/or isolated teens. Fans, like the band, were usually out for escapism, whether from school, home, a prospectless future, an empty or isolated small town, or simply boredom, alienation and despair. *Generation Terrorists'* sole and somewhat incongruous cover version, 'Damn Dog', may not have much to recommend it musically – particularly in view of how accomplished and well-judged a covers band the Manics would become, as evidenced on the 2003 compilation *Lipstick Traces*. However, the 1980 film the song is taken from, *Times Square,* was another cult chronicle of traumatised teens conquering through codependency and forming a band. There was a similar feeling of runaway adventure for fans in the day-long process of preparing for provincial gigs, following tours and poring over the weekly music press for news and reviews. Gigs offered a free space for self-expression where 'dressing up' could imply putting on a costume or a form of conscious play-acting. On one level what was 'believed in' by both the band and their fans was a conscious performance, an act, involving a suspension of disbelief – and this is also part of what makes their debut album work. There is no detectable fear of embarrassment, due largely to their fronting as a bulletproof 'last gang in town' (James Dean Bradfield, retrospectively, called their closeness 'an Enid Blyton nightmare'). The leap of faith involved in listening renders it a compulsive and compelling ride regardless of its artistic merits.

The band's longevity and current status as idiosyncratic national treasures can make it strange to think back to their early 'burn out not fade away' anti-ambition. *Generation Terrorists* may have conclusively failed to change the world, but hearing it changed the way many listeners saw and thought about the world. Given a chance, the album cannot fail to charm. Its slick and stylised aggression and despair are wrapped around a core of genuine emotion, and all of these things set it apart from its contemporaries. Even its expressions of alienation carry a sense of pent-up positive energy, a perverse joy, an exuberance and a boundary-pushing belligerence very different from *Gold Against the Soul*'s airless AOR and *The Holy Bible*'s prowling and restless claustrophobia.

Generation Terrorists is endearingly messy and sprawling, outrageous, bizarre, flamboyant and flawed, a fascinating failure and, because of all these things, a success. In addition to the disaffection and anger which they would continue to express in later work, a certain silliness which demands to be taken seriously is at the heart of the band's approach in this era, and of responses to them. Manic Street Preachers remain a band who perfectly represented where they came from. In their uses of literacy, uses of glamour, and uses of musical legacies, they also represented the sometimes preposterous methods of escape one had cause to employ. You have to go big if you don't want to go home.

Part Two

1992–1993

1992 (continued)

February 22
- *Generation Terrorists* enters the UK album charts at number 13.

March 6
- The Manics appear at their first major awards show, Dublin's Irish Republic Music Awards (IRMAs), performing 'You Love Us'. The band trash the stage, and James performs bare chested with 'YOU HATE US' written across his torso in lipstick. Afterwards they start a food fight at the awards dinner, and are promptly asked to leave. Nicky will later appear in the hotel bar stripped down to his underwear, while Sean goes clubbing with Dutch dance sensations 2Unlimited.
- Several UK shows are postponed after Nicky needs surgery on his knee. He completes the tour on crutches.

March 16
- **Slash 'N' Burn** (Sony/Columbia)
  Tracklisting:
  1. 'Slash 'N' Burn'
  2. 'Motown Junk'
  3. 'Sorrow 16'*
  4. 'Ain't Going Down'**
  * CD Only, ** CD and 12" only
  Formats:
  CD, 12", 7"

March 20
- The band appear on *Top Of The Pops* without the injured Nicky Wire, who is replaced temporarily with tour manager Rory Lyons wearing a pig mask.

March 23
- 'Slash 'N' Burn' peaks at number 20 in the charts.

April
- Richey tells *Smash Hits* journalist Sylvia Platterson that his advice for young people is 'never get past the age of 13'. Platterson interpreted this to her readers as meaning that they should try to remain child-like. The full quote, as Platterson would reveal in her memoir *I'm Not With The Band*, was substantially more nihilistic: 'on your thirteenth birthday, kill yourself'.

- The Manics begin fighting their long defeat in the US, starting with a show at the Limelight, New York, on April 26. Their debut North American tour consists of six carefully selected cities: New York, Cambridge, Toronto, Chicago, San Francisco and, finally, a show at the Whisky A Go Go in Hollywood – all either college towns or cities with strong music scenes. They are met with generally positive reactions, but it's notable how little excitement they are generating. Manics biographer Simon Price will later speculate that their timing had just been off; pedalling glammy hard rock when grunge sulking was the flavour of the month.
- Columbia release a truncated and remixed version of *Generation Terrorists* in the US, excising several songs and dubbing four tracks with live drums played by a session drummer, apparently to give them added radio punch. Responses are muted, though 'Motorcycle Emptiness' becomes a minor rock radio hit.
- LA's KROQ station uses 'Slash 'N' Burn' in a segment about the Rodney King riots, still happening as the band arrive in town. Richey is absolutely distraught at the association.

May 12
- MSP make their debut in Japan, at Club Citta in Kawasaki. They are stunned to find an almost Beatlemania-like reaction when they arrive at the airport in Tokyo ('we were looking behind us expecting to see The Black Crows or someone' said Nicky later). A five-night tour of 3,000-capacity venues is totally sold out. They will film a new video while they're there, shooting guerilla-style on the streets of Tokyo and Osaka.

June 1
- *Motorcycle Emptiness* (Sony/Columbia)
  Tracklist:
  1. 'Motorcycle Emptiness'
  2. 'Bored Out Of My Mind'
  3. 'Crucifix Kiss (live)'*
  4. 'Under My Wheels (live)'**
  * CD only ** CD and 12" only
  Formats:
  CD, 12" picture disc, 7", cassette

June 17
- 'Motorcycle Emptiness' charts at 17. It will stay in the top 40 for another three weeks – their most successful single yet.

June 19
- The biggest Manic Street Preachers headline show so far takes place at London's 2,300-capacity Town and Country Club (now known as The Forum, Kentish Town). The show is sold out. Nicky finishes the gig by announcing 'this is the last fucking gig we'll ever do', referencing Bowie's famous farewell to his Ziggy Stardust days. He's lying.

June 21
- Having been asked by *NME* to contribute a cover song for a charity compilation called *Ruby Trax*, marking the magazine's 40th birthday, the band, again marshalled by Steve Brown, book a days' recording at a cheap demo studio in Cardiff at the cost of £80, where they track a version of 'Theme From M*A*S*H (Suicide Is Painless)', the title music from the 70s TV show.

July
- The official Manic Street Preachers fan club is formed.
- Work begins on the next Manics album at Outside Studios, Wales.

August 29
- The band play the main stage at the Reading Festival. Nicky accidentally belts a security guard with his heavy Rickenbacker bass, causing concussion and a broken arm. The band agree to forfeit part of their fee.

September 5
- First tour of Germany begins. The Manics claim they hate it.

September 7
- *Theme From M*A*S*H (Suicide Is Painless)* (Sony/Columbia)
  NOTE: Double A-side with Fatima Mansions
  Tracklist:
  1. 'Theme From M*A*S*H (Suicide Is Painless)'
  2. Everything I do (I Do It For You) - by Fatima Mansions
  3. 'Sleeping With The NME' (recording from the *NME* office the morning after the '4-Real' incident)
  Formats
  CD/7"

September 13
- 'Theme From M*A*S*H' becomes the Manics first UK Top 10 single, entering the charts at number nine. The next week, following a *Top of the Pops* appearance, it will climb to seven. It will be four years before they reach such dizzying heights again.

November 16
- *Little Baby Nothing* (Sony/Columbia)
  Tracklisting:
  1. 'Little Baby Nothing (7″ version)' (featuring Traci Lords)
  2. 'Dead Yankee Drawl'*
  3. 'Suicide Alley'
  4. 'Never Want Again'
  5. 'R.P. McMurphey (live)'**
  6. 'Tennessee (live)'**
  7. 'You Love Us (live)**
  * CD 1 only, ** CD 2 only
  Formats:
  CD1, CD2, 7″

October 5
- The second leg of the *Generation Terrorists* UK Tour begins at Exeter University. The band are now playing bigger venues, usually holding between 1,000 - 2,000 people.

December
- Phillip Hall of Hall or Nothing, the band's manager, is diagnosed with cancer. It will later become clear that the disease has progressed too far, and that Hall's diagnosis is terminal. The band are devastated.

December 11
- The last UK show of the *Generation Terrorists* era takes place at the Kilburn Ballroom, London, starting an occasional tradition of Manics Christmas gigs. The band debut a new song for the first time since 1991; 'Patrick Bateman'. Nicky caps the year by saying on stage 'In this season of goodwill, let's all hope Michael Stipe goes the same way as Freddie Mercury pretty soon'. The comment will go down in Manics lore as one of Wire's lowest blows. It keeps the letters pages of *NME* and *Melody Maker* busy for several weeks. Nicky will take many years to either justify or fully apologise for the comment ('I might be pushed into showing a morsel of regret', was his late-90s line), though he would later explain that anger and fear over Hall's illness was the real motivating factor behind his desire to lash out. He will eventually apologise unequivocally to gay lifestyle magazine *Attitude* in 2009, saying 'We all know the Michael Stipe thing was a tragic, fucking stupid, insane, pathetic, maddening thing to say.'

1993

January 3
- Bradfield, Moore, Wire and Edwards begin demoing songs for their second album at the House In The Woods studio in Surrey, where much of *Generation Terrorists* had been recorded.

January 25
- Recording sessions for the album which will become *Gold Against The Soul* begin in earnest at the palatial Hook End Manor, built into a country retreat near Reading and complete with a swimming pool and four-poster beds, at the cost of somewhere between £1,500 and £2,000 a day (sources disagree on this). Dave Eringa, who engineered the group's recording sessions for Heavenly, is given the job of producing, having steered the band through the demo process already.

March
- Alarmed at his heavy drinking and self injury issues, the band book Richey Edwards into a 'private health farm' to recuperate before their rigorous promotional schedule begins.

April 1
- Mixing begins on *Gold Against The Soul*. The album is completed by April 20, and is delivered to Sony, in contrast to their debut, under budget and ahead of schedule.

May
- The Manics return to Japan for another sell-out tour.

May 29
- *Melody Maker* publishes the first proper Manic Street Preachers interview of the year. Nicky admits that he thinks Richey and James have both become 'confirmed alcoholics', and calls David Bowie 'the most decadent, crap person of the twentieth century'.

June 7
- *From Despair To Where* (Sony/Columbia)
  Tracklisting:
  1. 'From Despair To Where'
  2. 'Hibernation'
  3. 'Spectators of Suicide (Heavenly Version)'*
  4. 'Starlover (Heavenly version)'**

* CD only, ** CD and 12″ only
Formats:
CD, 12″, 7″

June 14
- 'From Despair To Where' charts at a disappointing 25.

June 19
- During an *NME* interview, Nicky causes outrage by saying that he wouldn't mind if New Age Travellers were 'rounded up and put on an island' and that they 'deserve total hatred and contempt'. The magazine is deluged with letters of complaint, and prints a follow-up piece a few weeks later.

June 20
- *Gold Against The Soul* (Sony/Columbia)
  Tracklisting:
  1. 'Sleepflower'
  2. 'From Despair To Where'
  3. 'La Tristesse Durera (Scream to a Sigh)'
  4. 'Yourself'
  5. 'Life Becoming A Landslide'
  6. 'Drug Drug Druggy'
  7. 'Roses In The Hospital'
  8. 'Nostalgic Pushead'
  9. 'Symphony of Tourette'
  10. 'Gold Against The Soul'
  Formats:
  CD, 12″ Vinyl, Cassette

Gold Against the Soul

By Laura Kelly

'An attempt at selling out that didn't sell'

Sat between the sparkling small-town escape fantasy of *Generation Terrorists* and *The Holy Bible's* towering takedown of all humanity, 1993's *Gold Against the Soul* is the unloved middle child of the four-piece Manics' trilogy of albums. A year earlier, fresh-faced and flushed with heady arrogance, the band had promised to sell 16 million copies of their debut album and then set fire to themselves on *Top of the Pops*. Whatever it was, *Gold Against the Soul* wasn't that.

The NME, still then a preeminent tastemaker, had given *Generation Terrorists* full marks. *Gold Against the Soul* got a mere six out of ten. *Q* gave it a measly two out of five. Though the album saw them break the top ten for the first time, coming in at number eight, overall sales were lacklustre, retreating from rather than building on their debut.

Flirting with hair metal, funk rock, grunge and classic rock, I'll grant you that *Gold Against the Soul* is an oddity. Musically, it has neither the spiky exuberance of its predecessor nor the cutting precision of its successor. They'd signed to Columbia and were under the traditional major-label, second-album pressure. Unsurprisingly, the production is big, radio-friendly and slick. Laden in strings, expansive. A more-is-more maximalism to fill stadiums. Indeed, promo duties for the record saw the band support Bon Jovi on their *Keep the Faith* tour. *Gold Against the Soul* is no punk's idea of cool.

It wore its American rock influences proudly… right at the moment when the UK press had started to turn their attention to the more Albion fare offered by the likes of Suede and Blur. It was the wrong record at the wrong time. If we're being unkind, we might say it was an attempt at selling out, that didn't sell.

In the decades that followed, a cloud of embarrassment, bordering on shame, has hung around the record's enormous riffs, like smoke on the water. When, in 1996, *Everything Must Go* eventually achieved the commercial success they'd pitched for three years earlier, *Gold Against the Soul* was further confirmed as the runt of the litter. The band have repeatedly named it their least favourite of their early albums. For a number of years in the 2000s, wags at Manics gigs would jokingly shout requests for album opener 'Sleepflower', knowing the band would tell them to fuck off.[3] (In typical Manics fashion, the band eventually took the jokesters at their word and transformed the song into a punch of a live thrill.)

Where both *Generation Terrorists* and *The Holy Bible* would get loving reissues for their 20th anniversaries – the *Bible's* second reissue, following a gorgeous 10-year retrospective – 2013 would come and go with barely a murmur for the Manics' overlooked second record. It would be 2020 before it got the deluxe treatment. Arriving in the middle of a global pandemic, a shut-down of society, and a crisis for creatives everywhere, the already lower-key 27th (because apparently that's a thing) anniversary edition was once again shat on by history. It didn't even get a gold vinyl version, which to my mind is a travesty.

So why are we here talking about it? Why, after the guts of three decades devoted to this band, have I chosen a record they don't like for a deep dive?

Well, don't tell Nicky I said this, but it is absolutely possible for a band to be just plain wrong about where their finest hours lie. Here's the secret: for all its production pomp, *Gold Against the Soul* is the most relatable record the Manics have ever made. The last album to truly feature the brief but luminescent lyric-writing partnership of Richey Edwards and Nicky Wire (*The Holy Bible* being so predominantly Richey), it has a bruised, beating heart in there. It's why – much to the band's consternation – there is a significant slice of Manics fans who will go into battle for this record. Like Radiohead's masterpiece of ennui, *OK Computer*, *Gold Against the Soul* captures the existential crises that stalk everyday life. It's Sartre with guitar solos. De Beauvoir with a beefed-up rhythm section.

Most of us are lucky enough to never find ourselves in the extremity of experience exposed in *The Holy Bible*, but a huge number will look at ads all day and wonder why we're '*so lame*', as on 'Yourself'. At one point or another, faced with grief or failure, we will feel our life become a landslide. *Gold Against the Soul's* concentration on the personal, its scope defined in ordinary lives, makes this an album that matures with the listener through mortgages and drugs, self-doubt and insomnia. To borrow a comparison straight out of the Manics 'suggested reading' list, *Gold Against the Soul* is the *Keep the Aspidistra Flying* to *The Holy Bible's* *1984*.

---

3. 'This one's called 'Sleepflower" said James at a 2003 festival to cheers, '… not really, ya soft metal mutherfuckers'.

The existentialists teach us the terror of freedom. As Sartre wrote: 'Man is condemned to be free; because once thrown into the world, he is responsible for everything he does. It is up to you to give a meaning.' On *Generation Terrorists*, the Manics had already realised that *'anxiety is freedom'*. On *Gold Against the Soul*, they face the wider world, and we all have to live as our decisions. Looking within, each choice takes a toll and forms a person.

Before I unpick further, first, an admission. I have a bit of skin in the game here. If Manics records worked like *Doctor Who*, *Gold Against the Soul* would be *My* Manics Album in the same way Sylvester McCoy is *My* Doctor. Sure, I might know that David Tennant and *The Holy Bible* are objectively better, but your first love will never really leave you.

*   *   *

I'd been introduced to the band in 1992, through the pages of my beloved *Smash Hits* – in which Richey and James did a memorable fashion shoot, resplendent in white jeans and crucifixes, and Nicky Wire was attacked by a biscuit tin. By the time *Gold Against the Soul* came around, I finally had enough pocket money to achieve record shop autonomy. It was on a Guides' trip to the Northern Irish seaside town of Bangor, in the summer of 1993, aged 11, that I bought my first Manic Street Preachers cassette.

I was meant to be doing a 'fun' treasure hunt that in my memory had clues to do with Bible verses, though in that I may have retrospectively done a disservice to the poor buggers trying to entertain a bus full of pre-teen girls. Bible verses or no, instead of completing the prescribed activity I'd sloped off, escaping sweaty heat into the cool, exhilarating dim of the record shop. This, I thought as I flipped through the cassettes, is what people who are actually religious (and not just here for the campfires) must feel like in church. The possibility in the plastic cases beneath my fingertips was proximity to God. I vibrated with the sense of something bigger than myself.

In a not altogether unrelated turn of events, I was ejected from the Guides very soon after this seminal moment for (among other crimes) wearing band t-shirts to weekly meetings and refusing to close my eyes during prayers. As a typically self-aggrandising Manics fan – for, if you can't learn intellectual over-importance from the Manic Street Preachers then you are simply not paying attention – I took it to mean that my searing critique of organised religion was too much for them. I had supped my pain-in-the-ass, bookish rebellion from the best.

Anyway, back to that summer's eve in Bangor. My mum had given me a few quid to buy some dinner from the chippy. It was enough for two singles.

Leaving my musical hideaway in time to get the bus back home, I had From 'Despair to Where' and The Cure's 'Friday I'm in Love' in a wee plastic bag. As I clutched my resolutely inedible cassingles, the vinegar fumes off the rest of the troupe's chips provoked an immediate pang of regret. But I was to get more sustenance from those songs than ever has come from soggy newspaper-wrapped potatoes.

A Belfast kid growing up in, what we did not yet know, was the fag end of the Troubles, there was a jolt of familiarity in the question of where you could feasibly get to, given a starting point of despair. From the late 60s until the late 90s, more than 3,500 people were killed in the Northern Irish conflict. 1993 was a year that saw the Warrington bomb attacks, in which two children were killed by the IRA; the Castlerock killings, in which the UDA shot dead five people at a building site; the Bishopsgate bombing in London, which injured 44 people and killed a news photographer; the Shankill Road bombing, which killed nine people at a west Belfast fish shop; and the Greysteel massacre, a gun attack on a bar that killed eight and injured 12. At that time, peace seemed a pipe dream. We presumed we'd live that way forever. Despair was worked into the very texture of existence.

As has recently been captured in the sublime novel *Milkman* by Anna Burns – and more light-heartedly by *Derry Girls'* blackboard-list of religious stereotypes – Northern Ireland's protracted conflict created an atmosphere in which everything was tribally coded. There was *usuns'* place to go on holiday and *themmuns'*. *Their* football team, and *Yours*. Every conflict throughout time and space had a goody and a baddie, depending on the side you were born into at home. Step outside those tribes and you'd find yourself beyond the pale.

From my place beyond the pale, the Manics were Polaris – a bright point to aid navigation. But it doesn't take an armed conflict to make a wilful teen feel adrift. The UK is awash with towns and cities that can make a person of alternative sensibilities feel utterly alone. There's a beautiful bit of early TV footage of the band that shows them walking through the streets of their hometown of Blackwood in south Wales. Wrapped in charity-shop glamour, they look utterly alien. And spectacularly beautiful. Around the country they gave thousands of little weirdos a life raft. A way to feel that the things that made you different could be the things that make you better. A different tribe to belong to. Pre-internet, this was a lonely tribe that played out primarily in the inky pages of the music weeklies, yet it was still something to believe in. Through the pages, and in the music, there was a glimpse of a better place that awaited.

Gold Against the Soul asks the vital question: what happens when your escape fantasy comes true? What then? Who will you be when you get that Sartrean level of freedom?

The Manics have always been a band of Big Emotions. *Gold Against the Soul* is no exception, inviting everyone whose emotional register, along with their amps, has a tendency to run to 11. In 'From Despair to Where', misery is a badge of honour setting the narrator apart from the *'open mouthed crowds'* going by outside. The song references Richey's preoccupation with the idea that adulthood steals away the innocent joys of childhood and the sense that despite our relative luxury in the West, we are still mostly unhappy.

Yet the question of the title, powerfully lifted by James Dean Bradfield's voice in an anthemic chorus, also looks to the future. Vitally, the fist-in-the-air melody of the chorus changes the words on paper. Despair isn't the end point, but a start. Though the Manics are unfairly caricatured as self-centred misery, there is still a responsibility here for how you behave in the world. A sense that who you are is what you do.

Empathy is not traditionally understood as one of the Manics' principal virtues, but *Gold Against the Soul* has several striking examples of their deep care for others. Like a young idealist politician faced with the everyday concerns of their constituents, they've developed the sloganeering certainty of *Generation Terrorists* into a politics of lived experience. The phenomenologists would be proud.

Prime among these imaginative leaps is 'La Tristesse Durera (Scream to a Sigh)'. The title is taken from a biography of Van Gogh and means 'the sadness will last forever' but it has little to do with Dutch post-impressionism. Instead, the lyrics focus on an aging veteran, abandoned by the country he fought for, forced to sell his medals to pay the bills. The only recognition he gets is performative and patronising, once a year to be wheeled out and sat before the cenotaph for Remembrance Day.

Now, I'm going to guess that most of *Gold Against the Soul*'s fans are not that imagined elderly veteran. Since the 90s, the generation wars have, if anything, got more bitter. Millennials and Generation Z blame Baby Boomers for ruining the world, while Boomers blame the younger generations for being too much of a bunch of snowflakes to cope with real life. These battlelines were not yet drawn so specifically in 1993; even so, at least since the invention of the teenager in the 1950s, young people have been supposed to feel a generation gap between themselves and their parents.

It's a chasm that Richey insisted the band didn't recognise. Taking an early – and surprising – side on the culture wars to come, they claimed to feel closer to the self-reliant and dignified older generations. Their own cohort

– having turned their backs on trade unions and collective responsibility for their communities – had embraced the solipsistic, capitalistic selfishness on import from America. 'La Tristesse', then, is a corrective, a plea for cross-generational understanding. Whatever the classic lefty Manics lover might make of militaristic Armistice commemorations or fighting for one's country, the song's empathy for the veteran draws out our own. We can internalise that sense of loss, of being discarded, lied to and misunderstood.

If 'La Tristesse Durera' is an example of the best of the Manics empathetic leanings, 'Symphony of Tourette' is a notable misfire. It's absolutely clear that it's meant to be a sympathetic portrayal of the condition, which was certainly less known in 1993 than it is now; the liner notes even include an explainer telling the curious that Gilles de la Tourette syndrome is 'a condition that produces multiple motor and vocal tics'. But here, the attempt to inhabit the sufferer doesn't land. Never a pinnacle, for all its good intentions, the song has only got more troublesome with age. Let it be a lesson that nothing – bar *The Holy Bible* – is perfect.

From the ridiculous to the sublime… In 'Sleepflower' and 'Life Becoming a Landslide', the elevation of visceral above the intellectual gets even more physical. The former goes beyond the obvious to entirely inhabit insomnia – the fuzzy teeth, the shot concentration, the restlessness. There's nothing theoretical in this shattering account of sleeplessness, recognisable to anyone who's felt that way. Three years before *Fight Club* came out, *Gold Against the Soul* presages many of the book (and more famous film's) cultural critiques, albeit offering a less explosive solution. As for Chuck Palahnuik, insomnia lifts the veil of modernity to reveal the meaninglessness of a capitalist existence.

Whilst surely fully half of popular music (if not more) concerns itself with the way babies get into the womb, 'Life Becoming a Landslide' opens with a rare and muscle-tearing scene of how they exit it, inviting us to see the mother as torn flesh at the same time as secular saint. It's a hint towards the most surprising thread running through the album – its radical feminism.

Popularised by a 1969 essay by feminist Carol Hanisch, a member of New York Radical Women and a prominent figure in the Women's Liberation Movement, the phrase 'the personal is political' is the defining slogan of second wave feminism. It underscores the link between personal experience and overarching social and political structures. Prior to the feminist movement of the 60s and 70s, everything that went on in the home – sex and childcare, dissatisfaction and oppression – was considered a private matter. The convenient dividing line between the public sphere, where men live and politics happens, and the private excluded personal struggles and marginalised women. So, in its insistence that the personal is political – and its emphasis on personal struggle – *Gold Against the Soul* is, arguably, the Manics most feminist record.

Its feminism is not merely a philosophically technical point. Grappling with domestic life, porn, the male gaze, how advertising shapes body image, and – as we've already mentioned – childbirth, the record touches on many of the key concerns of contemporary 90s feminism in its brief (for the Manics) 43-minute run time. It's feminism through the lens of men in their early 20s, yes, and comes with many of the caveats that implies. But coming from a rock establishment with a long and storied history of misogyny, it's a proud step in the right direction.

To the sometime consternation of the blokes in the music press, the Manics always provided a welcoming home for female fans. Back in one of their very early *Smash Hits* interviews, speaking to Sylvia Paterson – a women who really got them in all their glorious mixture of earnestness and playfulness – Richey had bemoaned the widespread tendency to think that young women couldn't take music every bit as seriously as their male counterparts. Later in the 90s, the music press condescension towards a certain demographic of the band's followers would find its comedy home in *Melody Maker* column 'Diary of a Manics Fan' – supposedly written by a female teenage fan who admired the group for their 'intense intensitude' but in fact written by a bloke named David Stubbs. Look down on us they might, but we knew the Manics themselves never would. To many of us, it meant the world to have them as allies.

* * *

As is my wont, I'm aware that I've now spent the vast majority of this chapter obsessing over the lyrics (another common malady of the Manics fan). I have a deep and abiding passion for this record, but even its lovers may allow that *Gold Against the Soul* is a sonically odd fish. The sheer expansive power of the music – Big Music for Big Emotion – is certainly arresting, but the fact remains that it is a bit all over the place. Nicky has pointed to inspiration from Alice in Chains and, disconcertingly, Red Hot Chili Peppers, which probably explains some of *those* funk rock sections.

Although James would later complain that the band was musically unfocused at this time, this omniverous appetite resulted in some of the best B-sides of their career. If I could go back and make one change to *Gold Against the Soul*, it would be to ditch 'Symphony of Tourette' (those Chili Peppers influences don't improve the troublesome lyric) to find room for the sublime 'Hibernation'. (Ok, ok, gun to my head, maybe I'd also swap 'Drug Drug Druggy' out for 'Donkeys'.)

Found on the flipside of my Bangor-bought 'From Despair to Where' cassette, 'Hibernation' is the most underrated song from the Manics' most underrated period. If I can persuade you of nothing else, take three and half minutes right now and settle into this delicate cry for help, delivered from a leafy street in the suburbs. It's all those 1950s bottles of gin under the sink, updated. Finally widely accessible, thanks to that aforementioned 2020 album reissue, you can easily get it on Spotify. It's a gorgeous, heart-rending study of the hidden hopelessness of conventionality. Never has the lie of keeping up with the Joneses been more subtly exposed.

Arriving on the reverse of 'Life Becoming a Landslide', 'Comfort Comes' is one of the most important tracks of the era – and the clearest sign of things to come. Angular, harsh and dark, it is an unembellished premonition. Remorselessly driving away from the strings, organ and piano that had given *Gold Against the Soul* both its radio-friendly sound and its warmth, it's a sonic step into the cold clarity that would soon give us the untouchable, unreachable genius of *The Holy Bible*.

Yet it's not the most widely loved of the era's B-sides. That honour surely goes to cult fan favourite – and perennial delicious live bonus – 'Donkeys'. A particular favourite of Dave Eringa, frequent Manics collaborator and the producer who gave *Gold Against the Soul that* sound, it also boasts Nicky's favourite bass part. Soaked in battered grandeur and building to a huge, Slash-esque solo, it's absolutely spiritually at home in the big brush strokes of the rest of the album. And it's all the better for it.

I'll be the first to confess that absolutely nothing I've said here makes *Gold Against the Soul* any cooler. What I'm here to tell you is that there's an alternative to cool – and this album is it. To this day, there's something heroic in this record's resolute refusal to be fashionable. There's also something profoundly and, to me, attractively Manics about contrarily choosing to stan an album the band themselves disdain. Who wants to be cool and remote, anyway, when you can be present and *care*? *Gold Against the Soul* is better than cool. I guess what I'm saying is – credibility? I'm yawning.

Part Three

1993–1994

1993 (continued)

June 23
• The *Gold Against The Soul* tour begins at the Marquee, London, and will last until July 18.

June 28
• *Gold Against The Soul* charts at a respectable number eight.

July 1
• Support band Blaggers ITA's singer, Matty Blagg, gets into a fight with *Melody Maker*'s Dave Simpson at an aftershow party over a bad review, prompting allegations of bullying and demands for the band to be dropped from the tour. Though unhappy with the incident, the Manics allow them to complete the planned dates.

July 18
• The inaugural Phoenix Festival takes place. Despite having opted to play the event over Glastonbury due to disputes about their billing, the band take the stage in an underwhelming 4pm slot. They will spend the summer bouncing around Europe's festival circuit, complaining most of the way about how much they hate festivals.

July 19
• *La Tristesse Durera (Scream To A Sigh)* (Sony/Columbia)
  Tracklist
  1. 'La Tristesse Durera (Scream to a Sigh)'
  2. 'Patrick Bateman'
  3. 'What's My Name (Live)'*
  4. 'Slash 'N' Burn (Live)'*
  5. 'Repeat (Live)'**
  6. 'Tennessee (I Get So Low)'**
  * CD only, ** 12" only
  Formats:
  CD, 12", cassette

July 26
• 'La Tristesse' charts at 22, a slight improvement on its predecessor but still a low showing for a band with such a high profile.

July 29
• Confirming their mainstream appeal, the band play one of Radio One's faintly cheesy out-door Roadshow events in Margate.

Aug 7
- Manic Street Preachers play their first ever festival headline set at the free-entry Heineken Festival in Swansea. A heavily inebriated crowd which includes factions of rival sports fans, pelt them with bottles and cans, one hitting Nicky Wire in the head. He's taken to hospital after the show, complaining of dizziness (and about ungrateful hometown crowds).

September 5
- MSP tour Germany again. Concerns grow over Richey's mental health as he adds stubbing cigarettes on his arms to his catalogue of self injury habits.

September 18/19
- MSP play support slots with Bon Jovi at Milton Keynes Bowl. Jon Bon Jovi would later get the band's name wrong ('The Maniacs') while thanking them onstage. The Manics don't enjoy the experience, and are relatively sure Bon Jovi's audience feels the same way.

September 20
- *Roses In The Hospital* (Sony/Columbia)
  Tracklisting:
  1. 'Roses In The Hospital'
  2. 'Us Against You'
  3. 'Donkeys'
  4. 'Wrote For Luck'*
  * CD only
  Remixes (12″ only)
  1. 'O G Psychovocal Mix' (Ashley Beedle)
  2. 'O G Psychomental Mix' (Ashley Beedle)
  3. '51 Funk Salute Mix' (Ashley Beedle)
  4. 'Filet-O-Gang Mix' (Charlie Smith and John Davies)
  5. 'ECG Mix' (Charlie Smith and John Davies)
  6. Album version
  Formats:
  CD, 12″, cassette

September 25
- Nicky marries his childhood sweetheart, Rachel in Cardiff.

September 27
- 'Roses In The Hospital' charts at a far-more-respectable number 15.

September 30
- The band perform 'Roses In The Hospital' on *Top of the Pops*. For the second time in three years Nicky, currently enjoying a honeymoon, is

replaced on the show by a member of the road crew wearing a mask (this time, Minnie Mouse).

October 20
• Another hectic tour of Japan kicks off. Much of the tour is filmed by the band and crew. The footage will be released online to coincide with a special edition of the album in 2020.

December 7
• A year on from his diagnosis, the Manics' manager and friend Phillip Hall, to whom they owe much of their success, dies from lung cancer. Out of respect and struggling with their grief, the band pulls their sold out show at Brixton Academy later that week, a gig which would have been their biggest headline show so far.
• Martin Hall, brother of Phillip, becomes the band's sole manager, a position he still holds at the time of writing.

December 14
• Phillip Hall's funeral.

1994

January 26
• The Manics embark on a short UK tour, including a rescheduled show at Brixton Academy in London.

February
• The band head to Soundspace Studios in Cardiff, the cheap studio in the city's red light district where they had recorded 'Suicide Is Painless', to work on material for their third album.

February 2
• The four Manics grace the inaugural *NME* BRAT! Awards with their presence. Richey describes Damon Albarn and Justine Frischmann's arrival at the awards as like 'Liz Taylor and Richard Burton at the Oscars', calling it 'over-professional', 'sickening' and 'very tiresome'.

February 7
• *Life Becoming a Landslide* (Sony/Columbia)
  Tracklisting:
  1. 'Life Becoming a Landslide'
  2. 'Comfort Comes'

3. 'Are Mothers Saints'*
4. 'Charles Windsor'**
* CD only, ** CD and 12" only
Formats:
CD, 12", cassette

February 14
- 'Life Becoming a Landslide' limps into the singles chart at 36; their worst showing since 'Stay Beautiful' in 1991.

March 2
- A tribute to Phillip Hall is held at Clapham Grand in London. The Manics headline the show, and are joined for the finale by Suede's Bernard Butler, whose own father had recently passed away from cancer. The indie supergroup performs Suede's 'The Drowners', The Faces' 'Stay With Me' and closes with MSP's own 'Motorcycle Emptiness'.

April 8
- Kurt Cobain of Nirvana dies after shooting himself in the head at his home in Seattle. The band are all deeply affected by the incident.

April 22/23
- The Manics play two sold out nights in Bangkok, Thailand, where both *Generation Terrorists* and *Gold Against The Soul* have been a huge success. They are the first western rock band below stadium-level to play in the country. 3,000 people attend each show in a room built to house just over half that. The stomping of the overstuffed crowd actually cracks the ceiling of the restaurant below the venue.
- Despite the fierce loyalty shown to the country's monarchy by many Thais, the band play their anti-Royalty anthem 'Repeat' on both nights, with Nicky saying of the king 'May he reign in hell'. He spends the rest of the trip convinced he will be arrested.
- Richey is gifted a set of knives by a fan, and uses them to slash his chest backstage, meaning he is bleeding freely throughout the first show. In an interview with the *NME*'s Barbara Ellen the other Manics play the incident down, saying that those who know him 'understand'. Ellen notes with surprise in her article that Richey admits to paying for the services a of sex worker during the trip. When pressed by the writer he talks about the 'transactional' nature of his sex life, and how he prefers it if groupies don't even stay for a kiss after they visit him.
- That spring Richey finds out that a close university friend, Nigel, has died by suicide.

May 28
- Two new tracks, 'Faster' and 'PCP' are premiered during the band's set at the Rock Against Racism Carnival, in South London's Brockwell Park. The event is intended to raise awareness of the dangers of the far-right British National Party (BNP), on the rise again in London, and is the culmination of a march through Brixton by the Anti-Nazi League. The Manics share the bill with The Levellers, a band they have been less-than-complimentary of in the past. Richey tells *NME* that this particular cause is above such petty concerns, and that taking a stand against racism was 'a central part of being a good human being'.

June 6
- *Faster/PCP* (Sony/Epic)
  Tracklisting:
  1. 'Faster'
  2. 'PCP'
  3. 'Sculpture of Man' *
  4. 'New Art Riot (In E Minor)'**
  * CD and vinyl only, ** CD only
  Formats
  CD, 10″ vinyl, cassette

June 9
- During a performance of 'Faster' on *Top of the Pops*, James wears what the press will refer to evermore as an 'IRA-style balaclava' (with 'James' written not-especially-threateningly across his forehead in tippex). IRA terrorism and the Northern Ireland Troubles are still serious issues in the UK, and James' choice of knitwear generates between 17,500 and 25,000 complaints (sources vary on the exact figure, however either would still be the most the show had ever received for a performance.)

June 16
- 'Faster'/'PCP' enters the UK singles chart at 16.

June 24
- Glastonbury's Other Stage plays host to the Manics debut at the festival. The military-chic look they had teased on *Top of the Pops* would also dominate their touring aesthetic for the remainder of the year, and the Glastonbury set establishes the template. The stage is draped in army netting and each of the band is sporting a different militaristic outfit, with Sean in a UN peacekeeper's beret and James wearing a white US Navy

sailor's suit (plus, briefly, his *Top of the Pops* 'JAMES' balaclava). A bracing, vicious and extremely well-received performance is marred somewhat by Nicky Wire's mouth, which proclaims at one point that someone should 'build some more fucking bypasses over this shithole'.

June
- During a short tour of Portugal concerns grow over Richey's behaviour, as he becomes increasingly incoherent and frequently tearful. His alcoholism also continues to worry the band, who book him another stay at a health farm. According to Nicky Wire, Richey, obsessed with keeping his stomach flat, is barely eating at this time.

July
- Nicky receives a worryingly incoherent phone call from Richey in the early hours of the morning. Fearing something isn't right he alerts his friend's parents, Graham and Sherry, and together they investigate Richey's Cardiff flat. They find him in a horrible state, having been drinking alone and self-injuring to an extent that Nicky would later say went well beyond the '4Real' incident, or the cutting of his chest in Thailand. According to Wire, by this point burgeoning anorexia had taken Richey's weight down to just six stone.
- Richey is admitted to an NHS hospital, The Whitchurch, in Cardiff where he is placed on a ward with twelve other alcoholics and addicts and given Valium and Librium to ease his anxiety and help him sleep. The band are appalled at his care, describing the hospital as somewhere patients are kept 'in stasis'. After eight days his friends and family agree that he should be discharged.
- During his time in the hospital it is agreed that Richey will become a non-touring member of the band, acting as a lyricist and contributing to artwork and visuals. However, he will change his mind about this arrangement almost immediately, later telling a *Select* journalist that he felt that it would be somehow 'cheating'.
- In late July, Richey is moved to a private clinic, The Priory, in London; which at the time charged up to £300 per day. He begins the 12-step Alcoholic Anonymous programme and is prescribed Prozac. Sinead O'Connor is also a patient at the facility at the time. The press is told that he has 'nervous exhaustion'. He will spend ten-weeks in psychiatric care at the cost of nearly £20,000. At one point recovered addict Eric Clapton, who volunteers at the clinic, offers to pop round which his guitar to jam. Richey is horrified.

July 30
- The Manic Street Preachers play Scotland's T In The Park festival as a trio. They will play several European festivals over the course of the summer while Richey recuperates in The Priory. Aside from the need to promote their upcoming album, the gigs are essential to help pay for Richey's hospital bill.

August 1
- *Revol* (Sony/Epic)
  Tracklist:
  1. 'Revol'
  2. 'Too Cold Here'*
  3. 'You Love Us (Heaven version)'*
  4. 'Loves Sweet Exile (live)'*
  5. 'Drug Drug Druggy (live)'**
  6. 'Roses In The Hospital (live)'**
  7. 'You Love Us' (live)**
  * CD1 only, ** CD2 only
  Formats
  2 x CD

August 30
- *The Holy Bible* (Sony/Epic)
  Tracklist:
  1. 'Yes'
  2. 'Ifwhiteamericatoldthetruthforjustonedayitsworldwouldfallapart'
  3. 'Of Walking Abortion'
  4. 'She Is Suffering'
  5. 'Archives Of Pain'
  6. 'Revol'
  7. '4st7ib'
  8. 'Mausoleum'
  9. 'Faster'
  10. 'This Is Yesterday'
  11. 'Die In The Summertime'
  12. 'The Intense Humming of Evil'
  13. 'PCP'
  Formats:
  CD, Cassette, 12″ vinyl, 12″ vinyl picture disc

The Holy Bible

By Emma O'Brien

'You may never be coming back'

In the late 90s there was a particular breed of Manics fan that became kind of a byword for the species – usually an angsty, bookish teenager who had still been at primary school when *The Holy Bible* came out, and inevitably came at the lore and dramatic backstory that shadowed the later albums secondhand, kind of like a *Star Wars* prequel if it included 'Suicide Is Painless' and pissing off Michael Stipe. It was a good era to come of age – plenty of fresh produce to keep you invested and still time to dig down into the darker stuff.

In 1999 I had an official Manics calendar with a suitably lofty literary quote for every month. I memorised them all and worked as many as I could into my GCSE English papers. I'm sure a lot of people might consider me the wrong person to discuss this album, that this should be the domain of someone who was at uni when Richey disappeared and still has a carefully preserved file of *NME* Letters Page arguments to use as research, who can talk us through the sad drama and the black glamour that came to surround this album as an objective narrator, who probably detested girls like me, as we crunched boa feathers and Claire's Accessories tiaras under foot with the plastic beer glasses as we left the gigs. And if that's you, I'm sorry. But not really, because I think the black velvet mist that came to surround *The Holy Bible* tells us something about the album, and the people who love this band, and the girls who got so invested mining album cover quotes for their GCSEs who are now musicians, and writers, and mothers and teachers and professors, and I think it's worth saying. It probably needs a whole book to do it justice, and more eloquent people than me have written them (reading list at the end) but on behalf of all those girls, and the women they are now, I'll tell you how *The Holy Bible* sounds to me.

Before we go any further, let me make it clear that in any number of cases of Interestingly-Mentally-Ill-Manics-Pixie-Dream-Fans, the cart and the horse went the wrong way round. I didn't believe then, and I don't believe now, that anyone saw that horrific 4REAL image and thought 'yep, that's what's been missing for me, and it's cheaper than copying his tattoos.' I had a self-harm habit well under my belt by 1995, and eating issues going on even further back than that. What I didn't have until a few years later, and I suspect this is true for many of us, was a language to explain and understand these urges. In 2000, when I was mostly playing *The Holy Bible*, I'd leave sixth form in the middle of the day and spend an hour staring helplessly at the psychologist who talked at me about depression and cognitive behavioural therapy, obsessional thoughts and personality types; shrugging in response to direct questions, with a hurricane battering the back of my throat – because if I said these things they'd sound wrong, or stupid, or like I'd made them up; because I *was* frequently wrong, and stupid, and made up of any number of things that scared me. Luckily, then, I had a lot of material to quote from.

We all read the books and the authors that were on the sleeves and in the lyrics (and let me just say here, if you're of the weak stomach crew you may wish to skip over J.G. Ballard) and made them our screen names and wrote them on folders.[4] This is, of course, eminently less painful than carving it into your skin. '*Can't shout can't scream,*' indeed. And everyone needs an album to cry to and a myth to take comfort in. It's been that way forever, and evermore shall be. In 2007, in response to a typically dreck *Daily Mail* outrage bait piece about 'EMO SUICIDE CULTS', a group of My Chemical Romance fans held an actual demonstration in the middle of London protesting against this theft of their narrative and explaining how sharing their pain actually kept them alive and together. I don't think anyone did this in 1995 but, really, I think the people I met online at the turn of the Millennium should do that for *The Holy Bible* when we all turn 40.[5]

I once tried to explain to a boyfriend who was immersed in the American emo of the early noughties and a few years younger than me, that back in dial up days we didn't have acceptable outlets for our teenage self-loathing with cute vocalists on MySpace; we didn't all have online journals (yet), *Hollyoaks* wasn't doing a yearlong study of someone's descent into anorexia – you either went full goth or, if you liked a good book and a bit of glitter,

---

4. My best friend once mis-spelled my Manics lyric MSN Messenger name and spent three months talking to a complete stranger thinking it was me. This is really true. They're still mates.

5. I've just remembered with tremendous affection a LiveJournal community (yes that's how old I am) dedicated to Manics shitposting that once infiltrated the online sharing community PostSecret with fake secrets culled from Manics lyrics and anecdotes and caused absolute mayhem in the comments for weeks. Those girls were my sisters, and I write for them.

you got into the Manics. And of course, though obviously I wasn't there, back in 1995 the original Cult of Richey – if there ever actually was such a thing (and I'm sceptical) – didn't even have the internet. It's hard to imagine a great rock 'n' roll breakdown playing out weekly in the pages of a music magazine now that we've got it all on Twitter every time we unlock our phones. It's hard to imagine how it must feel, now, to the people who stood and watched as Richey Edwards fell apart and had to gather up the ends of the whole mess into some kind of memory of who he actually was. This didn't play out without an eyebrow raised knowingly to the camera, either: as Simon Price documented at some length in his book, the band were aware enough of the staying power of a good myth not only for Richey to pose for the damned 4REAL photo in the first place, but to then use a recording of the anguished *NME* staff debating their culpability in publishing it as a B-side. To a charity single. About suicide being painless. Come on, lads.

As much as all this dark, bloody drama was meat and drink to me as a teenager, something about the whole episode really sets my teeth on edge. Self-harming in front of someone, in my mind, is several levels more explicit than stripping naked in front of a total stranger. I'd rather have died than done it for a camera. And although the remaining Manics did allude later to feeling they had, in Sean's words[6], 'done a lot of harm rather than good' in playing up to the myth, I still grit my teeth when I remember Nicky Wire calling it a great punk rock statement. Because it isn't, at any level, a statement or a manifesto or a rationale or an iconic image, it isn't anything but the act of someone who is desperately, desperately ill and is losing the logic that tethers them to the world the rest of us live in. And I think about this a lot. And I wonder how it sounds, now, to the people who had to watch someone go.

I was mildly surprised a few years ago when I read that 'This Is Yesterday' was actually a Nicky Wire contribution, written in his loved-up honeymoon state (Richey was presumably busy rolling around on the floor with the Holocaust, the inherent racism of America and something to do with Myra Hindley and crochet[7]) because it always sounded a bit like a farewell note to me, as *Journal For Plague Lovers'* 'William's Last Words' would become. But

---

6. From an NME interview, via Simon Price, again. Did I mention I referenced that book every assignment for three years of a degree?
7. At the 30 year anniversary gigs Wire could change into a white leather jacket and smirk as he tuned up for a chorus listing serial killers and laugh when we all joined in on the 'STERILISE RAPISTS' bit, and to be frank I think he has earned that.

then I watched a documentary about Amy Winehouse, about how at the end of her life she couldn't bear to sing the songs that made her name because of the pain she'd poured into them, and I played *The Holy Bible* again, and I played some more of my favourite grief songs and I realised that it could *only* have been Nicky Wire, because 'This Is Yesterday', like so many of the songs he would write later, in pain, in grief, in memory, in a context I'll never understand, is the sound of a sadness that is tethered to this world. It's about regretting, and wishing things were different, and loving someone, and maybe leaving them through death or by simply moving on with life. It's a hymn to someone. It's a song about how it hurts to love another person. The rest of that album isn't tied to the world in that way. 'This Is Yesterday' isn't the sound of someone who's going to cry in bed then remember to pay the council tax. It isn't turning over a razor in your hands for a few minutes, then hearing the door open and realising your partner is home. It isn't leaving your battered copy of *The Bell Jar* on the ward for the next sad girl to get her membership card as you go back to your life, whatever is left of it, outside a hospital. The rest of the album is, though. It's the sound, as Jarvis Cocker would describe it later, of *someone losing the plot*. It's the contents of a mind that's burning itself out, burning in horrible pain, screaming and spitting and fucking and vomiting and dying and starving; the mind of someone who is so hungry they are digesting their muscles and they think *yes, yes, this is good, this is as it should be*. It's sitting and waiting to see what will become of you; if you will die after all, like that poor girl[8] at the opening of '4st 7lb'[9] (numbers, Richey? You're going to give *numbers*, to an *anorexic*? It's like that, is it?) and maybe you should, because what else can you do, when everything is so awful, other than to wait, sick and sad and shivering, until you're brave enough? What can you tell people, when they ask 'what is so bad?' other than to point at how terribly human beings have treated each other and ask how do you brush your teeth and get a bus knowing all of this? *The Holy Bible* is,

8. Caraline Neville-Lister died from anorexia in 1994, shortly after filming the documentary the album samples from. Her friend Claire Jackson set up a support group in her name for people with eating disorders, having promised that she wouldn't 'die for no reason'. Caraline is now a service that provides therapy and support to people with eating disorders across the Bedfordshire area.

9. Richey explained at the time that '4st 7lb' is 'the weight at which an anorexic faces death.' This, for a number of reasons, is bollocks. Maybe that was his touchstone, or maybe he just pulled it out of a magazine, but he put it on a record knowing damn well that the anorexic brain sees a number and goes: CHALLENGE ACCEPTED. I cannot reconcile why someone would do this.

essentially, the sound you get when somebody goes so insane they're never coming back. There are shrines to the ones who don't come back, and books about them, and *Newsnight* polls in which their albums are described by people who don't know how it feels to think you may never be coming back.

I am writing this surrounded by books and playing an endless playlist through my phone, and I am 37 years old as I type, which is a full decade older than Richey Edwards was ever known to be. Richey, and Amy, and Kurt and all the rest of them who, in one way or another, swapped life and pain and love and council tax and just knowing you've survived for being immortalised at their lowest; for being the picture that hangs on a million sad girl's walls, for the song that streams over and over again on the pro-anorexia playlist (they exist. Don't check, it does nobody any favours), for being cold and stopped and perfect and maybe even a great punk rock statement, all checked out at 27. There are any number of theories, and indeed books, examining why this age is the nadir for the beautiful broken ones. Personally, I wonder if since you tend to have your first ride on the Fun-With-Self-Destruction Bus when you're starting secondary school, there's only so much a body and mind can be expected to take before they just crash and 27 is the limit?

It's important to note that according to the oracle that is phonomancer Dave Kohl from Kieron Gillen and Jamie McKelvie's comic series *Phonogram*, Richey is neither dead nor alive; he's just gone. The character, who can bring music to life, explains this to his Manics fan ex-girlfriend at the Severn Bridge, which he describes as an entry point to a myth, and expounds upon the price of becoming one, of believing one, essentially; what it costs you and everyone around you if you never come back.

I've made you a list of the books I read when I was planning this essay. They're far more complete and more eloquent than anything I have the space to offer you, but I think it's important for those of us who came back, who eventually replaced the ten circles of the Inferno, the locked ward and the '*beauty of self-abuse*' (sic) with jobs and degrees and lovers and babies and automated checkouts and 'Top Ten Breakdown Album' listicles and things that are painful and just being here, just living, just that – I think we should share the songs and the books and the slogans that tied us to the world. In the words of another twenty something songwriter, 'the things that know who we are when we've lost ourselves[10].' Because the thing about coming

---

10. Easyworld, 'Bleach'. 2001. Not streaming, but the videos on YouTube. Thank me later.

back is that you won't ever be able to get away from yourself and the best trick is to learn to pick up all the lovely little bits of themselves that other people leave with you. The books, the plays, the albums, the old online diaries. Take them and pass them on and tether yourself to the world. Get used to the good kind of pain, and maybe you'll even write your best friend a love song that ends up tattooed on someone.

Or at the very least you'll still be there at 37 to remind them of it and thank your stars that LiveJournal deleted its archive.

Reading list

Simon Price: *EVERYTHING: A book about Manic Street Preachers*, Virgin Books, 1999

Sarah Chaney: *Psyche On The Skin*: A history of self harm, reaktion books, 2017

Kieron Gillen, Jamie McKelvie: *Phonogram vol 1: Rue Britannia*, Image Comics, 2007

Hannah Ewens: *FANGIRLS: Scenes from Modern Music Culture*, Quadrille Publishing, 2019

Rhian E Jones, Daniel Lues, Larissa Wodtke: *Triptych: Three Studies of the Manic Street Preachers' The Holy Bible* Repeater Books, 2017

Howard Sounes: *Amy, 27: Amy Winehouse and the 27 Club*, Hodder Paperbacks, 2014

David Evans: *33 ⅓: The Holy Bible*, Bloomsbury, 2019

Part Four

1994–1996

1994 (continued)

September 4
- *The Holy Bible* charts at number six, the band's highest ever album chart placing. However, by the following week it will have slipped to 25. By the week after, it will have vanished from the top 40 altogether.

September
- Richey leaves The Priory in early September. He is insistent that he wants to stay with the band and joins the group in rehearsals for their upcoming tour.

September 20
- The Manics embark on a tour of France supporting Northern Irish grunge trio Therapy?. For the first time on a Manic Street Preachers tour, Richey takes his guitar playing seriously. He chooses the set each night, decorating the band's setlists with religious imagery.

October 4
- *She Is Suffering* (Sony/Epic)
  Tracklisting:
  1. 'She Is Suffering'
  2. 'Love Torn Us Under'*
  3. 'The Drowners (live)'**
  4. 'Stay With Me (live)'**
  5. 'La Tristesse Durera (Scream to a Sigh) (Vocal Mix)' - The Dust Brothers (AKA The Chemical Brothers)***
  6. 'La Tristesse Durera (Scream to a Sigh) (Dub Mix)' - The Dust Brothers (AKA The Chemical Brothers)***
  7. 'Faster (Dub mix)' - The Dust Brothers (AKA The Chemical Brothers)***
  * CD1 and Cassette only, CD1 and 10" only, *** CD2 only
  Formats;
  CD1, CD2, 10", cassette

October 5
- The next leg of *The Holy Bible* tour begins at Glasgow Barrowlands. Sleeper and Dub War support.

October 11
- 'She Is Suffering' charts at 25 before slinking away.

November 7
- The Manics begin a tour of mainland Europe with Suede. Richey's behaviour once more causes concern. At one point, according to Manics biographer Simon Price, he buys a meat cleaver and threatens to butcher his fingers to avoid going on stage. He begins to self injure again, and eats very little. The band decides that life on the road isn't helping Richey and decline offers to extend the tour any further, cancelling a run of shows in Japan planned for January 1995. This would give Richey a clear month to recover and prepare for a US tour, due to begin in February.

December 4
- The final date of the tour with Suede takes place in Munich, Germany. After the gig Richey is seen banging his head against a wall proclaiming 'I want to go home' over and over again. A member of the band's road crew quits, fearing he may one day be forced to discover Richey's body.

December 20/21
- The Manics play the final shows of the *Holy Bible* era, a pair of sold-out dates at London's Astoria. The brutal volume is so loud that Nicky gets a nosebleed. At the climax of the final show all four proceed to smash both their own and the venue's equipment in a display that is both cathartic and nihilistic for all concerned. They cause £8,000 worth of damage.

1995

January
- At some point in early January, Richey presents his bandmates with a folder of lyrics he has been working on over the Christmas holidays. When asked in an interview about the direction of the band's fourth album he suggests he would like it to sound like 'Pantera meets Nine Inch Nails meets Screamadelica'.
- The band head to one of their favourite demo studios, The House In the Woods in Surrey, to begin the writing process for their fourth album and work on a recently-secured and potentially lucrative movie tie-in. They record a new song, 'Judge Yr'self', for the soundtrack of the new *Judge Dredd* film, starring Sylvester Stallone, due to be released later in the year. A handful of scratch demos are also recorded for their fourth album proper, intended to be released in 1996. These include Edwards-penned tracks 'Kevin Carter', 'Elvis Impersonator: Blackpool Pier', and 'No Surface All Feeling', a song influenced by Smashing Pumpkins recent album *Siamese*

Dream, a favourite of both Richey and Nicky. Richey records guitar on the latter track, a rarity for him at the demo stage (or indeed at all).
- Following the session Nicky, James and Sean are alarmed when Richey appears to be missing. Much to their relief he resurfaces the next day.

January 14
- Richey's beloved dog, Snoopy, dies. He had been with the family since Richey was a child. On several occasions he had told journalists that his dog was his prized possession. Richey is devastated. Around this time he shaves his head.

January 23
- A journalist, Midori Tsukagoshi of Japan's *Music Life* magazine, interviews Richey at his Cardiff flat.

January 29
- The Manics rehearse at the House In The Woods for an upcoming US tour, intended to push the soon-to-be-released US version of *The Holy Bible*, which has been specially remixed for the American market by the label. The band – much to their surprise – love the remix.

January 31
- James and Richey, who are heading to the US the following morning to do radio promo and interviews in advance of the tour, check into the Embassy Hotel in London. Richey is given room 516.
- Richey withdraws £200 in cash from his bank account. It will later transpire that he has been withdrawing £200 daily for the past ten days.

February 1
- Richey quietly leaves the hotel at around 7am without checking out. James and Richey are supposed to meet in the morning to travel to the airport, however Richey is nowhere to be found.
- There is no sign of Richey. James contacts Martin Hall, the band's manager, who tells him to get his flight as planned, and that he'll track down Richey and put him on the next flight. Martin heads to the hotel and asks the hotel to check Richey's room, where he discovers a packet of Richey's antidepressants and a still-packed suitcase of his clothes. Also present is a box of books and videos, gift-wrapped in home-made wrapping paper, addressed to Richey's on/off girlfriend, Jo. Inside is a note saying 'I love you'.
- Since Richey had seemed in good spirits everyone assumes he will resurface soon – Martin waits in the room for Richey to return until it becomes clear that he isn't coming back to the hotel.

- Later that day it is fairly certain that Richey visits his flat in Cardiff, where he leaves his passport and medication.

February 2
- With no sign of Richey, a concerned Martin Hall files a missing persons report with the police; the reference number for Richey's case is 9500–823.
- Richey's family – his parents, Graham and Sherry, and sister Rachel – place an advert in a local paper which reads 'Richard, please make contact. Love Mum, Dad and Rachel'. It runs for three days, but yields no response.

February 5
- A fan by the name of David Cross claims to spot Richey at a newsagents by a bus station in Newport, Wales. He introduces himself as they have a mutual friend, a US Manics fan called Lori Fidler. According to Cross, the man he believed to be Richey asked how she was. There will later be reports that Richey had contacted or even visited Fidler during this period, but none can be confirmed.

February 7
- A Newport cab driver by the name of Anthony Hatherhall says he picks up a man fitting Richey's description from a local hotel at around 7am. He speaks in a faux-cockney accent but, according to the driver, occasionally slips into a Welsh one. The man asks if he can lie down in the back seat, and asks to go to Uplands, where he says his boss's lorry has broken down. The driver asks for £40 up front. They drive around South Wales, including the Manics' hometown of Blackwood, building up a fare of £68, which is paid in cash. Eventually Hatherhall drops the man off at a motorway service station, Aust Severn, on the English side of the river Severn. Later, James will dismiss the story as unlikely, calling it a 'mythical tour around the valleys'.

February 14
- Richey's car, a Vauxhall Cavalier technically owned by the whole band, is issued a parking receipt at Aust Severn service station. Toll records show that the car had crossed the Severn Bridge at either 2.55 am or 2.55 pm that day, though as the receipt system doesn't use a 24-hour clock, it is impossible to say which. Staff at the services are not aware at this point that there is anything unusual or important about the car.

February 15
- Official statements are released regarding Richey's disappearance by the Manics and South Wales Police. Richey's father, Graham, appears on

local radio asking his son to get in touch and appealing for help. The band cancels all upcoming appearances. The statement stresses that that the band, their management and the Edwards family are all unavailable for comment, asking the press to 'respect their privacy' and for their 'help and sensitivity regarding this matter'.

February 17
- Police discover Richey's car at Aust Services. A run-down battery and food wrappers imply someone has been sleeping in it. It is securely locked, with a steering lock bar covering the steering wheel. It is speculated that Richey may have attempted suicide at the nearby Severn Bridge, jumping into the river below. Press articles point out that the bridge is a 'notorious suicide spot'. The River Severn is searched by police, but no body is found. Years later, Richey's sister Rachel will point to the steering lock as evidence that her brother intended to return to his car.
- At the time of writing – April 20, 2021, – despite endless speculation and many reported 'sightings', no-one has been able to reliably confirm the whereabouts of Richey Edwards after 7 am, February 1, 1995, nor has a body been recovered. Though he has now been legally presumed dead, police say they will continue to investigate any new information.

April 8
- *Melody Maker* runs an article, 'From Despair to Where?', convening a panel of bands and readers, including members of Sleeper, the Boo Radleys and Pulp, to discuss a 'culture of despair' in rock 'n' roll, prompted by Richey's disappearance as well as Kurt Cobain's suicide the previous year. The music press is flooded every week with letters from readers struggling with their mental health and empathising with both Richey and Kurt. Nicky will later refer to such fans as 'The Cult of Richey'. The article prompts follow up pieces in *The Times* and *The Guardian*.

May 8–13
- Having discussed the band's future with Richey's family and gained their blessing to continue, the three Manics meet for rehearsals at Cardiff's Soundspace Studios. They continue working on the songs demoed before Edwards' disappearance, including those he had written the lyrics for and worked on himself (among them, 'Elvis Impersonator: Blackpool Pier', 'Small Black Flowers The Grow in the Sky' and 'Kevin Carter'.) They decide against using any of the more recent lyrics left with them in January, and consider publishing Richey's final works as a book instead. Several new Nicky Wire-penned tracks are worked on. One song, 'A Design For

Life', a paean to working class culture, is strong enough to convince the trio that they have a future as a band in Richey's absence.
- At some point in the first half of the year Columbia records agrees to take up their option of a fourth Manic Street Preachers album, though there are some at the label who feel the band are no longer commercially viable. Label boss Rob Stringer passionately argues that the Manics deserve another shot.

June 30
- The *Judge Dredd* movie hits theatres in the US without the Manics intended contribution, which was abandoned after Richey's disappearance. The movie is critically panned.

August 26
- *NME* runs a news story confirming the band's intention to continue without Richey. James and Nicky give a brief interview, saying they won't be rushing the process and will be going into the studio to 'see how things go'. The story stirs a fierce debate in the magazine's letters page.
- Around this time the band begin sessions for their fourth album, recording with Stephen Hague at Peter Gabriel's Real World studio, however they find the studio overly sterile and the sessions are abandoned. Only one song from the recordings done with Hague, 'The Girl Who Wanted To Be God', will make the album.

September 4
- The Manics record a cover of Burt Bacharach's 'Raindrops Keep Falling On My Head' for inclusion on *The Help Album*, a charity record recorded in a single day, raising money for children displaced by the war in Bosnia in collaboration with the charity, War Child. The song is recorded at producer Mike Hedges' studio in Chateau de la Rouge Motte in Normandy, France, where the band have decamped to continue work on their fourth album.

September 5
- Easy listening covers out of the way, the Manics begin the recording sessions for their much-anticipated post-Richey album, to be titled *Everything Must Go*. Mike Hedges is in the producer's chair.
- Toward the end of the year recording will move to Abbey Road in London, where orchestral parts will be tracked for four songs.

September 9
- *The Help Album* is rush-released, featuring the Manics first post-Richey music. Also featured are Oasis, The Boo Radleys, Paul Weller, Blur,

Radiohead, Massive Attack, the Stone Roses, Sinead O'Connor and Suede. The release is turned around so quickly that the liner notes are printed in the music press for fans to cut out themselves and place inside the case.

December 22
• A TV documentary, *Missing At Christmas*, is broadcast on ITV (coincidentally on Richey's 28th birthday) and features a segment on Richey Edwards. As a result, several new 'sightings' are reported, though the police, the band and Richey's family are not able to reliably confirm any of them.
• Around this time the band set up a trust fund to collect Richey's future royalties.

December 29
• The Manic Street Preachers play their first show in over a year, opening for The Stone Roses at London's Wembley arena. Now a trio (augmented by keyboard player John Green) they deliberately keep a gap stage right where Richey would normally stand. Half of their ten-song set is comprised of new material; 'Elvis Impersonator: Blackpool Pier', 'A Design For Life', 'Enola/Alone', 'Australia' and 'Everything Must Go' all receive their live debuts. Reports of the audience's reactions vary. In his book *Nailed To History* author Martin Power claims they receive an overwhelming standing ovation upon taking the stage, to which they look 'genuinely humbled'. Meanwhile, Simon Price in *his* Manics biography, *Everything*, claims that the band's emergence is met with indifference from Stone Roses fans and a sort of stunned awe from the tiny hardcore of Manics fans who have turned out for the event. Both report Nicky Wire as remarking 'What's up? It's only us!', although with very different intonation depending on the account. Paul Moody, writing in *Vox* calls the performance 'Frantic and huge-hearted'. *Melody Maker*'s Everett True writes a passionate, despairing review of the show, in which he points out that several Britpop celebrities including Noel Gallagher of Oasis, Mark Morriss from the Bluetones and Danny Goffey from Supergrass, stay in the VIP bar and don't bother to watch.

1996

February 24
- *NME* reveals details of a new Manic Street Preachers single, with lyrics penned by Nicky, called 'A Design For Life'. The song quickly picks up radio and TV plays.

March 19
- The band open for Oasis at Cardiff International Arena. They will be one of the Gallagher brother's go-to support bands throughout 1996. The Cardiff gig is followed by two shows at Dublin's Point Arena.

April 8
- The first Manic Street Preachers headline show since December 1994 takes place. The band play the Town & Country club in Leeds as part of Radio 1's Sound City event. Nick Neysmith joins as touring keyboard player. He will be part of the band's set-up, on and off, for the next two decades.

April 11/12
- The Manics perform their new single, 'A Design For Life' on *Top of the Pops* and *TFI Friday*.

April 15
- *A Design For Life* (Sony/Epic)
  Tracklisting
  1. 'A Design For Life'
  2. 'Mr Carbohydrate'°*
  3. 'Dead Passive'*
  4. 'Dead Trees and Traffic Islands'°*
  5. 'A Design For Life (Stealth Sonic Orchestra Version')°*
  6. 'A Design For Life (Stealth Sonic Orchestra instrumental version')**
  7. 'Faster (vocal mix)'**
  8. 'Bright Eyes'***
  * CD1 only, ** CD2 only, °CD and 12", *** cassette and 7" only
  Formats
  CD1, CD2, cassette, 12", jukebox 7"

April 21
- Championed by Radio 1, notably on Chris Evans' Breakfast Show, 'A Design For Life' charts at number 2 having sold 93,000 copies in its first week; by quite some distance the band's biggest hit to date. It will stay on

the charts for 14 weeks and eventually sell upwards of 200,000 copies. It is kept from the number one spot by Mark Morrison's 'Return of the Mack', a smash hit that summer, which beats the Manics' single by just 7,000 copies.

April 26
• The Manics warm up for two massive stadium shows with Oasis by playing the tiny downstairs bar at Manchester's Haçienda

April 27/28
• Oasis duty again, this time supporting the band for two nights at Maine Road stadium, Manchester. With a genuine hit single to their name the shows are a far cry from opening for Bon Jovi in Milton Keynes. 'A Design For Life' is greeted by the crowd as enthusiastically as many of the headliner's hits.

May 20
• *Everything Must Go* (Sony/Epic)
  Tracklist:
  1. 'Elvis Impersonator: Blackpool Pier'
  2. 'A Design For Life'
  3. 'Kevin Carter'
  4. 'Enola/Alone'
  5. 'Everything Must Go'
  6. 'Small Black Flowers That Grow In The Sky'
  7. 'The Girl Who Wanted To Be God'
  8. 'Removables'
  9. 'Australia'
  10. 'Interiors (Song For Willem De Kooning)'
  11. 'Further Away'
  12. 'No Surface, All Feeling'
  Formats:
  CD, cassette, 12" Vinyl

Everything Must Go

By Phoenix Andrews

'There were so many girls who wanted to be God'

It's not unusual to be terraformed by the music and aesthetics that hit you at 15. 1990s Britain was a hostile environment for an LGBTQ+ teenager. We didn't have the words for what we were. We certainly didn't have the support. Margaret Thatcher's government was followed by John Major's, and Section 28[11] was in place before I turned eight. Puberty happened during packed lessons in 'temporary' classrooms that lasted for a generation, where sexuality and gender were ever present but a banned topic of discussion. By 15 I'd already been listening to bands like the Manics, alongside pop and R&B, and reading *Smash Hits* and the other weekly music papers since I was 11 years old, but 'A Design For Life' hit different. A conservative rural upbringing and habit of borrowing CDs and tapes from the Carnegie library in the nearest town was slashed through to the glittering red innards with that opening guitar swoop. This, this is how being a writer, politics obsessive and wannabe pop star, with nobody like me around me, was made liveable.

The dynamic and emotional range of *Everything Must Go*, as well as its place in the band's history and canon, elevates it above all of their other records. It's a perfect execution of their intentions at the perfect time. Or the perfect time for me, anyway; rising through my teens and both embracing and fighting the Britpop orthodoxy. For the first time, the band were really looking out at the world and trying to tell broader stories that let everyone in, while still rooting the songs in personal experiences and vivid obsessions. Musically, the accessible pop-rock of their first two albums returns and is lent depth rather than merely frills with the synths and strings that swell its epic sound. Other guitar bands of the period experimented with string sections for expensive-sounding cheap emotion. Here it was more cinematic, of a piece with the guitar solos of their debut.

---

11. The cruel policy originating in Thatcher's government that banned teachers from telling children that queer lifestyles were normal or healthy. They fuck you up, your Tory Mum & Dad. – MB

As both pivot and pin in their canon, it is not an album that – despite its own claims – can escape history. *Everything Must Go* is not the last long player to contain Richey Edwards' lyrics, (that's *Journal for Plague Lovers,*) but it is the last record he really contributed to before his disappearance. His rhythm guitar on 'No Surface All Feeling'[12] reminds us that he was more than a lyricist and icon, he was (honestly) a musician and a lifelong friend. He may not have been the most proficient strummer ('La Tristesse Durera (Scream to a Sign)' is apparently the only other track in the band's canon where his playing made the final edit), but his presence on the stage was as important as other members of the band's presence on a recording. Suddenly there was a space stage right (the left side for the audience) where he once stood with a mic and a Telecaster Thinline. While Nicky Wire's lyrics and themes dominate the album, Richey's songs provide an interior life; a creeping dread that remains true to his character while pointing at the anxiety and neuroses underlying the tracks he *didn't* write. Wire and Edwards were brothers of a kind, whose internal struggles took them in different directions but fundamentally were deeply entwined. And those struggles were equally inseparable from mine, with this album the constant comfort through an unpleasant adolescence and traumas that were more than teenage strife. I had four breakdowns before the age of 25. I wanted to disappear. I'm still here.

There were some benefits to being a 90s misfit. Instead of basing my tastes on what my peers liked, I fed myself on the newspapers (*Guardian, Independent, Times, Financial Times*) and music papers (*NME* and *Melody Maker*) and reference books inexplicably available to read in my state school library; as long as you never took them home. I regularly bought *Smash Hits, Select, Vox* and *Q* with my various earnings from retail, paper rounds, babysitting and cleaning work. Whenever a band I'd heard on the radio or on a compilation (thanks as much to the *NOW That's What I Call Music* series, a mad, grab-bag of genres, as to 'indie' mixes like *Shine*) or a comedian I'd seen, made a reference to another band, album, comedian, book or film, then I'd chase that up and get lost in it like a *Wikipedia* or *TV Tropes* loop. One thing infinitely leading to another. I understood the literary quotations, the Bowie riffs, the 1960s obsession, Monty Python jokes, Morrissey's Victoria Wood theft and history of racism, Public Enemy and their samples … on it went. The Manics hit my radar early thanks to

---

12. The song's outro is said to include guitar Edwards recorded when the band first demoed the song, in the months before his disappearance. The fact it's a relatively easy part gives this some credibility. - MB

all of this, as well as *Smash Hits'* tendency to cover any musicians they found interesting. The band's hyperlinked culture smash was so rich that my spider brain was overwhelmed. So yes, I heard the earlier singles and owned the albums. But they didn't feel like they were MINE, my own band, the one that changes your life. Not until 'A Design For Life'. I'm not basic, I was just 15.

The strangeness of that period in politics and life is hard to explain to those who weren't there, especially if they're a few years younger or older than me or outside the UK. This was an experience unique to Xennials or elder millennials, too young for Generation X and too old to have been online as teenagers. In the past, I've called my micro-generation 'the Blair Generation' – we grew up under Thatcher and Major, were excited by Cool Britannia and the 1997 General Election but weren't old enough to vote or go to gigs or meaningfully take part as anything other than a consumer. We didn't have the internet at home – the first time I went online was in 1998 at a friend of a friend's house where she promised she'd show us the forums on *manics.co.uk*. We didn't have mobile phones or broadband, let alone smartphones and social media, and our homework was usually handwritten (yet our first proper jobs required IT skills. Go figure). In this context, the accessibility of *Everything Must Go*, a proper, mainstream album, was a good thing. It being sold in the supermarkets and the singles showing up on the *Chart Show* on ITV was important. For teenagers living outside cities and without hugely supportive parents, that was how we got into music.

The album brought about an acceleration of my journey in fandom, a perfect storm combining my age, access to fanzines via adverts in music magazines and neurodivergent desire to research and consume as much of the band and their past and present as possible. At one point most of my friendships came via Manics fandom, with many of us intensifying our fannish behaviours as the band got bigger. Within a few months of the album being released, I was hitting up charity shops and Topman sales to dress like James Dean Bradfield and Nicky Wire. I sent off for poetry books from Wire's brother Patrick Jones and went to see his plays in Cardiff. I visited Blackwood and had a toastie in Dorothy's café.

It is hard to talk about the fandom at the time, which swelled massively in numbers following *Everything Must Go*, even if you don't count the casual buyer, without using the old memes; 'FMF' ('fucking Manics fan') and 'intensely intense'. Laughing at ourselves was a key part of being a fan. David Stubbs of the *Melody Maker*, known at the time for his sweary 'Mr Agreeable' column, even created the recurring feature 'Diary Of A Manic Street Preachers Fan' as a fond nod to the common tropes of Manic Fandom. This titular Fan loved the band for their 'intense intensitude' but also shared some impressive fantasies about the band members. I shall never forget reading aloud a poem about James Dean Bradfield involving the line 'pumping pistons – yes, yes!' Being, and indeed dressing like a dedicated Manics fan involved a certain amount of knowing self-parody. I think that's why I enjoyed it so much. Yes, I love clashing animal prints and shiny plastic trousers – I'm non-binary so such finery is a way of life – but it's a semi-ironic and self-aware style – I'm aware of the clichés inherent in such an aesthetic. Putting the outfit on for the gig and being recognised by your kind is still a thrill.

My first gig was in April 1997, part of the *Everything Must Go* tour. Not just my first Manics gig, but first ever, proper gig. It was at Doncaster Dome, previously best known to me as the leisure centre with the wave machine and outdoor rapids. I had no idea of gig etiquette, how to manage my bladder or navigate crowd surges. I was somewhere in the middle, towards the front, and got crushed, having not yet found my preferred spot, at the far left or right, near the barriers. I ended up near the back and had to find my friend at the end. It was a rush all the same and I spent all of my meagre money on merch. I quickly realised that, though the crowd was a mix of the band's old and new audiences, it was still heavy on the old fans and their cultural kin, the eyelinered teenage newbies. There were rather fewer of the beige Mondeo men and beery Oasis fans than would characterise the move up to bigger gigs in arenas and stadia. Everyone got on, to my neophyte eyes.

I was able to check my memories of the setlist with others and reproduce it here:

'Australia'
'From Despair to Where'
'Faster'
'Kevin Carter'
'La Tristesse Durera (Scream to a Sigh)'
'Elvis Impersonator: Blackpool Pier'
'Removables (Song For Willem De Kooning)'
'Theme from M*A*S*H (Suicide Is Painless)'
'The Girl Who Wanted to Be God'
'Motown Junk'
'Motorcycle Emptiness'
'No Surface All Feeling'
'Small Black Flowers That Grow in the Sky (Acoustic)'
'Raindrops Keep Fallin' on My Head (Acoustic)'
'Enola/Alone'

'Everything Must Go'
'Stay Beautiful'
'A Design for Life'
'You Love Us'

It is hard to imagine a song like 'Removables' being played live after 1997 (and indeed it wasn't, until the 20th anniversary tour in 2017.) A brittle anthem of self-harm, it is not the strongest track musically or lyrically on the album and was reputedly a one-take recording, earning its inclusion by providing a little messy Richey space in a set full of radio-friendly bangers. It must have felt cathartic for Bradfield to sing; a dirgey howl that didn't try to cram in awkward phrasing, difficult notes or excess words. Fans remember it for the mondegreens (misheard lyrics) and nihilistic statements that quickly became screen names in the early days of the internet: 'I bronze my thighs easily' was a particular classic. This period was also the start of proper reality television in the UK and the MDF and bright shirts of *Changing Rooms* would one day become the varnish and veneers of *The Only Way Is Essex*. A tanning joke via a minor Manics song helped bridge the gap in my pop culture-addled mind.

Yes, my early steps onto the internet involved the Manics, watching as those screen names and email handles sprang to life. The unlimited internet access of a university computer lab coincided with the release of *This Is My Truth, Tell Me Yours*, and my feelings were processed alongside fans on the official site's web forum. I made lifelong friends in Manics forums and chat rooms and some of them I will always think of as their old MSP-inspired handles. There were so many girls who wanted to be God.

Everything Must Go opens with 'Elvis Impersonator: Blackpool Pier' and the lyrics are solely credited to Edwards, though it reminded Bradfield of past Wire-Edwards co-writes. It isn't as bleak as some Richey songs, though its attack on a UK in thrall to American culture is a familiar topic. Two decades later, critiques of the US are common; anti-imperialist sentiments, attached to particular presidents or foreign policies. Back in the Nineties, Britain really had the everyone-drinks-Coke-Yankophilia that is being mocked here, over and above neoliberalism or the Thatcher-Reagan relationship or first Gulf War. This was also common across Europe, a hangover from Cold War obsessions and the desirability of American consumer goods to many behind the Iron Curtain. Our television and cinema were dominated by US imports, be it prestige dramas and comedies or teen favourites like *Saved By The Bell* and the TV adaptation of the *Sweet Valley High* books. We were all encouraged to be Californian high school dudes eating McDonald's. The Manics, for their part, had spent enough of their time in white Levi 501s

playing US-inspired rock riffs. Even *The Holy Bible* shared a kinship with
the nihilistic end of American grunge. All that considered, to kick off with
Blackpool, home of the illuminations and a very British alternative to Las
Vegas, and pull in musical themes from *American Trilogy* by Elvis Presley
himself, is especially audacious. It sets the tone for the Manics' own take on
Brit(ish)pop, and does so with a knowing wink, as well: Nicky Wire and the
band's fans were – and are still– often to be found in second-hand sequins,
dyed hair and make-up of dubious quality and application skill.

'Enola/Alone' spoke to the sparkly yet depressed teen in me as if I'd
written it myself. The Smiths CDs I dutifully taped from the library copies
always felt cleverer and more contrived than this song's paean to keeping
buggering on. It's what these days we would call 'relatable', a Nicky Wire
lyric matched to a soaring and aching melody. Both spoke of the sadness
and anxiety I was feeling all the time, matched with an ambition to survive
and thrive and a kind of unrequited romance typified by the lift in the very
second chord. When you're too scared to do more than go to the local shop
and buy the same thing every day, you need a mantra – and here it was. Sorry
about all the terrible poetry I wrote as a result.

As an album, *Everything Must Go* is less frantic than the band's previous
three, with more space to breathe and to think and dream. Lyrics and
arrangements were curated with more care. The post-Gallagher brand
of 'indie' recruits liked these songs for the driving guitar and crashing
drivetime drums, and there is more space for people nothing like Richey
and Nicky to find themselves in the stories told. 'Kevin Carter' is about a real
person, and is treated less like the abstract documentary footage and interior
examination of a song like 'Yes' than as a lost friend who deserves respect.
Sean Moore's trumpet returning from their earliest demos is another voice,
like the role that instrument plays in jazz, and the cornet does in brass band
music, making its case with images and sounds, rather than words.

While 'Enola/Alone', like its near namesake in synthpop, 'Enola Gay',
tempers its melancholy with an upbeat brightness, 'Small Black Flowers That
Grow In The Sky' is all the way down in inescapable misery. It takes the
breathing, almost-theme of the album to another level, stripping away words
and musical elements to give James Dean Bradfield an opportunity to really
sing from the heart. I feel as fetal and caged in pain listening to this track as I
did at 15. It wasn't my mental state, it was Richey's, but the empathy hurt, then
and now. The break that the title track provides between these two songs is
needed. Catharsis and celebration before bringing us into that tiny crawlspace.
I saw Patrick Jones' play of the same name on several occasions and it produced
the same emotions. Something of 'Never Forget' by Take That creeps into

'Everything Must Go' – these young men have not forgotten where they came from, but they need to move on with their lives and music to survive.

The band were not wrong to fear rejection. There were plenty of old skool Manics fans who pulled a Comic Book Guy with every album from *Everything Must Go* onwards – 'This is the worst album ever...Manic Street Preachers died today'. Uncomfortably, musicians grow up at a different rate from their listeners and lead different lives. They don't want to fossilise, their themes and styles calcified. MSP could have changed their name when it was clear Richey was not returning, like New Order springing from the ashes of Joy Division after Ian Curtis took his life. They certainly made some allusions to New Order in the design and typography of the album sleeve and the singles derived from it. Fundamentally, though, they were still the same band. Nicky had always written many of the lyrics, James and Sean all the music, Richey's guitar parts were mostly played by James on records and so on ... their sound had not substantially changed in the way that some alleged at the time. New Order went from a guitar-led band fronted by Curtis to a synth-led band with Gillian Gilbert as a new member and their guitarist, Bernard Sumner, on vocals. Manic Street Preachers dropped from a four to a three piece, with some support from musician friends live, and the sound of the post-Richey albums all had clear roots in their previous work.

By 1996 the Manics had become used to rejection by the masses. They had thrived, often by necessity, on being oppositional and obnoxious. Their music had been orthogonal to the dominant British music scenes as each album was released, though curiously from a 2020s viewpoint they sound perfectly of their time. They *enjoyed* not fitting in, riling people with their aesthetic and interviews. With *Everything Must Go,* they suddenly fit. Guitar music was popular, not just in the music press and specialist radio shows, but actually fashionable. Britpop had made rock into pop once more. The songs were radio-friendly unit shifters. Manic Street Preachers had to get used to being loved and get comfortable with it. High chart positions! Brit Awards! Triple platinum discs! Pop magazines! Saturday morning children's television!

The album was released during the Nineties peak for physical music sales and since May 1996, it has sold over two million copies. At the time, 'multiformatting' and releasing four or five singles from an album was normal, driving radio and TV airplay and chart success. Most singles were released as two different CD formats, plus cassette and the occasional 7"+×,

---

13. The 70s sold less, but were considered a nice item for the purists. Blur won the 'Battle of Britpop' because 'Country House' came out on two CDs and a tape, while 'Roll With It' was two CD's and a 70: Blur's tape outsold the Oasis vinyl. - MB

encouraging fans to buy multiple copies. At least one of the CDs would be sold at a very low price in chart return shops, to register more sales as buyers took a risk on a 99p release, heavily promoted with point-of-sale material around the store. 'A Design For Life' hit the UK singles chart at number 2, the first of a run of five consecutive Top 10 hits[14] – four of these singles taken from *Everything Must Go*. It was available as two different CDs, a cassette and 7" vinyl issued for pub jukeboxes (where the humble 45 still thrived).

The *Everything Must Go* singles followed the common guitar band pattern of the time: CD1 containing new songs as B-sides and CD2 featuring remixes of the single by popular and credible electronic music acts, with the cassette's flipside containing cover versions from recent live sets. This approach to chart-gaming fitted with both the original Manics vision of success and a handy point in my life and income. I had multiple jobs as a teenager and not much in the way of an active social life, living in a rural area as an unpopular bullied kid. A few quid a week on CD singles and music magazines was a normal way to spend my earnings. Remixes from Chemical Brothers and Jon Carter won't have scored them any club plays (a reason, alongside the separate club charts, why pop artists continued to commission dance remixes of their ballads and up-tempo tunes into the Noughties), but they might have sold to, or at least intrigued, fans of those acts. The Stealth Sonic Orchestra remixes, on the other hand, were not just a synthetic orchestral outlet for Apollo 440 but iconic in their own right. Anyone who has listened to the intro tape for Manics gigs or heard their music running under the football on television has heard these versatile and epic versions of the *Everything Must Go* singles and 'Motorcycle Emptiness'. Our own personal cinematic soundtrack.

Having that soundtrack made me feel important. *Everything Must Go* is an album of transition, and not just for the band. I was growing up, dealing – without the language to describe it – with my transness, being a teenager, negotiating my relationship with the Establishment, undiagnosed disabilities and how queerness worked. Nobody at school was out as gay, lesbian, bisexual or transgender – but here was this band transgressing gender conformity and not caring about not fitting in or being too much for other people. It's okay to be intense. Not only was Section 28 an ever-present thing, meaning we just didn't talk about sexuality and gender in public, gay

---

14. And also a run of No. 2s – the Manics have topped the charts only twice, while four of their singles and six of their albums have taken the silver medal. It is their natural state. - MB

men and trans people were still dying en-masse of AIDS. HIV was still considered a death sentence. If I said I fancied a girl, it would be a *thing* and I would be even more outcast than I had been. I started crossdressing in sixth form and that got enough grief. It wasn't identity politics, it was policed identity. The importance of shouting along to 'Australia', as a form of release, even as it provided theme music for kids TV shows like *Renford Rejects* and the cricket, wasn't lost on me. Oh, so *this* is an acceptable way of expressing myself but *that* is not? It's heavy, it builds … oh, not my sense of shame, but this song about freedom and trying to run away from your emotions. Those *interiors*, that other song about reaching out to a friend and failing, are things you can't show.

I didn't really get 'Further Away' until I grew up and fell in love properly, requitedly, was treated well. It's one of those songs like 'Something Changed' by Pulp, that suddenly, quietly, click into place and find a whole new level of meaning. The band couldn't have written it before this album either. It's not a pose or a pastiche, it's a real love song. When I was listening to the album in the 90s, I thought I understood. I had been in love. I had been happy. I felt sad. I wanted other people to understand. But I hadn't been loved back and trusted. I hadn't been awake and listening to your breathing and worrying what I'd do if you never woke up. I had had too much emotion a hundred times, but never felt that deeply.

'No Surface All Feeling' is how I have always been, a layer of skin missing. It's a song about losing a friend, presumably Richey, and the guitar comes over you live like tidal waves from the introduction onwards; sanding off another layer to the quiet verses and chorus screams to sighs. Every line is delivered with sincerity. If you've never screamed the words 'junk' or 'truth', I'm not sure you're one of us. One of the broken believers of the Manic Street Preachers. At the end, everything must go and we have to let it.

Part Five

1996–1998

1996 (continued)

May 5
- Heavenly Records release the debut album by Northern Uproar, co-produced by James Dean Bradfield and Dave Eringa.

May 23
- A show at Glasgow's Barrowlands kicks off the first Manic Street Preachers headline tour in two years. The band will be on the road for much of 1996 and a good deal of 1997, including a brisk trot around most of Europe's major summer festivals.

May 18
- The band appear on BBC Two's *Later ... With Jools Holland*. Nicky is absent from the performance after 'straining a muscle in his arm while answering the phone'. The band borrows the bass player from Pete Townshend's band, who is also appearing on the show, for performances of 'Everything Must Go' and 'A Design For Life'.

May 26
- *Everything Must Go* charts at number 2, selling 60,000 copies in its first week. This would usually be a comfortable number one, but that position is blocked by *Outside*, the much anticipated come-back of George Michael, inconveniently released the same week. *Everything Must Go* will go on to achieve Triple Platinum status (three million sales), and would still be in the top 5 of the album charts a year from its release.

June 17
- Manchester dance act 808 State release their album, *Don Solaris*. James Dean Bradfield contributes vocals to a song called 'Lopez', with lyrics written by Nicky Wire.

July 22
- *Everything Must Go [single]* (Sony/Epic)
  Tracklisting:
  1. 'Everything Must Go'
  2. 'Back Garden'*
  3. 'Hanging On'*
  4. 'No-one Knows What It's Like To Be Me'*
  5. 'Everything Must Go (Chemical Brothers Remix)'**
  6. 'Everything Must Go (Steal Sonic Orchestra Version)'**

7. 'Everything Must Go (Stealth Sonic Orchestra Soundtrack)'**
8. 'Raindrops Keep Falling On My Head'***
* CD1 only, ** CD2 only, *** cassette only
Formats
CD1, CD2, cassette

July 26
- 'Everything Must Go' charts at number five.

August 3
- The first of three massive dates with Oasis, beginning with a show at Balloch Castle Country Park by Loch Lomond castle in Scotland

August 4–5
- Oasis host two gigantic, festival-sized shows at Knebworth Park in England. The gigs are seen by many as the peak of the 90s' Britpop era and the pinnacle of the Manchester band's career. A combined audience of 250,000 people attend across the weekend. The Manics are the only band besides the headliners to play both shows. They will later complain that they found the experience to be somewhat joyless, and little more than an opportunity to sell CDs.

August 23
- The Manics begin a short North American club tour to warm up for a run of dates opening for Oasis in the US. The tour begins at Montreal's Club Soda.

August 27
- Opening night of the Oasis tour in Rosemont, Illinois. Oasis singer Liam Gallagher fails to appear for the show. The gig goes ahead with guitarist Noel Gallagher taking vocal duties.

August 30
- Despite rumours of a rift, tonight's Oasis gig goes ahead with Liam Gallagher present on vocals once more. The Oasis/Manics tour proceeds as planned.

September 10
- Noel Gallaher quits the Oasis tour and all subsequent dates are cancelled. The Manics hastily organise a club tour so as not to waste their work visas, and play a further thirteen shows at small venues across the country. The tour sells poorly, averaging 500 tickets per night, a ludicrous contrast

to home, where Manic Street Preachers are becoming one of the biggest bands in Britain. LA's 500-capacity Troubadour does sell out, though *Kerrang!*'s Lisa Johnson notes that the venue felt much fuller at other recent gigs, and that the band take a while to warm up.

September 27
• The underwhelming US dates come to an end at Casbah in San Diego, California. The band fly home to promote a new single and prepare for a tour of the UK and central Europe.

September 30
• *Kevin Carter* (Sony/Epic)
  Tracklist
  1. 'Kevin Carter'
  2. 'Horses Under Starlight'*
  3. 'Sepia'*
  4. 'First Republic'*
  5. 'Kevin Carter (Busts Loose Remix)'**
  6. 'Kevin Carter (Self Sonic Orchestra Version)'**
  7. 'Kevin Carter (Self Sonic Orchestra Soundtrack Version)'**
  8. 'Everything Must Go (acoustic)'***
  * CD1 only, ** CD2 only, ***Cassette only
  Formats
  CD1, CD2, cassette

October 5
• The Manics begin their UK tour in Aberdeen, graduating from 1,000–2,000 capacity clubs to 3,000–5,000 seater theatres, with a handful of enourmo-dome arena shows planned for the end of the year. 40,000 tickets are sold for the tour in advance. The band choose to highlight Welsh talent for the support slots, which are divided between Catatonia, Super Furry Animals and the Stereophonics. MSP will be on the road continually until the end of the year.
• Capitalising on the success of *Everything Must Go*, Channel 4 broadcast a new documentary, *The Vanishing of Richey Manic*, examining the ongoing mystery of Richey's fate, nearly two years on from the day he had disappeared. The show features interviews with Deborah Curtis (the widow of Ian Curtis, Joy Division's late singer), Steve Lamaq and Manics-authority Simon Price. Less appropriately, it also features Shaun Ryder and Boy George. The Manics decline to participate.

October 6
- 'Kevin Carter' charts at number nine, which is very respectable for the third single from an album everyone in the country appears to already own.

November 1
- A nine-date tour of Germany, France and the Netherlands kicks off in Frankfurt.

November 11
- Nicky contributes lyrics to a song called 'Waiting For Today To Happen', for the new Lightning Seeds album, *Dizzy Heights*.

December 2
- *Australia* (Sony/Epic)
  Tracklisting:
  1. 'Australia'
  2. 'Velocity Girl'*
  3. 'Take The Skinheads Bowling'*
  4. 'Can't Take My Eyes Off You'*
  5. 'Australia (Lion Rock remix)'**
  6. 'Motorcycle Emptiness (Stealth Sonic Orchestra Remix)'**
  7. 'Motorcycle Emptiness (Stealth Sonic Orchestra soundtrack)'**
  8. 'A Design For Life (live)'***
  * CD1 only, ** CD2 only, ***Cassette only
  Formats:
  CD1, CD2, cassette

December 5
- The first ever biography of the Manic Street Preachers, Paula Shutkever's *Manic Street Preachers – Design For Living*, is published by Virgin Books.

December 7
- 'Australia' charts at number seven, the band's fourth consecutive top-10 entry.

December 12
- The Manics play the sold out 6,000-capacity Cardiff International Arena, the site of their first show of 1996, when they had opened for Oasis as a cultish indie band.

December 14
- A three-night run of headline shows in London's biggest theatres begins at Brixton Academy. All are sold out.

December 15
- The London run continues at Shepherds Bush Empire. The band are joined onstage by Kylie Minogue for 'Little Baby Nothing'. Kylie had been Nicky's first choice to duet on the song back in 1992.

December 16
- The final Manic Street Preachers show of the year. The band are briefly joined by Liam Gallagher during their set at Kentish Town Forum, though he spends more time prowling the stage and trying to play-fight with Nicky than actually performing in any way.
- *Everything Must Go* and 'A Design For Life' both claim the number two spot in *NME's* end of year reader's poll (appropriately mirroring their chart positions). Meanwhile *Melody Maker* readers crown *Everything Must Go* album of the year, as does *Select*, though *MM* relegates 'A Design For Life' to number three. They do, however, dub James 'Sexiest Man of the Year'. *Kerrang!* name the album the second best of the year, while the more serious musos at *Mojo* place it way down at 29. Perhaps more notable, both *The Guardian* and *Sunday Times* gift the band 'Writer's Album of the Year' awards.

1997

- The Manics sign a new £1 Million publishing deal with Sony/ATV.

January 28
- 808 State's 'Lopez', which features vocals by James and lyrics by Nicky, is released as a single, remixed by Brian Eno and The Propellerheads.

January 28
- The annual *NME* BRAT! Awards are held in London. The Manics walk away with gongs for 'Best Album', 'Best Single' and 'Best Live Act', though lose out on 'Best Band' to tour-mates Oasis. They also win an award for 'Best Song Including The Name Kevin'. Nicky dedicates their awards to Arthur Scargill, while saying the audience are 'all London Tories'.

February 24
- The Manics win awards for 'Best British Group' and 'Best British Album' at the Brit Awards, arguably the most prestigious prizes at the UK's most prestigious music awards. Nicky dedicates one of the wins to Britain's comprehensive schools. It is the first time the band have even been nominated at the Brits.

March 3
- Several newspapers run a story about an alleged sighting of Richey Edwards in Goa, India. Richey's family investigate the claims but can find nothing to suggest he had ever been in the country.

April 2
- A short UK tour begins at Blackpool's Empress Ballroom. Support is from the Boo Radleys. The tour will culminate at London's Royal Albert Hall on April 12.

April 5
- James guests with The Beautiful South on a special episode of *Later … With Jools Holland* dedicated to the band, contributing guitar and vocals to the song 'Old Red Eyes Is Back'.

May 10
- The Hillsborough Justice Concert takes place at Anfield, raising awareness for the victims of the Hillsborough Disaster a decade earlier, who were still awaiting justice at that point. The Manics are a last-minute addition to the bill, and are profoundly moved by the event.

May 17
- James plays a solo acoustic spot, opening for The Charlatans, at a charity gig raising money for the National Missing Persons Helpline.

May 24
- The band play their biggest headline show to date at Manchester's NYNEX Arena (later known as the MEN Arena, the AO Arena, or just 'Manchester Arena'). All 20,000 tickets sell out in a single day. The show is broadcast live on BBC Radio 1, and filmed for later release on video.

May 29
- 'A Design For Life' wins 'Best Contemporary Song' at the Ivor Novello Awards.

August
- The Manics begin work on their next album at London's Whitfield Street Studios, with Apollo 440's Howard Gray, whom James admires for his work with Simple Minds. Among the songs recorded is 'Black Holes For The Young', a duet with Sophie Ellis-Bextor (then singer with indie band Theaudience). It will later surface as the b-side to 'The Everlasting'. No tracks from the session will make it to the eventual album.

August 22
- The Manics unveil two new songs, 'Ready for Drowning' and 'Born A Girl', at a small warm-up gig at Newport Centre, Wales; 'Ready For Drowning' and 'Born A Girl'

August 23
- Manic Street Preachers headline the Reading Festival, their first mainstream festival headline spot. Both *NME* and *Melody Maker* run full-page photos of Nicky wearing a see-through camouflage dress on their respective covers the following week.

August 24
- The band play their final gig of 1997 at the rain-soaked Féile Festival in County Durham. Some reports of the show suggest a lacklustre response, though Nicky will describe it as one of his favourites of the year, calling it 'magical'. The rest of 1997 and much of 1998 will be taken up with writing and recording their fifth album.

September 1
- Capitalising on the band's recent success, Sony reissue the six *Generation Terrorists* singles, 'Stay Beautiful', 'Slash 'N' Burn', 'You Love Us', 'Loves Sweet Exile', 'Motorcycle Emptiness' and 'Little Baby Nothing'. All six chart just outside the top 40.

September 7
- Work on the new Manics album picks up with producer Greg Haver at Cardiff's Soundspace (now renamed Big Noise), a favourite haunt of the band, where they had originally recorded 'Theme From M*A*S*H' and worked on songs for *The Holy Bible* and *Everything Must Go*. Many of Sean's drum performances on the album will come from these sessions. Recording will then move to Mike Hedge's Château de la Rogue Motte, where the band and Hedges will spend the remainder of the year.

September 8
- Kylie Minogue releases 'Some Kind of Bliss', a song co-written with James Dean Bradfield and Sean Moore. The track will peak at a lowly number 22 in the UK charts. Later, James will worry that he had 'failed her'.

September 29
- *Everything Live*, a concert film of the show at NYNEX Arena is released on VHS.

October 22
- Kylie Minogue's latest album is released, initially intended to be called *Impossible Princess* but retitled (and delayed) following the death of Princess Diana. As well as 'Some Kind of Bliss' it contains another Minogue/ Bradfield collaboration, 'I Don't Need Anyone', this one with lyrics by one Nicky Wire. It initially charts well, but sales will quickly tail-off. She will be dropped by her label, Deconstruction, as a result.

November
- Nicky tells the Japanese fanzine *Crossbeat* that the new album will have 'a melancholy feel, like the rain falling in Tokyo'.

December
- Nicky tells Manics fanzine *Iconoclastic Glitter* that his highlights of 1997 – a year in which he had headlined Reading, sold out huge arenas and won every major UK music award – were 'Glamorgan winning the county championship, Joe Calzaghe and the British Lions'. When another fanzine, *Aspire For Life*, asks him to summarise the year, he says, simply 'tiring'.

1998

January
- Work on the album moves to Rockfield's Quadrangle Studio in Monmouthshire, (where Queen had recorded 'Bohemian Rhapsody') working again with Dave Eringa. The band intend to record b-sides for their forthcoming single. It soon becomes apparent that one new track, 'If You Tolerate This Your Children Will Be Next', far from a b-side, is actually a potential hit. They then move the short distance to Monnow Valley studios, in which Oasis had recorded their debut, *Definitely Maybe*. The final flourishes would be added at London's Air Studios, where the album will be mixed.

January 19
- The Edwards family arrange for Richey to be included in the 'missing' section of the Welsh edition of the *Big Issue*, as the third anniversary of his disappearance approaches.

June
- The band deliver their finished fifth album, *This Is My Truth, Tell Me Yours*, to their label.

July 20
- Jo Wiley hosts the world-wide first play of the new Manic Street Preachers single, 'If You Tolerate This Your Children Will Be Next' on her BBC Radio 1 show.

July 28
- Stories circulate about a song on the new Manics album about the Hillsborough Disaster, entitled 'South Yorkshire Mass Murderer'. *NME* reports that South Yorkshire's Assistant Chief Constable, Ian Daines, finds the idea of the song 'in bad taste' and 'likely to cause offense to many people'. The title will later be abbreviated to 'S.Y.M.M', though it's unclear if that decision has anything to do with the comments from her Majesty's constabulary.

August 20
- The Manics play their first live show in almost a year, performing a secret gig in Copenhagen's Freetown Christiania, the city-within-a-city commune in the Danish capital. Several songs from *This Is My Truth, Tell Me Yours* are played live for the first time, including 'If You Tolerate This Your Children Will Be Next', 'The Everlasting', 'You Stole The Sun From My Heart' and a rare outing for 'S.Y.M.M'.

August 24
- **If You Tolerate This Your Children Will Be Next** (Sony/Epic)
  Tracklisting:
  1. 'If You Tolerate This Your Children Will Be Next'
  2. 'Prologue To History'*
  3. 'Montana/Autumn/78'*
  4. 'If You Tolerate This Your Children Will Be Next (Massive Attack Remix)'**
  5. 'If You Tolerate This Your Children Will Be Next (Class Reunion o the Sunset Marquis mix)'**
  6. 'Kevin Carter (live)'***
  * CD1 only, ** CD2 only, ***cassette only
  Formats
  CD1, CD2, cassette

August 29
- An article in *Music Week* reveals that the Manics have parted company with their US label, Epic records, after a growing frustration from the band's management about their failure to make any headway in the country. *Everything Must Go* has sold only 3,000 copies there. James Dean Bradfield will later describe Epic's US promotion of the album – a huge hit

the world over but ignored in the States – as 'a farce'. The magazine asks Nicky Wire for a comment, who responds 'we don't give a shit – we've only done 20 gigs in the States – the psyche between us and them doesn't exist.'

- The Manics play support at The Verve's gigantic Slane Castle gig in Ireland. Before the show they talk to Northern Ireland secretary Mo Mowlan, who has asked to meet the band. She is surprised when Nicky talks politics.
- Former Manics bass player Miles 'Flicker' Woodward gives a rare interview to *The Western Mail*, in which he says how much he misses his old friends. He goes on to talk about how their early gigs ended in violence and that he thought his drinking would get out of control if he stayed.

September 6
- 'If You Tolerate This Your Children Will Be Next' enters the UK Charts at number one, narrowly beating Steps' 'One For Sorrow'. The single sells 176,000 copies in its first week but then is knocked off its perch a week later, replaced by All Saints' largely-forgotten 'Booty Call'.

September 12
- *NME* reports that punk band The Stranglers suspect the Manics of plagiarism, pointing out similarities between their 1979 single 'Duchess' and the band's own 'If You Tolerate This …'. The Manics say that, though they recognise the similarity, any resemblance is purely coincidental.

September 14
- *This Is My Truth, Tell Me Yours* (Sony/Epic)
  Tracklist:
    1. 'The Everlasting'
    2. 'If You Tolerate This Your Children Will Be Next'
    3. 'You Stole The Sun From My Heart'
    4. 'Ready For Drowning'
    5. 'Tsunami'
    6. 'My Little Empire'
    7. 'I'm Not Working'
    8. 'You're Tender And You're Tired'
    9. 'Born A Girl'
    10. 'Be Natural'
    11. 'Black Dog On My Shoulder'
    12. 'Nobody Loved You'
    13. 'S.Y.M.M.'
  Formats:
  CD (initial quantities the title embossed in silver lettering on the jewel case), 12″, cassette, minidisc.

This Is My Truth Tell Me Yours

By Marc Burrows

'When you're six-foot-three, you can see a long way backwards'

The fifth Manics album was the band's commercial peak – a monster hit of a size and scope bestowed rarely on a British rock groups in the years since; launched in the final, decadent gasp of the music industry's imperial pomp. In terms of record sales, for literally everyone involved, it was all going to be downhill from here. *This Is My Truth Tell Me Yours* spent three weeks at number one, and was eventually certified triple platinum; spending over seventy weeks in the charts. The band's mainstream beautification was sealed with Brit Award wins for 'Best British Band' and 'Best British Album', while a swept-board at 1999's NME BRAT! Awards (best band, single, album, video and live act) proved they'd held on to their critical and outsider clout as well. In 1999, they would top the bill at Glastonbury and the V Festival, and cap the era off by headlining (and selling out) a stadium show for the first and only time in their career. They had finally fulfilled the promises they'd made as mouthy punks in 1990: they were the biggest band in Britain. And they did it with the weirdest, bleakest, most introverted and nakedly despairing album they would ever write.

To understand just how strange and remarkable this is, we have to widen the lens. 1998 was a weird time, not just for the Manic Street Preachers, but in guitar music in general on both sides of the Atlantic. The nineties had hurtled along at an alarming and exciting pace as Generation X felt its oats, eyed a new millennium on the horizon and started to gallop carelessly, as hard as they could toward the finish line. That youthful rush manifested as alternative rock in America. 'Smells Like Teen Spirit' kicked open the door and everyone else, Pearl Jam, Soundgarden, Smashing Pumpkins, Hole, Alice In Chains, Red Hot Chilli Peppers and a thousand more wearers of flannel and ripped tights, had tumbled through. Of course, anyone running too fast and too carelessly will eventually stumble and fall – by 1998, almost all of those bands were haunted by heroin or suicide or both.

Over in the UK, British bands had started to revel in their own cultural identities and, as in America, rushed forward to define a new cool. We would come to know it as Britpop. There's various arguments for where the movement began, but most will agree that its first proper – if slightly limp-wristed – flourish came in 1992 when Suede's glamorous Sashay onto the scene coincided with Blur's reinvention as oiky London mods with their retrospectively-beloved-but-underperforming single, 'Popscene'. Suede would have a hit with their self-titled debut album the following year, while Blur's *Parklife* and Oasis' debut, *Definitely Maybe*, both marked a genuine cultural touchpoint in 1994. That same year Kurt Cobain's suicide had ended US Alt-Rock's age of innocence, but it couldn't halt its popularity. On both sides of the Atlantic record companies realised that boys (and the occasional girl) with guitars were the in-thing and hastily signed up anyone that could hold one more-or-less the right way around. Suddenly rock n' roll was where it was at. What united most of the British bands, especially the ones snapped up by the majors in the immediate post-*Parklife* era, was a shouty, spiky mod-meets-post-punk style and the impression of a dizzying good-time party happening constantly, harking back to an imagined swinging London of the mid-60s. Sharp suits, great hair, witty lyrics sang in your accent and flicking the v's on *Top of the Pops*. Britishness was a celebrated commodity and, pushed by the indie mags and a revamped Radio 1, a celebratory excitement seemed to fill British guitar music. It wouldn't last. Like in America, everyone was running too fast and no-one was looking where they were going. There was too much money, too many drugs, and too much existential meltdown as the weirdo outsiders of the 1980s found they'd become the 90s' in-crowd and didn't know what to do with it. A lot of the biggest bands; Blur, Suede, Pulp, to an extent Oasis, started to doubt who they wanted to be as the pressures of being bona fide popstars ran head-first into an expectation from within that they should be making great art. As Tony Blair swept into power in 1997, ending well over a decade of Tory rule, Britpop started its meltdown.

This has both everything and nothing to do with the Manic Street Preachers and *This Is My Truth, Tell Me Yours*. The Manics were never a Britpop group as such; they didn't fit the mould. *Generation Terrorists* and *Gold Against The Soul*, released concurrently with Blur's first two albums and Suede's debut, had been precision-tooled for the rock market – the inkies loved the band for their indie roots, their aesthetic and because they gave good quote, but musically they sat more comfortably in rock weeklies like *Kerrang!* and *Raw*. No Manics album shares DNA with the great Britpop party records of the mid-nineties boom: Suede's *Coming Up*, Oasis' *Definitely Maybe*, Blur's *Parklife*, Pulp's *Different Class*, Supergrass' *I Should Coco* or a half dozen more we could reel off. As the Britpop bubble was bobbing to the surface in 1994, the Manics were stepping the other way with *The Holy Bible*;

an album notable for its lack of knees-up-ave-a-bananaisms or classic rock n'roll. While the band's dark masterpiece did indeed make contact with their Britishness in a way their first two records hadn't, it was the Britain of Wire, Joy Division, The Cure, PiL and The Fall, rather than the Beatles/Bowie/ Kinks/Stones/Jam/Smiths axis of the *Select* magazine mainstream. The Manics were holding themselves aloof and apart from their *NME* peers, happier to be bunged in with The Wildhearts and Therapy?, or American acts like Nirvana or Mudhoney than Sleeper or Cast.[15]

No-one looking at the indie rock landscape of 1994 could have predicted the way 1996 and 1998, the respective years of the next two Manic Street Preachers records, would play out. Alternative rock and Britpop, the yin and yang of transatlantic populist guitar bands, began to twitch and contract. In America it was probably The Smashing Pumpkins' *Mellon Collie and The Infinite Sadness* that did it; the category-defying double album released in 1995 that showed one of the biggest post Nirvana alt rockers breaking out of genre conventions. In the UK the fault was with Oasis who actually did the opposite; doubling down on the classic rock wing of the indie rock 'n' roll boom. With their second album, 1995's *What's The Story? (Morning Glory)*, Oasis became comfortably one of the biggest bands the UK had ever seen. They transcended genre – maybe not in musical style (Oasis had less sonic variety than most of their peers), but certainly in popularity: *What's The Story* was one of those albums almost everyone seemed to own. You'd hear it on *EastEnders* and at football matches. They played it in the hairdressers. The effect on the music industry was predictable; Britpop still ruled the roost, but the focus was now on solid, button-shirted everymen: Ocean Colour Scene, Hurricane #1, The Verve. The spiky fun seemed to drip away. Instead there was an emphasis on 'classic' songwriting, 'proper' guitar music that could be stripped back to acoustic guitars, mid-paced classic rock, veneration for The Beatles (which largely ignored their experimental edge) and epic-sounding string sections. Everyone sounded a bit like Wings[16]. The music your Dad liked was now cool. Some wag at the *NME* nicknamed it 'Noelrock' after the senior Gallagher brother, whose workmanlike songwriting had, somehow, defined an era.

The metamorphosis in the Manic Street Preachers was happening independently of, but also somehow in-step with Britpop. Richey had wanted

---

15. The band did tour Europe with Suede in 1994, but it was the bloodied, battered Suede of Dog Man Star, not the bum-slapping, chart smashing version that came both before and after.

16. Only the band the Beatles could have been.

to take the band in a darker, heavier direction, but he was no longer around to steer the ship, and after the intensity of the last few years, of touring a brutally punk album, becoming a byword for self-destructive angsty intellectualism, and the utter despair of losing a friend, the remaining band members wanted room to breathe.[17] The result was *Everything Must Go* and 'A Design For Life', music full of space and clarity with lyrics that actually scanned. The songs called for some orchestral oomph, as well as some mid-paced, straight forward drive-time indie rock. Working largely without a manifesto for once, the glamourpuss provocateurs-turned-militant-post-punk-existentialists had released a record that could sit comfortably next to *What's The Story? (Morning Glory)*, and sell to the same audience. Which it did. In droves. The band toured with Oasis on and off throughout 1995 and 96, appearing at their giant shows at Maine Road and Knebworth, and following the Gallagher circus (which occasionally took place without one or the other Gallagher brother) around the US. *Everything Must Go* went to number two and would hang around the top five for over a year, while the band graduated to arena shows of their own for the first time, and triumphantly headlined 1997's Reading Festival. By accident or by design – and in all honesty it was a bit of both – the band had caught the zeitgeist at the right time, abandoning their military chic or DIY punky glamour in favour of sensible shirts and hair cuts, and releasing a classic sounding, accessible rock record at the exact point that classic sounding, accessible rock records made by ordinary looking blokes in button-down shirts were selling. The Manics had gone Noelrock. They had also, alongside Blur, Oasis, The Verve, Pulp and Radiohead, re-formed the UK's indie front line.

And that's where 1998 comes in. Four of the biggest bands of the alternative rock/Britpop era would drop new albums that year: Ash, Pulp, Smashing Pumpkins and Manic Street Preachers. Two others, Blur and Oasis, had released records the previous year. All of them, to one extent or another, had felt the extraordinary pressure of following up a giant global hit, of balancing the needs of a newly acquired mainstream fanbase with a cultish hardcore that had come with their earlier success; of the demands of major record labels keen to capitalise on their latest cash cows with the instincts to drive forward that had gotten them into this position in the first place. And they had to do it in the intense glare of the media, and in many

17. The change actually crossfaded with Richey's vanishing – the musical palette of Everything Must Go was already evolving in that direction in late 1994, months before he made his exit.

cases while dealing with internal trauma. Of the bands listed, only Oasis made an obvious attempts to remain commercial[18], making their overblown cocaine classic *Be Here Now*, which in its own way is quite, quite mad. The others all stamped down deliberately on any expectations to produce cookie-cutter hits. Ash's *Nu-Clear Sounds* was a harsh-sounding alt-rock record, fairly uncompromising and uncomfortable, from a band scared of being typecast as Britrock's pretty boys; Jarvis Cocker drove Pulp to new levels of seediness with the downbeat *This Is Hardcore*; its title track one of the finest singles of the era, but at six minutes and 23 seconds hardly a sure-fire radio hit. The album is an introspective, somewhat decadent response to getting everything you ever wanted and being expected to give more. As Cocker said on 'The Fear', it was *'the sound of someone losing the plot'*.[19] Blur were working hard at scaring their teenybop audience off altogether with their self-titled fifth record, which owed far more to American college circuit bands like Pavement than it did to The Kinks and early Bowie. Its lead singles were the drugged-up, slurred 'Beetlebum' and the Nirvana-aping punk rush of 'Song 2'. To their label, Parlephone/EMI, it was the sound of commercial suicide[20], which just goes to show what some record execs know – 'Song 2' was the biggest hit Blur ever had. It was Smashing Pumpkins and the Manics that went all-in on the anti-commercial misery, though. Their 1998 records *Adore* and *This Is My Truth, Tell Me Yours*, were musical left turns from earlier work, replacing big guitars and anthemic choruses with downbeat electronica; channeling tragedy and pain (the Pumpkins' had sacked their drummer, Jimmy Chamberlin, after a heroin binge that nearly killed him and left their touring keyboard player, Jonathan Melvoin, dead, while the Manics had lost Richey) into the most interesting and patently uncommercial music of their career. Both records have commercial moments ('Ava Adore', 'You Stole The Sun From My Heart') but such cracks in the clouds never define their parent albums in the way earlier hit singles ('Tonight Tonight', 'A Design For Life') had. The Manics managed something else though, something that Pulp, Smashing Pumpkins and Ash couldn't manage – their existential crisis actually made them bigger than they had been to begin with.

Looking back, it is absolutely absurd that *This Is My Truth*, which – and let's get this straight – is a mostly grindingly slow, extremely melancholy record

---

18. Their comeback single, 'Do Ya Know What I Mean' is just 'Wonderwall' with the words changed. It's exactly the same chords. Seriously, go and check.
19. The second time this gets quoted in this book.
20. Execs visiting the studio apparently heard both songs and asked them to write some singles.

about grief, aging and depression, became the defining indie rock album of the year. It makes virtually no sense at all. Its lead single, 'If You Tolerate This Your Children Will be Next', despite being released in a sweltering summer, is chilly and remote rather than anthemic and accessible. There's an acoustic guitar buried under there somewhere, and a minimalist guitar solo toward the end, but other than that 'Tolerate' is a record that goes out of its way to alienate the casual listener. It's a rich and wonderful song but, with its strange washes and stately chord progression, it sounds, with the exception of the more extreme ends of *The Holy Bible*, less like a hit single than any Manics track before it. The wordy title forms the song's chorus and though it's melodically nagging, lyrically it's a strange and unrelatable slogan. Nicky is no longer declaring the extent to which he either talks about love or wants to get drunk. No-one is flying and running to Australia. Its opening lines aren't about the pride and power of literacy, as with *Everything Must Go*'s big single, instead they're about being cold, alone and afraid. The song's title was inspired by the Welsh socialists that fought facism in the Spanish Civil War, its line '*if I can shoot rabbits then I can shoot fascists*' a direct lift from Hywel Francis' *Miners Against Facism*. Its lyrics are openly pro-war. A curious choice for lead single from a band currently cresting a wave of popularity. And yet, 'If You Tolerate This Your Children Will Be Next' went straight in at number one; surely one of the least likely hit singles of the decade?

So how did they manage it? How did three men in boring clothes and ordinary haircuts doing a mid-paced slow-burner about the Spanish civil war achieve one of the smash singles of the year, and follow it up with a Brit Award-winning mega selling album about misery and boredom?

There are, for me, three reasons.

1) 'If You Tolerate This' and *This Is My Truth* synced with the mood of the indie record buying public in general. Gone was the 'cool Britannia' optimism that had set in across the country somewhere around 1995 or 96, with its genuine sense of freshness and knock-about optimism. The music of the mid-decade had captured that excitement: there's real shit-slinging, carefree fun in many of the big Britpop songs, especially when Oasis revved themselves up properly or Blur and Pulp hit the disco button. That wave of optimism and mild euphoria peaked with Tony Blair's landslide victory in 1997, finally ending a Tory run that had lasted, anagramically, since 1979. A wave of change, excitement, freshness and a new broom brought genuine giddiness. By 1998 though, that had faded. People had begun to realise that New Labour were less *new* broom and more Trigger's Broom. The Blair government's abandonment of

Liverpool's dockers, engaged in a Union-led dispute over severance pay, was seen as Labour turning on its own left flank, and was emblematic of how the party had drifted from its party-of-the-working-man roots. The death of Princess Diana in 1997 had left the national mood sadder, and more aware of the toxic culture of celebrity it had created. The biggest bands in the country found themselves alienated and scared by their own fame, stretching right up to the pop behemoths like Take That and the Spice Girls, a feeling that trickled down to fans. There was a general feeling throughout the scene that a bubble had burst, that the world was more complicated and sadder than perhaps many of us had thought. 'If You Tolerate This Your Children Will Be Next' synced in with that mood; melancholic, almost defeated but also somehow resilient. It was a record that told you that the future was now and that, actually, it might not be all it was cracked up to be. You can hear the same tone of resignation in other indie hits of the year – Placebo's 'Pure Morning', Embrace's 'Come Back To What You Know', Garbage's 'I Think I'm Paranoid', UNKLE's 'Rabbit In The Headlights'. Even Robbie Williams' 'No Regrets'. There was sadness and a strangeness in the air as the century creaked toward its end point. 'Tolerate' nailed that tone.

2) The Manics were, by now, massive. *Everything Must Go* had been one of those albums that transcended a usual indie band audience. At one point it was playing in the background on BBC One school drama *Grange Hill* as a student pulled an all-nighter. We checked back on him every once in a while, and the fact that a different song from *Everything Must Go* was playing each time was used to mark the passage of time. It was assumed enough of the audience would own the album to get the point. That is one hell of a penetration. Arguably *any* new Manic Street Preachers record was going to be a hit. It was well marketed too – Slow burn it might have been in mood, but due to the band's high profile, 'Tolerate' received plenty of radio play. An excellent, faintly disturbing video got heavy MTV rotation too, and back in the 90s that *mattered*. Its bleak tone was given plenty of opportunity to seep into the more receptive mindsets. In the late summer of 1998 you could hardly miss it.

3) 'If You Tolerate This Your Children Will be Next' is *a really good record*. It may not be immediate, but it *is* effective. In its own way (a very different way to, say, 'A Design For Life' or 'Motorcycle Emptiness') it's even anthemic. The choruses build, the bassline pumps, and there's a creeping intensity that rises as the song progresses. It goes 'whooooooooaaaaaaa-oooooooaaaah' at the end. 'Tolerate' *deserved* to be a hit. The Manics now had the profile to make it one.

'If You Tolerate This' was, in its own way, the perfect introduction to the latest evolution of the Manic Street Preachers and distilled the themes of the album to come nicely: mournful, tired, a little defeated, very Welsh. Lyrically these are themes that Wire, writing an album's worth of lyrics by himself for the first time, would embed into almost every song.[21] Thematically, it's an extension of a journey he began on an album more usually associated with Richey, as *The Holy Bible*'s 'This Is Yesterday' – the one song on the record Wire had written alone – is pretty much the blueprint for everything he's doing here. In many ways, *This Is My Truth ...* is Nicky's *Holy Bible* – the album in which his worst self is illustrated through his best, his lyrical abilities pulling a tight focus on his pain. We find a miserable, grieving Nicky looking into the past; and when you're six-foot-three and standing at the peak of your fame, you can see a long way backwards. 'The Everlasting' sets out the stall, addressing happier times when people (himself, the band and society in general) had genuine smiles. He was mourning the loss of community to the soft corporate power and isolation of late-era, post industrial capitalism (a theme the Manics would come back to on several future records), and mourning the passing of his (and the band's) youth. Nicky Wire, it should be noted, was at this point still just 29 years old; yet the sense of someone exhausted, whose best years are behind him, pervades the record. It's there on 'You Stole The Sun From My Heart', where he admits that '*I have got to stop smiling, it gives the wrong impression*' (for my money the best line he has ever written), it's there on 'My Little Empire', in which he channels the sheer misery of misery itself – how painfully, horribly boring it is to be depressed, stuck in your own world. On 'Black Dog On My Shoulder' he addresses that depression head on, on 'I'm Not Working' writer's block gives way to despair, on 'Be Natural' he is sick of playing his own role and on 'Born A Girl' he's sick of being himself on any level. The Nicky Wire of *This Is My Truth, Tell Me Yours* is heartbreakingly, desperately unhappy. Or at the very least, very, very good at writing about how that would feel.

It's also an album about absence. Although Nicky said at the time that 'Nobody Loved You', the brittle, *In Utero*-tinged rocker found towards the end of the record[22] was the only song the band had recorded that was *directly*

---

21. Wire has actually only written three Manics albums in their entirety, This Is My Truth, Lifeblood and Send Away The Tigers, the rest of their records have been co-written with (or entirely written by) Richey Edwards, or feature a token song by James Dean Bradfield.
22. Controversially excised from the 2018's 20th anniversary reissue in favour of the more sprightly b-side 'Prologue To History'.

about his missing friend, Richey Edwards' presence – or rather the lack of it – hangs over the entire album. 'Ready For Drowning' begins by quoting a real conversation Wire had had with an unwitting taxi driver about 'that missing lad', and it's not clear if the urge to 'put it out of its misery' is a reference to the suffering Edwards or the excruciating driver. On 'Tsunami' Nicky is the twin suddenly alone and finding his voice. Even when the reference is less direct, Richey is defined by his absence – Nicky's presence has had to swell to fill the creative gap left, and he partly uses those spaces to talk about how unhappy his friend's disappearance has made him.

One aspect of the band's thematic arsenal that slotted into a space previously occupied by Richey's eloquent screaming was literally closer to home: Welshness. *This Is My Truth, Tell Me Yours* is the most Welsh record the Manics had released. In their early years the band had both resented their Welshness (their home town of Blackwood was a 'boring shithole', a place to escape from, not celebrate), though they weren't above leveraging it to highlight their outsider status when it suited them. Still, the dismissive attitude of the music press, who couldn't resist headlines like 'The Newport Dolls' and 'You Sexy Merthyr Fuckers' (both *NME*), 'Dai Harder' (*Select*), or 'The Boyos Are Back In Town' (*Kerrang!*) had always rankled, and any writer making a crack about the Valleys in print usually gained a black mark against their name; something which came back to haunt a few hapless hacks once the band broke big, finding their services weren't required in for future campaigns. Perhaps wary of being dismissed, or maybe out of indifference or even an unconscious shame, the Manics had never self-consciously been a *Welsh* band. James' accent on record was as transatlantic as his guitar solos. Things began to change in the post-Richey era, though Bradfield's voice would always hover somewhere between LA and Llamedos. Wire would occasionally hang the Y Ddraig Goch of Wales on his bass amp, name dropping RS and Dylan Thomas in his interviews. *This Is My Truth*, from cover, shot at Black Rock Sands near Porthmadog, to subject matter, is soaked in Welshness. Those communities that no longer smile at one another in *The Everlasting* are Welsh mining towns, 'Ready For Drowning' is about a Welsh village flooded to provide a reservoir for Liverpool, the 'silent twins' of 'Tsunami' were Jennifer and June Gibbons, who had grown up in Haverfordwest. 'If You Tolerate This Your Children Will Be Next' was inspired by the Welsh volunteers who went to Spain to fight the fascists. The record unlocked a fixation with their homeland that would stay with them for the rest of their career with songs like 'This Stubborn Welsh Heart' and 'Cardiff Afterlife', and duets with Welsh singers like Cate Le Bon, Georgia Ruth,

Catherine Anne Davies and Gwenno Saunders. In 2010 Bradfield and Wire wrote 'The Girl From Tiger Bay' for Shirley Bassey. Catatonia were chosen to open the *This Is My Truth* UK tour, while the band's enormo-dome Millenium Stadium gig featured Super Furry Animals and Feeder. The Manic Street Preachers were no longer a band from Wales, they were a *Welsh* band. In one respect this was an of-its-time celebration of their heritage, in another it was just another way in which Wire was now focused inwards, at himself, his history, his homeland.

What's interesting is that while lyrically the record looked backwards and inwards, sonically, marshalled by James and Sean (and also Nicky, whose musical contribution to the band is often overlooked), it was throwing to the future. It would be easy to take these songs down a folky, deconstructed, soft-rock direction, a sort of darker, softer, *Everything Must Go*, and if you listen to the rehearsal and studio demos of the tracks you can see the shadow of a very different record – just as melancholic, but simpler, folkier, warmer, rooted mostly in the acoustic guitar. 'My Little Empire', for example, built around a melancholy, elegant electric riff played in an E-A-E-F-A-E tuning on the record, in demo-form strums along like *Harvest Moon*-era Neil Young. 'You're Tender and You're Tired', driven by reverby piano on the album, has a demo that sounds like something from The Verve's *Urban Hymns*. The chords and tempo are the same, but the feel is very different. Instead of the MTV Unplugged route, the Manics, alongside producers Mike Hedges (who'd helmed *Everything Must Go*) and Dave Eringa (whose association went back to 'Motown Junk') opted for retro-futurism, and a cold pallet of electronic washes and offbeat analog instruments (sitar, accordion, tin whistle, mellotron, omnichord, tambura), heavily treated. The electric guitar remains the key instrument, but its use is often at a right angle to expectation, moving into colder, stranger dimensions, James experimenting with tunings and effects, stepping away from his traditional white Les Paul in favour of more varied tones. Even the record's most straightforward rockers, 'You Stole The Sun From My Heart' and 'Tsunami', turn in oddball ways; the first powered by a tinny beat sampled from a pinball machine, the second using a sitar as its primary shade, staying in a sturdy mid-pace when it so clearly wants to push ahead and gallop. 'Born A Girl' is lonely, desolate, 'S.Y.M.M.' a gloomy drone, 'The Everlasting' shimmers and twinkles in the way a glacier would in the heat of the sun. *This Is My Truth, Tell Me Yours* has never really got the respect it deserves for being so musically weird at a time when it would have been so easy to turn the amps up and make another Noelrock album. It has more in common with Radiohead's *OK*

Computer than *Urban Hymns* or *Be Here Now*. Alienation was in the air, and the Manics broadcast it back better than most.

And that's what makes this record so oddly fascinating, sticking out like an icicle in the heat of summer when played in the context of the Manics albums either side of it on the rack. *Everything Must Go* had seen the trio – still in many ways a quartet – standing their ground, regrouping, getting through it. It's a record of bravery and compassion. Their next step couldn't be more of the same, because *they* were no longer the same. They were learning to live in the new world order, learning to accept its disappointments and its tragedies. In some ways *This Is My Truth, Tell Me Yours* is an album at odds with everything, that always freezes when you expect it to flow, and drifts away just when you think you've pinned it down. It's alienated, disappointed, sighing. Sifting through the detritus of Britpop, watching the optimism of the mid-decade flake and crumble … that's very 1998.

Part Six

1998–2001

1998 (continued)

September 15
• The *This Is My Truth, Tell Me Yours* UK tour begins at Kettering Arena. It will stretch to the end of the year, and is the band's first bona-fide arena tour.

September 20
• *This Is My Truth, Tell Me Yours* enters the UK Album charts at number one and will follow *Everything Must Go* to triple-platinum status within a year. It will go on to out-sell its predecessor.

September 21
• James Dean Bradfield provides a remix of Massive Attack's 'Inertia Creeps', returning the favour for the Bristol group's own take on 'If You Tolerate This', featured on the recent CD single.

September 23
• BBC Two dedicates an episode of its *Close Up* series (which documents interesting cultural figures like Dennis Potter, Jackson Pollock and Germain Greer) to the Manics. Entitled *From There To Here*, it is one of the few Manics documentaries that the band themselves have participated in. Nicky Wire grants producers access to his personal video archive, and all three members are interviewed. Inevitably, much of the programme focuses on Richey. The episode features footage from the Slane Castle show with The Verve, and contains a new live performance of 'Black Dog On My Shoulder'.

October 30
• At the annual *Q* awards in London, the Manics are named 'Best Band In The World Today'. Meanwhile, tourmates Catatonia dedicate their 'Best Single' award to New Labour's Welsh Secretary, Ron Davies, who has recently resigned after being caught apparently soliciting sex on Clapham Common. Davies had agreed to 'go to dinner' with a man and had subsequently been mugged and had his wallet and Commons pass stolen.

November 2
• *The Sun* reports that Nicky has written to Prime Minister Tony Blair asking if he could be named Minister for Wales in Davies' place.

November 13
• Several newspapers report yet another Richey sighting, this time on Fuerteventura in the Canary Islands, where he is apparently spotted

drinking in a bar, running away when recognised. Graham and Sherry Edwards travel to the island to investigate, but find no evidence that Richey had ever been in the area.

November 30
- *The Everlasting* (Sony/Epic)
  Tracklisting:
  1. 'The Everlasting'
  2. 'Black Holes For The Young' *
  3. 'Valley Boy' *
  4. 'The Everlasting (Deadly Avenger's Psalm 315)'**
  5. 'The Everlasting (Stealth Sonic Orchestra Remix)'*°
  6. 'Small Black Flowers That Grow In The Sky (live)'°
  7. 'The Everlasting (Deadly Avenger's Psalm 315 instrumental mix)'***
  8. 'The Everlasting (Deadly Avenger's 69th St. Mix)'***
  9. 'The Everlasting (Deadly Avenger's 69th St. Instrumental Mix)'***
  * CD1 only, ** CD2 and 12″ only, ***12″ only, *°CD2 only, °Cassette only
  Formats:
  CD1, CD2, 12″ vinyl, cassette

December 6
- 'The Everlasting' charts at number 11, ending the band's two-year run of top-10s.

December 15/16
- The Manics play two sold out nights at London's Wembley Arena.

December 22
- The band cap off the year with a triumphant homecoming show at Cardiff International Arena.

December 23
- The music mags publish their end-of-year lists. *Kerrang!* Puts this *This Is My Truth* at number 12 in its' Albums of the Year', *Melody Maker* at 29, and *NME* at 24. 'If You Tolerate This Your Children Will Be Next' is named sixth best single of the year by *Melody Maker*, and fifth by *NME*. Probably to counter James' 'Sexiest Man' award the previous year, *Melody Maker* readers name Nicky 'Unsexiest Man of the Year' and 'Fool of the Year'.

1999

January 22
• A rare tour of Australia gets underway, starting at the Metro Theatre, Sydney.

January 25
• The annual *NME* BRAT! Awards are held in London. The magazine's writers may have placed *This Is My Truth* fairly low in their end-of-year lists, but its readers, who voted for the awards, had other ideas. The Manics achieve a clean sweep, taking gongs for 'Best Band', 'Best Album', 'Best Single', 'Best Live Band' and 'Best Video'. Nicky Wire is also given two special awards for 'Pop Personality Who's Brain Should Be Kept Alive For Posterity' and 'Pop Personality You Would Most Want As Prime Minister'. The band, currently on the wrong side of the world, accept their awards in absentia.

February 5
• The tour moves on to Japan for a sold-out five nights.

February 16
• The annual Brit Awards are held at the Docklands Arena. The Manics take home statues for 'Best British Album' and 'Best British Group', and (having returned from their Pacific tour) perform 'You Stole The Sun From My Heart'.

February 27
• *The Daily Mirror* runs a rather sneery piece about Nicky Wire still living in a modest two-bedroom terrace house in the village of Wattsville in South Wales, despite being a 'millionaire rock star'. Nicky's neighbours are interviewed and talk about him in affectionate, if low-key terms. The piece will later inspire the song 'Wattsville Blues'.

March 2
• The Manics embark on a tour of mainland Europe taking in Sweden, Finland, Denmark, Norway, Switzerland, Belgium, Germany, France, Spain and the Netherlands.

March 8
• *You Stole The Sun From My Heart* (Sony/Epic)
Tracklist:
1. 'You Stole The Sun From My Heart'
2. 'Socialist Serenade'*

3. 'Train In Vain (live)'*
4. 'You Stole The Sun From My Heart (David Holmes' A Joyful Racket Remix)'**
5. 'You Stole The Sun From My Heart (Mogwai Remix)'**
6. 'If You Tolerate This Your Children Will Be Next (live)'***
* CD1 only, ** CD2 only, ***cassette

March 14
• 'You Stole The Sun From My Heart' charts at number 5.

March 23
• The band's new American label, Virgin Records, releases *This Is My Truth, Tell Me Yours* in the US. Virgin president Ray Cooper says the Manics 'could go all the way to the top' (they never do).

April 26
• The band declines an invitation to perform at a concert to mark the opening of the Welsh Assembly, the country's newly-devolved parliament, due to the attendance of the Queen. However, the event does include a performance of Patrick 'Brother-of-Nicky-Wire' Jones' poem, 'The Guerilla Tapestry' set to music scored by James Dean Bradfield.

April 30
• James performs a short acoustic set at Blackwood Miners Institute. It is the first time any of the Manics have performed in their hometown in a decade. The show is organised by Patrick Jones to raise money and awareness for victims of the war in Kosovo.

May 11
• The band gift an unreleased mix of 'She Is Suffering' to a benefit album, *No Boundaries,* raising money for Kosovan war refugees. Ironically, though the mix had been created specifically for the US market (via the indefinitely-postponed American release of *The Holy Bible*) the version of the CD featuring the Manics is only available in Europe.

May 20
• *Melody Maker's* Simon Price, one of the band's biggest champions in the press, publishes his exhaustive Manics biography, *Everything (A Book About Manic Street Preachers).*

May 23
• The Manics play the first of eight European festival headline slots at Germany's Rock Am Ring. Later in the year they will sell t-shirts bearing the legend 'TOO MANY FESTIVALS' on the reverse.

June 13
- The band's forthcoming US tour is cancelled after James' mother becomes seriously ill. It will later transpire that she is battling cancer. She will succumb to the disease later in the year.
- The *NME* runs a piece on the so-called 'Curse of the Manics', pointing out that each time the band attempt to tour America something happens to stop it going ahead properly (Richey's disappearance, Oasis pulling their shows, James' mum's illness).

June 17
- *NME* reports that the band have offered to gift the Football Association of Wales £30,000 in order to hire former England manager Terry Venables to coach the Welsh squad. The Manics also pledge to record the official anthem should Wales ever qualify for the Euros.

June 26
- Manic Street Preachers headline Glastonbury Festival, arguably the most prestigious gig a British band can ever play. Their set is briefly halted due to worries of a crowd crush during 'Yes'. A minor scandal erupts after it is revealed that the band have toilets backstage reserved for their personal use. Protest Pop legend Billy Bragg writes an open letter to the *NME* sniping about the band's hypocrisy. Nicky will later claim the band were 'just as bored with [their performance] as everyone else was', seeing it as something of a nadir for 1999.

July 5
- *Tsunami* (Sony/Epic)
  Tracklisting:
  1. 'Tsunami'
  2. 'Buildings For Dead People'*
  3. 'A Design For Life (video)'*
  4. 'Tsunami (Cornelius Remix)'**
  5. 'Tsunami (Electron Ray Tube Mix)'**
  6. 'Motown Junk (Medley, live)'***
  * CD1 only, ** CD2 only, *** Cassette only
  Formats
  CD1, CD2, Cassette

July 10
- Rumours of a split circulate in the UK press after an appearance at Belgium's Werchter Festival is pulled at the eleventh hour. A spokesperson

for the Manics says the cancellation is due to James straining his voice at the recent Roskilde Festival.

July 11
• The Manics headline Scotland's T In The Park Festival. Nicky dedicates 'Tsunami' to Billy Bragg, saying 'I wouldn't let him piss in my toilet for all the money in the world. Get back to the army, you dickhead, and stop stealing Woody Guthrie's songs.' Nicky indulges in an orgy of destruction at the end of the set, and will claim that he has caused £28,000 of damage (festival organisers will later deny this). He tells the BBC that the band plan to take 'a few years off' from playing live, following a huge New Years Eve show in Cardiff.
• 'Tsunami' charts at number 11.

July 13
• *The Sun* runs another story about the band's potential split, quoting an inside source who claims that there is an ongoing feud within the group and that 'tempers are very frayed'.

July 19
• Patrick Jones releases his debut CD, *Commemoration and Amnesia*, featuring spoken word and poetry over musical backdrops created by the likes of James Dean Bradfield and Super Furry Animal's Gruff Rhys.

August 21/22
• The Manics headline their third major British festival of the Summer, V99, held at two locations in Chelmsford and Staffordshire. They premier their first new material in over a year, a punky tune called 'The Masses Against The Classes'. In comparison to Glastonbury, where some felt the band were going through the motions, the set at V99 is energetic and spiky, and Nicky once again indulges his destructive urges at the climax. The band will head into Rockfield studios shortly afterwards to record the new song.

September 11
• The delayed North American tour gets underway in Toronto. In the end the Manics will play just eleven shows in the US and Canada in 1999.

September 14
• A show at New York's Bowery Ballroom is cancelled, with fans informed 15 minutes after the band are due to take the stage that James Dean Bradfield has contracted laryngitis.

September 15
- The next night's show at Boston's Paradise Rock Club, is also cancelled after a storm prevents James from flying out from New York where he has been seeing a doctor about his illness.

September 16
- Tom Jones' latest record, *Reload,* is released in the UK. It features a duet with James Dean Bradfield on a cover of Elvis Presley's 'I'm Left, You're Right, She's Gone'.

September 17
- The US tour gets back underway at St Andrew's Hall, Detroit. The remaining eight shows go ahead without incident.

September 28/29
- The band's US tour culminates in two sold-out nights at LA's Troubadour.

October 1
- Nicky tells *Rock Sound* that he doesn't feel 'there is much longer left in us', and that the plans they have for their sixth album might be 'a good way to go out'.

October 5
- The Manics hold a press conference in Cardiff to announce details of their New Years Eve show, 'The Manic Millennium'. The event will take place at the Millenium Stadium, the gigantic home of Welsh Rugby that had opened earlier that same year. Tickets will be kept at an affordable £30, and the band claim they'd need to sell out the show just to break even. Nicky also says that their second set of the night, which will begin after midnight, will be their only performance of 2000. They announce a new single; 'Masses Against The Classes', due for release in January.
- James pours cold water on rumours that they plan to split up soon, however does stress that their next album might be their last. James says he 'can't see himself being in a band at 40', while Nicky notes that his passport is due to run out in 2002 'and I don't intend to renew it'. They hint strongly that their sixth album would be followed by a greatest hits package, potentially called 'Forever Delayed', which would draw a line under their career.

October 16
- *NME* ruffles feathers by running a report of the Manic Millennium press conference under the headline 'MANICS TO SPLIT'.

November
- Sessions for the sixth Manics album begin at Valley Studios, Monmouthshire. The band hopes to channel the energy they have tapped with 'Masses Against The Classes', into their new record.

November 30
- The Manics announce that all 54,000 tickets for the Manic Millenium have sold out, and that they are looking to expand the capacity of the venue by a further 6,000. Supports for the show are announced as Patrick Jones, Shack, Feeder and Super Furry Animals.

December 1
- Nicky tells *Select* magazine that the band now have five songs for their next album, including one about the American singer Paul Robeson, and another titled 'Pedestal'.

December 31
- The sold-out Millenium Stadium plays host to 60,000 Manic Street Preachers fans as the band play the biggest show of their career. The Manics play two sets, one leading up to midnight and one after, leaving the audience room to ring in the new century themselves. Both the opening 'You Stole The Sun From My Heart' and closing 'A Design For Life' are broadcast live on BBC One. The show is widely considered a triumph, receiving rave reviews. It is filmed for a planned DVD/VHS release.

2000

January 10
- *Masses Against The Classes* (Sony/Epic)
  Tracklisting:
  1. 'Masses Against The Classes'
  2. 'Close My Eyes'
  3. 'Rock 'N' Roll Music'
  Formats
  CD, 10" vinyl (numbered, limited to 10,000)
- 'Masses Against The Classes' is deleted on the day of release, meaning Sony will not press any more records or CDs when present stock has sold out. This has the planned effect of making fans rush out to buy their copy before the chance to get it disappears forever.

January 16
- 'Masses Against The Classes' tops the UK chart with 35,000 sales, becoming the band's second number one, and the first number one of the new decade.

February 1
- The fifth anniversary of Richey's disappearance prompts a raft of stories in the press raking over the still-unsolved mystery of his final known days.

February 20
- Sherry Edwards, Richey's mother, writes a heartbreaking open letter, published in the *Sunday Mirror*, urging her son to make contact. It concludes 'you are my precious son and I will never give up looking for you. All my love as always, Mum.'

May
- The band are once more working at Rockfield with Dave Eringa on the new album. They hope to release two albums simultaneously with very different feels.

June 1
- One-time Manics lead singer Jenny Watkins-Isnardi publishes a memoir about her time in the band, entitled *In The Beginning, My Life With the Manic Street Preachers*. The book is serialised across five days in the *Daily Mirror*.

July 3
- *Leaving The Twentieth Century*, the film of the Manic Millennium show, is released on VHS and, in a first for the band, DVD.

September
- The band have decamped to Spain's El Cortijo studios, built into a villa near Seville and Granada, to continue work on the album. Mixing and additional recording will take place at Abbey Road in London before the end of the year.

November 8
- *NME* prints a story speculating that the new Manics album would be called *Give Em Enough Rope*, lifting the title wholesale from the second Clash album. A spokesperson for the band refuses to confirm or deny the story.

November 12
- David Holmes gives an interview to *NME* in which he says he has been working with the Manics on three songs for potential inclusion on the new record. He describes their new material as 'the best Manics stuff I've heard'.

November 30
- 'Beautiful Mistake', a documentary about the Welsh music scene, is released. It features James performing a solo version of 'Ready for Drowning'.
- James tells *Melody Maker* that the band have recorded around 30 songs for the album and are in the process of mixing them, with three left to go. He firmly denies that the record will be called 'Give Em Enough Rope'.

December 18
- The band announce that their new album will be titled *Know Your Enemy* ('the enemy is what we've let ourselves become', says Nicky), and will be launched with a gig at the Karl Marx Theatre in Havana, Cuba, on February 21. They will be the first mainstream western rock band to play in the county.

December 21
- Rumours spread that Fidel Castro, Cuba's revolutionary leader, will attend the Havana concert.

2001

January 9
- *NME* reveals that the Manics plan to make chart history for a major band by releasing two singles simultaneously, 'So Why So Sad' and 'Found That Soul'. Plans to release two albums in the same way have been rejected by the band's record company, forcing them to combine the releases and whittle them down to a single LP's worth.

January 22
- The premier of the new Manic Street Preachers single, 'So Why So Sad', is held on *NME's* website. A short clip of the companion single, 'Found That Soul', is hosted on the band's official site, *manics.co.uk*

February 9
- Some tracks from the new album are leaked after a hack of Sony's website, and are shared on Napster. Sony threatens any fans downloading the songs

with legal action and pressures Napster to ban anyone using the service to access unreleased Manics material. The band distance themselves from the row, issuing a statement via a spokesperson saying they don't agree with punishing fans for downloading.

February 10
- The Manics appear live on Saturday morning show *CD:UK*, where they play a boisterous version of 'Found That Soul'. An online rumour spreads saying the band warmed up for the performance by delighting the teenybopper crowd with a rendition of 1993's blasphemous heavy metal b-side 'Patrick Bateman'.

February 14
- James, Sean and Nicky arrive in Cuba ahead of their show, and spend the next few days filming for a Channel 4 documentary and talking to the media – who have arrived in droves from the UK and the local foreign press. Over 70 tickets for the coming gig are given to the media.

February 17
- Shortly before the show the band is introduced to Cuban leader Fidel Castro, the now 74-year-old revolutionary who has ruled the country for almost half a century. Casto says he will attend the show if the band can start a little earlier, and is warned by Wire that 'it might be a bit noisy'. Fidel, always the iconoclast, replies 'it cannot be louder than war'.
- The show at the Karl Marx theatre is considered by the band to be one of the highlights of their career. A 5,000 strong audience of local rock fans, most of whom have no idea who the band actually are, headbang and dance their way through a Manics greatest hits, plus several new songs. At Castro's request James plays a hastily arranged acoustic version of a new song, 'Baby Elian', about a Cuban child abducted by An American family. They receive a standing ovation from Castro himself.

February 18
- Having been impressed the previous night, Castro and the Cuban Ministry for Culture arrange for various photo opportunities over the next few days, delaying the band's return to the UK. Later the Manics will say they felt like they were trapped in the country's propaganda machine.

February 26
- *Found That Soul* (Sony/Epic)
  Tracklisting:
  1. 'Found That Soul'
  2. 'Locust Valley'*

3. 'The Ballad Of the Bangkok Novotel'*
4. 'Masses Against The Classes (live)'**
* CD only, ** 7" only
Formats:
CD, 7"
Notes:
'The Ballad of the Bangkok Novotel' is the first ever Manics release to feature lead vocals by Nicky Wire.

• *So Why So Sad* Sony/Epic)
Tracklisting:
1. 'So Why So Sad'
2. 'So Why So Sad (Sean Penn Mix)' - The Avalanches*
3. Pedestal*
4. 'You Stole The Sun From My Heart (live)'**
* CD only, ** cassette only
Formats:
CD, cassette

March 2
• The band play a small show for Danish television, their first European gig in over a year.

March 4
• 'So Why So Sad' and 'Found That Soul' chart at eight and nine respectively. There is some speculation that the double release was an attempt to sabotage their ability to have a hit, signalling a rejection of their previous mass appeal and the pressures it brings.

March 8
• The band plays a tiny warm up at Cardiff Coal Exchange, broadcast live on Radio 1.

March 9
• The Manics appear on *Top of the Pops* and are granted the extremely rare honour of playing both of their current singles on the same show.

March 11
• Despite the exposure from the double *TOTP* appearance, 'So Why So Sad' drops to number 25 in the charts, and 'Found That Soul' just clings onto the top 40 at 35.

March 16
- The *Daily Mirror* runs an interview with Nicky in which they accuse the band of being 'intent on career suicide' following their unconventional double release, uncompromising new songs and trip to Cuba.

March 19
- *Know Your Enemy* (Sony/Epic)
  Tracklisting:
  1. 'Found That Soul'
  2. 'Ocean Spray'
  3. 'Intravenous Agnostic'
  4. 'So Why So Sad'
  5. 'Let Robeson Sing'
  6. 'The Year of Purification'
  7. 'Wattsville Blues'
  8. 'Miss Europa Disco Dancer'
  9. 'Dead Martyrs'
  10. 'His Last Painting'
  11. 'My Guernica'
  12. 'The Convalescent'
  13. 'Royal Correspondent'
  14. 'Epicentre'
  15. 'Baby Elian'
  16. 'Freedom of Speech Won't Feed My Children'
  17. 'We Are All Bourgeois Now' (unlisted)
  Formats:
  CD, cassette, 12″ vinyl, minidisc

Know Your Enemy

By Andrzej Lukowski

'The enemy here was themselves.'

Hello it's us again

As the millennium approached, a lot of people really wanted the Manic Street Preachers to make a rock record.

Strictly speaking, most of the million or so Brits who'd bought each of their last two albums would probably have been perfectly happy with more of the same, but to the band's sizeable hardcore of devotees – not to mention their champions in the press – the sober, sports casual-clad arena rock trio of the second half of the nineties was fundamentally indivisible from the provocative, preposterous, eventually-tragic punk quartet from the first. And the earlier band was more interesting.

Mega-selling fifth album *This Is My Truth, Tell Me Yours* had gently declined in favour since its release, and the band's credibility had taken a dive over an (in retrospect truly baffling) scandal over a private portaloo at Glastonbury[23]. It's not like there was serious ill will towards the superstar incarnation of the Manics, but a palpable sense of ennui had set in over the project, as amusingly manifested in a '99 tour t-shirt bearing the legend 'too many festivals'. Could they ever channel that old fire again?

Yes! Scabrous, self-referential non-album single 'The Masses Against The Classes' was the hardest thing they'd done since *The Holy Bible* and gave the band the first UK number one of the twenty-first century. It was one of the heaviest British chart-toppers ever, like The Stooges doing something

---

23. In order to avoid Glastonbury's infamous facilities which, according to an unknown wag quoted by The Guardian at the time, were 'the essential shared trauma that unites the megastars with the fans in the mosh-pit', the band had arranged their own private facilities as befitted their status as headliners. A sign on the door warned that they were for the exclusive use of the Manics only. Agit-folk legend and cheeky scamp Billy Bragg took a photo, and the press had a field day; teasing the avowed socialists for their elitism. At the time it was dubbed 'Toiletgate', presumably because no-one had thought of "The Portaloo Massacre". - MB

unmentionable to the Isley Brothers' 'Twist N Shout.' It also exhibited a sassiness missing from their oeuvre since probably the *Generation Terrorists* days: 'success is an ugly word, especially in your tiny world' sneered James Dean Bradfield, laying into what we would probably now call 'the haters'.

Rebuking those who'd lost faith while, crucially, *giving them exactly what they wanted*, it was a laser-guided missile of a song, proof the Manics could still tap into the band they'd once been while also retaining their commercial clout, telling wavering fans to go fuck themselves while also taking their money. If it had been their final release, it would have been a pretty perfect way to end things. Released just a few days after their sellout NYE enormogig at Cardiff's Millennium Stadium, it neatly wrapped up the second act of their career. They'd shown they could still rock. They'd shown they could still provoke. Now they were free to do something different.

It was a mixed blessing.

Went to Cuba to meet Castro

Not many people got to hear the Manic Street Preachers perform the ramshackle Nicky Wire-sung album track 'Wattsville Blues' live: it was only ever played six times.

One of those people was me! A second-year-student at Leeds University, I made the trip to see the band at the Manchester Apollo in March 2001.

Another was Fidel Castro: President of Cuba, a perennial thorn in the side of the US, Che Guevara's BFF, twentieth-century Marxist icon. He saw it at a different gig.

That the Manic Street Preachers played a show at Teatro Karl Marx in Havana on February 17 2001 – the first by a Western rock band – in front of one of the most notorious political leaders of the twentieth century has gone on to be a central plank of their legend, one of the strangest bits of their story, and uniquely adrift from the rest of their legacy. To put it another way: it has nothing to do with Richey, but it doesn't feel like it has much to do with anything else they did either.

In summary, the Manic Street Preachers, a band with barely any profile outside of the UK, who have never played another gig in Latin America before or since, whose splenetic early rhetoric belied the fact they were not given to extravagant rockstar gestures, and whose socialism was always heavily spiked with cynicism, decided to stage a gig halfway across the world to an audience that had never heard any of their music – broadly speaking out of a sense of socialist solidarity. Also, the actual Fidel Castro turned up, with his quip that the gig would be 'louder than war' giving the band a bona fide new slogan.

As I recall – and this seems corroborated by re-reading contemporary accounts from the various UK journalists who tagged along – it didn't seem like a *particularly* outrageous gesture at the time. The band's fanbase was young-ish and British, born years after the Cuban Missile Crisis and decades after the Cuban Revolution. Unlike Americans, Brits were free to visit Cuba. It was pre-9/11. It was not a concert *for* Castro, he just came along, and remember this was '00s Castro, an elderly head of state who hadn't done anything controversial in eons. Moreover, although it was apparent that socialism was a through thread, the fact is the Manics' politics had always felt somewhat opaque, and secondary to their interest in the human condition: they were never ideologues, and there was no sense that the trip was an attempt to preach to us about the joy of Marx.

What were they actually doing there? The band had presented the trip relatively humbly: several of the songs on *Know Your Enemy* referenced Cuba (as did the artwork to 'The Masses Against The Classes'), and they'd asked socialist MP Peter Hain if he might be able to arrange for them to play the country, which he did, and so they went. That doesn't feel like much of an explanation though: one does not simply play a gig in Cuba.

Perhaps the most fascinating thing about rewatching the accompanying C4 documentary *Our Manics in Havana* is the note of elegy, the idea that this was intended as one last great adventure for the band before they called it quits. The trip came almost precisely a decade after the release of 'Motown Junk': it had been an astonishingly tumultuous, incredibly prolific decade, full of traumas and triumphs that the band had barely stopped to process. But here both Bradfield and Nicky Wire seemed to be strongly suggesting that the Manics were winding down: Bradfield's view in the documentary is that the trip to Havana was a possibly ill-advised idea that was important to do, lest the band's final years see them stagnate ('People who say we spent the latter half of our career coasting, we can tell them we didn't' quoth he, 20 years ago); Wire meanwhile, seems to find a romantic kinship between the band and communist Cuba – he sees both as unfashionable, stubborn and living on beyond their time.

Did they give tacit support to a repressive regime? Probably, in a small way: they themselves commented that they were 'used' by the regime. There is no doubt watching the documentary that they were awed by Castro. The accompanying UK press corps asked some fair questions about Cuban human rights abuses which Wire, largely, grumpily, batted away by saying variants on 'yeah, we know all that' – it feels like a cop-out, but one suspects that he was holding his tongue somewhat about his belief that the West was as bad if not worse (it's not hard to extrapolate this given it's literally the subject matter of two of the songs played at the show, 'Baby Elian' and 'Freedom of Speech Won't Feed My Children').

Two decades on, though, and it's hard to see their meeting with the President as liable to affect how history judges him. And indeed, much as the band felt a kinship with ornery, out-of-time Cuba, their presence was surely part of its erosion. Castro had once banned and persecuted rock musicians – now he was welcoming back an act deemed ideologically appropriate. It was the thin end of the wedge, and just a few months before his death, in 2016, notorious non-socialists The Rolling Stones played their own Havana show – an event on some level enabled by the Manics' trip 15 years previously.

I think what ultimately springs out when reconsidering the Havana show is the strangeness of this most hermetically sealed of bands chaining themselves to any mythology beyond their own. Clearly, the story of global communism was vastly more significant and sweeping than their own (of course engrossing) tale, and it's surreal that they essentially cashed in their rockstar chips to hang out with Fidel Castro, to be the first Western rock band to play Cuba, to allow themselves to be part of another story, to be awed and uncynical about something. Maybe there were naive and ill-advised things about it, but as a gesture it remains pure: it's hard to look at the young men in the old documentary and say there was anything cynical or manipulative or malign about their actions. They never did set fire to themselves on *Top of the Pops*. But you sense that they were running from their success and their legend here, and they did finish the first, most vital phase of their career with a concert that wouldn't be forgotten in a hurry.

'It's definitely a victory,' comments Bradfield of the trip, 'but it's a close-run thing'.

Ba-ba-ba ba-ba-ba

I used to be fascinated by the record charts in Woolworths. The charts went up on Monday, and featured that week's releases, meaning that they weren't based upon sales figures, but presumably somebody or other at Woolies – which was sort of like a very big chain of very small department stores – was employed to take an educated guess at where the singles and albums would end up charting in the official top 40, which didn't come out till Sunday.

As I, for whatever reason, recall; the two, simultaneously-released advanced singles from *Know Your Enemy* – that's 'So Why So Sad' and 'Found That Soul' – were predicted to chart at two and three. Woolworths still reckoned them to be the biggest band in the country.

Why release two singles at the same time? Back then it seemed like a mix of rockstar brio, slightly playful gesture, and prosaic attempt to showcase two sides of a diverse record. Looking back, though, and I wonder if it wasn't more perverse than that; if not actively an act self-sabotage, it was certainly willfully flirting with risk for a band who'd previously chosen their singles carefully and successfully

'Found That Soul', with its pummeling guitar line, snarled lyrics about finding beauty at rock bottom and the wittily lo-fi video was in some sense a continuation of the back-to-basics mission of 'The Masses Against The Classes'. It had some echoes of the staccato assault of *The Holy Bible*'s heavier numbers, but with some more of that fuzzy, sexy Stooges swagger their recent chart-topped had had. Despite sounding far more quintessentially Manics than 'So Why So Sad', the general view was that 'Found That Soul' was the willfully difficult single, a wink to fans of the heavier records and a nod to the parent album's diversity, deliberately paired with a surefire hit. Fair enough: it's hardly what you call radio-friendly. But was it really the 'difficult' song?

'So Why So Sad' was viewed as the *real* comeback single, because it had an expensive video (it's the one where there's a war happening on a beach), far more radio play and was nominally more musically commercial. In fact, it seems blindingly obvious in retrospect that it was the weirdest single of the band's career, a sardonic, dreamily paced Beach Boys pastiche about faking happiness that sounded nothing like the music that had made the band popular, and nothing that was popular at the time. I know people who essentially view this song as the main reason for the band's decline in popularity, and maybe they're right: there are other tracks on *Know Your Enemy* that might have become bigger hits if they'd received the kind of push 'So Why So Sad' did.

Anyway. The songs came in at eight and nine, which was fine-ish, but short of Woolworths' expectations. With barely 200 sales separating them, it seemed fairly obvious that it was essentially the base buying both singles, and that 'So Why So Sad' had not, in any way, crossed over. But did the Manics seriously expect it to? Perhaps – after all, everybody else did. But looking back at it now, it's difficult not to conclude that the Manics prefaced their sixth album with not one difficult single, but two, released in a way that seemed guaranteed to provide maximum confusion. Certainly, that was nothing if not an accurate foretaste of the album.

What a mess

Although nine songs from *Know Your Enemy* featured at the Havana show – as many as they ever played on a given night – it's notable that *Our Manics In Havana* didn't heavily plug the new album, or even dwell on it at all, really. The band seemed convinced they were running out of time, but it's not immediately clear exactly why. Maybe they were feeling tired or fatalistic or just being self-deprecating? Or perhaps they were just pretty certain that *Know Your Enemy* was very, very unlikely to be another hit.

Let's be clear: *Know Your Enemy* is a mess. Not a disaster. But a mess. You can still look back on it fondly and note that many of the songs are criminally underrated. But it is a confusingly eclectic slog that makes even *Generation Terrorists* look like a model of formal restraint. A more positive way of looking at it: it's a great B-sides album, where the band and a small army of producers and engineers nail at least a dozen new styles. But it doesn't feel like all 17 of them were intended to be listened to in sequence, over and over again.

It is all over the shop. Perhaps the one musical style that could be reasonably expected from a guitar trio that's *not* present on *Know Your Enemy* is stately, bombastic AOR a la their previous two records. Other than that it's pretty must a free-for-all: Stooges proto-punk, gaudy Beach Boys-aping wall of sound, rasping lo-fi a la *Blur*-era Blur, disco, blipped-up techno-rock, screeching Sonic Youth guitar workout, early-R.E.M.-style jangle-pop ... the eclecticism is both impressive and exhausting as they try to sound like everything except themselves.

It starts brightly: the opening roar of 'Found That Soul', followed by the delicate, Bradfield-penned lament 'Ocean Spray', the electrifying *Daydream Nation*-alike 'Intravenous Agnostic', the surf-pop strangeness of 'So Why So Sad', the mature, wistful folk ballad 'Let Robeson Sing' and the gorgeous jangle-pop of 'The Year of Purification' is quite the rush. It could have got us most of the way through a ten-track-record or formed an absolutely terrific EP or mini-album.

If it had, we'd think of *Know Your Enemy* differently. Those six songs show a band growing up and broadening their palette in a deft, dexterous and frequently gorgeous fashion. They do heavy again, thrillingly – 'Intravenous Agnostic' is new territory, but *loud* new territory – while moving the wiser, more open-hearted spirit of their two big records forward in agreeably non-bombastic fashion.

But then there are 11 more songs. I like 'Wattsville Blues', the swampy, lo-fi, Wire-sung track, and I hope Castro did too: it's a strangely moving little gem of a genre experiment, a throbbingly abrasive paeon to staying at home and being boring with a beautiful interplay between Wire's untutored growl and a soaring, heavenly Bradfield. It's not, however, an easy segue from the soaring 'Year of Purification', and it's not an easy segue onwards to the glistening ersatz disco of 'Miss Europa Disco Dancer', and so on and so

Nicky Wire during the Generation Terrorists tour, The Roadmenders, Northampton, 1992. (*Photo: Lindsay Taylor-Fullman*)

Richey Edwards, James Dean Bradfield and Nicky Wire onstage during the Generation Terrorists Tour, Roadmenders, Northampton, 1992. (*Photo: Lindsay Taylor-Fullman*)

James Dean Bradfield onstage in Japan circa 1992. (*Photo: Masao Nakagami, Wikimedia Commons*)

Sean Moore, Richey Edwards, Nicky Wire and James Dean Bradfield backstage at the Reading Festival, 1992. (*Photo: IMAGO/Future Image*)

Finally in the biggest band in Britain, Nicky breaks out the animal prints at the NEC, Birmingham during 1998's December tour. (*Photo: Lindsay Taylor-Fullman*)

Nicky Wire "leaving the 20th Century" on stage at Millennium Stadium, Cardiff, New Years Eve 1999. (*Photo: Lindsay Taylor-Fullman*)

Fans resplendent in leopard print queue for a show at Manchester Apollo on 2001's Know Your Enemy tour. (*Photo: Emily Hyatt*)

James Dean Bradfield onstage at the Point Theatre, Dublin, Ireland, Dec 1 2002. (*Photo: Roger Woolman, Wikimedia Commons*)

Nicky Wire resplendent in khaki on stage at the Move Festival, Manchester, 2003. (*Photo: Lindsay Taylor-Fullman*)

A smiling Nicky Wire during the band's headline set at the 2004 Isle of Wight Festival, premiering songs from Lifeblood. (*Photo: Lindsay Taylor-Fullman*)

A miniskirted Wire onstage in Preston in 2007. (*Photo: Lindsay Taylor-Fullman*)

Nicky on stage in 2007 touring Send Away The Tigers. (*Photo: Lindsay Taylor-Fullman*)

Nicky displays some messages from the crowd in 2009. (*Photo: Lindsay Taylor-Fullman*)

Sean Moore in Melbourne during 2010'a Australian tour. (*Photo: Andrew Briscoe [East13 Photography]*)

Nicky Wire performs outdoors in Melbourne during 2010's Australian tour. (*Photo: Andrew Briscoe* (*East13 Photography*))

Nicky Wire onstage at the Õllesummeril Festival, Tallinn, Estonia. (*Photo: Ren Hekkons, Wikimedia Commons*)

James Dean Bradfield and Marc Burrows at the Classic Rock Awards, London, 2013. (*Photo: Marc Burrows, personal collection*)

James Dean Bradfield and Sean Moore onstage during one of the 2014 Holy Bible shows at the Roundhouse, London. (*Photo: Drew de F Fawkes, Wikimedia Commons*)

James Dean Bradfield in Cardiff, during the Brickstock event in 2016. (*Photo: Emily Hyatt*)

An airborne JDB at Chris Evans' Carfest event, 2017. (*Photo: Emily Hyatt*)

L-R Sean, Nicky and James on the red carpet for the 2017 Q Awards in London. (*Photo: Emily Hyatt*)

The never knowingly under-leoparded Catherine Anne Davies, AKA The Anchoress, on the red carpet at the 2017 Q awards, shortly before dueting with the band on 'Little Baby Nothing'. (*Photo: Emily Hyatt*)

James belts out 'Your Love Alone Is Not Enough' on the Resistance is Futile tour, Leeds, 2018. (*Photo: Greg Hildreth*)

James Dean Bradfield in Birmingham on the Resistance Is Futile Tour. (*Photo: Emily Hyatt*)

Manics fan Emily Hyatt and friends grab setlists from a show in Newcastle during the Resistance Is Futile tour. (*Photo: Emily Hyatt*)

James Dean Bradfield pictured outside the BBC's Broadcasting House in London, prior to performing on the One Show in 2018. (*Photo: Emily Hyatt*)

The band take part in a Q&A with fans at London's Rough Trade East record store around the release of Resistance Is Futile in 2018. (*Photo: Emily Hyatt*)

In full flight at London's Shepherd's Bush Empire in 2019. (*Photo: Emily Hyatt*)

A thumbs up from Nicky Wire onstage at Cambridge Corn Exchange, 2019. (*Photo: Lindsay Taylor-Fullman*)

forth, through the David Holmes produced techno-rock of 'Dead Souls', the restrained, moody folk-rock of 'His Last Painting', the fuzzed-out cosmic grunge of 'My Guernica', six-minute indie rocker of 'The Convalescent', the raw, Kinks-gone-to-the-dark-side character sketch of 'Royal Correspondent', the long, anthemic, E Street Band-esque 'Epicentre', the fizzing acoustic polemic of 'Baby Elian', the bizarre hard rock vaudeville of 'Freedom of Speech Won't Feed My Children'... and then a radiant, glistening hidden cover of an obscure McCarthy B-side, 'We Are All Bourgeois Now'.

The songs have real merits... but they just don't go together, don't give each other room to breathe, and aren't helped by busy production from a sprawling engineering team. There is a thrill to the constant breaking of new sonic ground, but the dazzle becomes tiring, like watching a firework display for 12 hours straight. It's the band's most international album, and the one with the highest number of political songs, but it's not Wire at his peak, lyrically, and the simpler stuff hits home harder: 'Let Robeson Sing''s simple, heartfelt tribute to US activist Paul Robeson is infinitely more affecting than the fiddly 'Baby Elian' and 'Freedom of Speech...', both desperately crying out for the uncluttered anthemicism of earlier records. Bradfield's lament for his mother, 'Ocean Spray', has an articulacy and directness that goes beyond Wire's more oblique, impressionistic writing.

In a sense, the most damning thing about *Know Your Enemy* is how good the McCarthy cover sounds 17 songs in; its shimmeringly melodic guitar lines are free of the sonic fuss of the tracks that proceed them, and I feel myself lifting out of the murk every time it kicks in. Malcolm Eden's brutally ironic lyric about the end of class conflict in Thatcherite Britain is magnificent, the sort of perfect narrative pop song that was never in the Manics' gift.

And yet. And yet. Those first six songs are sublime. I could listen to the beautifully melancholic squalls of sound on 'Intravenous Agnostic' all day, that howling lightning. Even when it goes off-piste it does so bravely and passionately. Like Castro's Cuba, it's perhaps sometimes a better thought than practical reality. But it represents a moment of genuine liberation for the band: from the shackles of their success, but also from the myth of Ritchey. The band's enemy here was themselves. They declared war. They won. And lost.

So go out and make your way in the world
After Cuba, the band played an 11-date tour of mid-size venues in Britain, Germany and Spain. When I saw them in Manchester, they seemed to be

having a ball hamming up the likes of 'Miss Europa' and 'Wattsville Blues', but even then they only managed seven of the album's 17 songs.

They played some summer festivals, with even fewer *Know Your Enemy* songs.

An autumn arena tour was announced and then didn't happen, for reasons never quite explained.

Know Your Enemy did not sell well, or, at least, it sold in line with the band's first three records, not their last two.

Instead of the *Know Your Enemy* arena tour, the Manics headed back into the studio and cut a couple of new songs for *Forever Delayed*, the big-selling 2002 greatest hits album that did come with an extensive arena and international tour, on which they would typically play a single song a night from *Know Your Enemy*, usually 'Ocean Spray'.

Like I said, I remember the band having fun with the more outré songs they played in Manchester, but that impression of *Know Your Enemy* as soggy and difficult is reinforced by the fact that so little of it has even been attempted in concert: at one point there is a run of six consecutive songs – 'Dead Martyrs', 'His Last Painting', 'My Guernica', 'The Convalescent', 'Royal Correspondent', 'Epicentre' – that have in live totality been represented by three acoustic performances of 'Royal Correspondent'. And that strangely shortened. The gems have been buried as well: 'The Year of Purification' only got six outings (at least Castro got to see it), 'Intravenous Agnostic' was attempted just once (August 20 2001, Llandudno, Wales, as a warm-up for headlining Reading and Leeds festivals, fact fans!), and 'We Are All Bourgeois Now,' never.

In a sense, it's difficult to see how it could have gone differently: the Manics have always been outspoken about the importance of playing the hits, and by 2001 they had an awful lot of hits to play. A 17-track album was never going to get a full airing, and many of the songs left unplayed were tricky for a three-piece to tackle live. Released into the wild, *Know Your Enemy* was just too damn awkward to live.

I got nothing to lose now baby

The band swiftly moved on: if the Manics never exactly threw *Know Your Enemy* under the bus, they remained standoffish about it in the years after, with it and follow-up *Lifeblood* the black sheep of their back catalogue, sandwiched awkwardly between their defining first decade and their successful reinvention as elder statesmen.

The Manics have reissued a number of their records, but in a strange, erratic order that seems largely based upon their personal fondness for them.

It looked like *Know Your Enemy* had been overlooked, with the reissues having skipped ahead to 2007's *Send Away the Tigers*. But somewhat surprisingly, the last word at the time of writing was a 2020 *NME* interview, in which Wire said that *Know Your Enemy* would receive a twentieth-anniversary reissue in 2021, possibly radically reformatted into two separate albums, with the addition of unused material from the sessions. (NB you have to imagine Wire meant a double album, as re-releasing it as two separate single albums would be preposterous).

The idea that *Know Your Enemy* was conceived as two shorter records had first been floated in interviews around the band's 2013/14 sister albums *Rewind the Film* and *Futurology*. It should probably be taken with a pinch of salt: the band never said anything about it at the time and would surely have been allowed to by a record label who'd clearly let them do everything else they wanted to.

Reissuing it as a double album is an idea that could go either way: with the best will in the world, I'm not sure *adding* tracks is the answer to this album. What's exciting, though, is the simple fact that its creators are reengaging with it. *Know Your Enemy* was a mad, fizzling folly that burned out quickly, leaving little imprint, overshadowed in our cultural memory by the gig that launched it. It is entirely understandable why this happened, but it means that there are some wonderful songs that have lain sealed away for two decades or more, barely acknowledged. Maybe even the boldest reissue won't change much in terms of public perception, but to a band for whom history is everything, it feels important that they welcome these wayward oddities home from a long exile.

Know Your Enemy was the album on which the Manic Street Preachers dared to try and be somebody else. It didn't really work. It was broken. But it was magical too.

Part Seven

2001–2003

2001 (continued)

March 25
- *Know Your Enemy* enters the album chart at number two. The following week it will drop down to six. Within a month it will have dropped out of the Top 40. To date, two decades on, *Know Your Enemy* has sold half a million copies; less than either of its two predecessors sold in a single year.

March 23
- The *Know Your Enemy* UK tour begins. Rather than the expected slog around the country's arenas, the band opt to play two night stands in three large theatres: Manchester Apollo, London's Brixton Academy and Glasgow Barrowlands, followed by a handful of dates in Spain, France, Germany and Ireland. Support in the UK comes from My Vitriol.

March 31
- A 20ft mural in Cardiff city-centre painted by *Know Your Enemy* cover artist Neale Howells to celebrate the release of the album is torn down by city officials after complaints that the piece, which includes swearing and stylised penises, is offensive.

June 1
- A trek around Europe's summer festivals starts at Germany's Rock Am Ring. The band will play sixteen festivals across the 2001 season, making it one of their busiest summers ever.

June 4
- *Ocean Spray* (Sony/Epic)
  Tracklisting:
  1. 'Ocean Spray'
  2. 'Groundhog Day'*
  3. 'Just A Kid'*
  4. 'Ocean Spray (video)'*
  5. 'Ocean Spray (live)'**
  6. 'Ocean Spray (Kinobe Remix)'**
  7. 'Ocean Spray (Medicine Remix)'**
  8. 'Ocean Spray (live video)'**
  9. 'Little Trolls'***
  10. 'Ocean Spray (Ellis Island Sound Remix)'***
  * CD1 only, ** CD2 only,***Cassette only

Formats:
Enhanced CD1, enhanced CD2, cassette
Notes:
The first Manics song since their very early days to feature lyrics written solely by James Dean Bradfield, who penned the words about his mother's final days.

June 10
• 'Ocean Spray' charts at number 15

July 27
• The Manics play outside of Europe for the second and final time of 2001, performing at the FujiRock Festival in Japan.

August 25/26
• The band return to the Reading Festival, which has now been rebranded 'The Carling Weekend', with an extra event in Leeds bolted on for good measure. The Manics' headline set is introduced by a video of "Karl Marx".

September 4
• *Let Robeson Sing* (Sony/Epic)
  Tracklisting:
  1. 'Let Robeson Sing'
  2. 'Masking Tape'*
  3. 'Didn't My Lord Deliver Daniel'*
  4. 'Let Robeson Sing (video)'*
  5. 'Let Robeson Sing (Ian Brown Mix)'**°
  6. 'Let Robeson Sing (Felix Da Housecat Mix)'**°
  7. 'Let Robeson Sing (live)'**
  8. 'Let Robeson Sing (live video)'**
  9. 'Fear of Motion'***
  * CD1 only, ** CD2 only, *** 12" only, **°CD2 and 12"
  Formats
  Enhanced CD1, enhanced CD2, 12"

September 16
• 'Let Robeson Sing' charts at number 19.

September 21
• A tour of UK and European arenas, including two-night stands at Wembley and Manchester, is cancelled without explanation. Some fans and journalists suggest that Nicky Wire's fear of flying has been stoked

by the September 11 attacks in New York, though that wouldn't explain the band's reluctance to tour the UK, which could be done by bus. The Manics won't perform again for almost a year.

September 24
- *Louder Than War*, the concert film and documentary covering February's trip to Cuba, is released on VHS and DVD.

October 2
- *NME* reports that Nicky Wire has donated a large amount of signed Manics merch to an online auction to raise money to stop the closure of a local animal shelter. Nicky's Mum, Irene, tells the magazine that she suspects her son privately donates money to animal organisations 'all the time'.

November 2001
- *Q* readers award the Manics 'Best Live Act' of 2001. In the accompanying interview Nicky admits to feeling dejected by the lukewarm reaction to *Know Your Enemy* and the hostility the band's trip to Cuba generated. He also says they are currently assembling a Greatest Hits package.

2002

January 22
- As the seventh anniversary of Richey's disappearance approaches, *NME* claims that the Edwards family are not planning to have their son declared dead. A police officer involved in the case is quoted as saying it was relatively unusual for a family to declare a missing person dead at the seven year mark; the earliest point it is legally permissible to do so. The piece carries no official comment.

February 1
- On the anniversary of the disappearance, the *Daily Mirror* interviews Graham and Sherry Edwards, who confirm that they intend to keep Richey's case open, saying they are more interested in finding their son than accessing the estimated £1.5 million in royalties accumulating in a trust fund for him.
- The band are currently in Monnow Valley studio recording new material and b-sides for their forthcoming greatest hits. Songs worked on include 'There By The Grace Of God', 'Automatik Technicolour', 'It's All Gone', 'Happy Ending' and '4 Ever Delayed'.

Late February
- Sean's daughter, Matilda Poppy, the first Manic baby, is born. Later in the year Nicky's daughter, Clara Enola Jones, will follow.

March 26
- The remains of a human foot are discovered in the River Severn leading to speculation that it could be part of Richey's remains, fuelled by the fact the unknown man was wearing size 8 trainers – Richey's size. His sister, Rachel, expresses her doubts (as do many Manics fans, well aware that their hero would be unlikely to be seen in Diadora trainers), but this doesn't stop a brief flurry of press interest. The *Daily Star* runs the news before the Edwards family have been informed, leading to tabloid journalists being labelled 'fucking cunts' by James Dean Bradfield. The remains are sent for testing and are found not to be a match for Richey.

July 27
- Nicky Wire announces details of the band's forthcoming hits package, *Forever Delayed*, and accompanying tour. He also, finally, puts to bed any suggestion that the Manics will be splitting up once the Greatest Hits was done, saying that though they had made no concrete decisions about the future, they had written around 14 new songs.

August 17/18
- The Manics return to live action for the first time in almost a year, headlining the *NME* stage at the V2002 festival.

September 2
- *NME.com* premieres one of two new Manics tracks to be included on the upcoming hits collection, 'Door To The River'; a song originally recorded for *Know Your Enemy* but left off the album.

October 12
- BBC Radio 2 broadcasts *Design For Life - Manic Street Preachers*, a career-spanning documentary featuring new interviews with the band and their associates and hosted by Kate Thornton.

October 14
- A charity album, snappily titled *NME In Association With War Child Presents 1 Love*, features the Manics covering the Rolling Stones' 'Out of Time'.

- *There By The Grace Of God* (Epic/Sony)
  Tracklisting:
  1. 'There By The Grace Of God'
  2. 'Automatik Technicolour'*
  3. 'It's All Gone'*
  4. 'There By The Grace Of God (video)'*
  5. 'Unstoppable Salvation'**
  6. 'Happy Ending'**
  7. 'There By The Grace Of God (Saint Etienne Mix)'***
  8. 'There By The Grace Of God (Starecase Mix)'***
  * CD1 only, ** CD2 only, DVD only
  Formats
  CD1, CD2, DVD

October 16
- The band return to The Millenium Stadium, this time to warm the crowd up before Wales' Euro 2004 qualifier against Italy. They perform 'You Stole The Sun From My Heart' and 'A Design For Life'.

October 20
- 'There By The Grace Of God' charts at number six.

October 28
- *Forever Delayed - The Greatest Hits* (Sony/Epic)
  Tracklist
  1. 'A Design For Life'
  2. 'Motorcycle Emptiness'
  3. 'If You Tolerate This Your Children Will Be Next'
  4. 'La Tristesse Durera (Scream To A Sign)'
  5. 'There By The Grace Of God'
  6. 'You Love Us'
  7. 'Australia'
  8. 'You Stole The Sun From My Heart'
  9. 'Kevin Carter'
  10. 'Tsunami'
  11. 'Masses Against The Classes'
  12. 'From Despair To Where'
  13. 'Door To The River'
  14. 'Everything Must Go'
  15. 'Faster'
  16. 'Little Baby Nothing'

17. '(Suicide Is Painless) Theme From M*A*S*H'
18. 'So Why So Sad'
19. 'The Everlasting'
20. 'Motown Junk'
Formats
CD, 2-disc CD with remix disc, 12″, cassette, DVD (featuring videos)

November 2
• A European tour in support of *Forever Delayed* kicks off in Berlin. It will see the band visit Germany, Poland, the Netherlands, the Czech Republic, and Austria.

November 3
• *Forever Delayed* charts at number four.

November 22
• An exhibition of photographs of the band by longtime Manics collaborator Mitch Ikeda opens at the Proud Galleries, Camden.

November 29
• A bafflingly condescending interview with Nicky Wire runs in the *Daily Mirror*, which calls the triple-platinum Brit-winning *This Is My Truth* 'poorly performing'. The piece ends by saying 'on February 1 this year, Richey had been missing for seven years, long enough for him to be declared dead. Surely, it can't be long before the band he made famous joins him.'

December 1
• The first full Manic Street Preachers tour of the UK and Ireland since, remarkably, 1998, kicks off at Dublin's Point arena. The band will be on the road until December 16, the tour will include two London shows (Wembley Arena and Brixton Academy) and will culminate with two sold-out shows at Cardiff International Arena. Support comes from Ian Brown.

2003

January 22–26
• The Manics cap off the *Forever Delayed* era with a four-show tour of Japan. These will be the last Manic Street Preachers shows until the summer.
• Plans to release a new song, '4 Ever Delayed', backed with a newly remixed and augmented 'Motorcycle Emptiness' are abandoned in the UK, though the tracks still enjoy a European release.

May 20
- The *Daily Mirror* reports that the band will be including 'Judge Yr'Self', the last song they recorded with Richey, on a b-sides collection called *Lipstick Traces* later in the year.

June 29
The Manics return to Glastonbury for the first time since 2000's Toiletgate, playing a well-received early evening slot on the Pyramid Stage. Nicky later says that the closing 'A Design For Life' was the first time of the three occasions the band have played the festival where he felt they were having a 'Glastonbury Moment'. 'Judge Yr'Self' is played live for the first time.

July 4
- Another macabre field day for the media as the skeleton of a young man is found in the river Severn. Subsequent dental examinations show that the body is not Richey. The band are told of the discovery after playing the Midtfyns festival in Denmark. Nicky will later tell *Hot Press* magazine 'I think it would have broken most bands, but we've tried to become anaesthetised to it.'

July 11
- The Manics headline Manchester's MOVE festival, held at Old Trafford Cricket Ground as part of a short run of European festival appearances.

July 14
- *Lipstick Traces: A Secret History of Manic Street Preachers* (Sony)
  Tracklisting:
  DISC ONE: ORIGINAL SONGS
  1. 'Prologue To History'
  2. '4 Ever Delayed'
  3. 'Sorrow 16'
  4. 'Judge Yr'Self'
  5. 'Socialist Serenade'
  6. 'Donkeys'
  7. 'Comfort Comes'
  8. Mr Carbohydrate'
  9. 'Dead Trees and Traffic Islands'
  10. 'Horses Under Starlight'
  11. 'Sepia'
  12. 'Sculpture of Man'
  13. 'Spectators Of Suicide'

14. 'Democracy Coma'
15. 'Strip It Down'
16. 'Bored Out Of My Mind'
17. 'Just A Kid'
18. 'Close My Eyes'
19. 'Valley Boy'
20. 'We Her Majesty's Prisoners'

DISC TWO: COVERS

 1. 'We Are All Bourgeois Now'
 2. 'Rock 'N' Roll Music'
 3. 'It's So Easy (live)'
 4. 'Take The Skinheads Bowling'
 5. 'Been A Son'
 6. 'Out Of Time'
 7. 'Raindrops Keep Falling On My Head'
 8. 'Bright Eyes (live)'
 9. 'Train In Vain (live)'
10. 'Wrote For Luck'
11. 'What's My Name (live)'
12. 'Velocity Girl'
13. 'Can't Take My Eyes Off You'
14. 'Didn't My Lord Deliver Daniel'
15. 'Last Christmas (live)'

Formats:

2CD (liner notes could be printed off from the band's website), double LP (limited edition, in furry cover).

Lipstick Traces (A Secret History of Manic Street Preachers)

By Dom Gourlay

'Paint a lucid picture'

Many people fail to realise – or conveniently forget – that the Manics came from an era where b-sides and non-album tracks were considered *as important* as those that appeared on their respective long players. Put simply, any artist worth their salt didn't do filler. It was either good enough, or it didn't get released. No ifs. No buts. No in-betweens. Quality control was at the forefront of every artist's mantra, and not giving their fans value for money is one thing that the Manics could never be accused of. Many of the band's b-sides and bonus tracks could easily have been lead singles in their own right. Go through the catalogues of their mid-90s peers, and they all had incredible b-side collections; Suede's *Sci-Fi Lullabies*, *The Masterplan* by Oasis and Sonic Youth's *The Destroyed Room* being three that immediately spring to mind.

Originally conceived as an alternative to the recently released greatest hits package, *Forever Delayed*, *Lipstick Traces* takes its title from Greil Marcus's 1990 social and cultural critique, *Lipstick Traces (A Secret History Of The 20th Century)* a book that says changed his life (he would go on to write a foreword for a twentieth-anniversary edition). The intention was to document the cream of the b-sides, cover versions and hard-to-find tracks left idle in the band's extensive vault which now contained a decade-and-a-half's worth of material. The selection process was always going to be difficult: by 2003 that vault contained six albums and thirty-five singles and EPs, and that was just the surface; beneath that was a layer of soundtrack contributions, collaborations, remixes, session tracks, cover songs and demos. Whittling it down to an (albeit-double) album's worth of songs meant popular fan favourites (hello, 'Starlover') were likely to be omitted.

The final record comprised thirty-five tracks spread over two discs. The first was reserved for original material, including two previously unreleased tracks, while the second focused on covers, again placing unreleased cuts among the more widely available b-sides and bonuses. One can imagine the sifting process being akin to an after-hours debating society rather than a placid focus group, with each of the band strenuously arguing the merits of what should be included or left out. The tracklisting was also put to a fan vote on the band's website, though a number of songs that featured highly in the ballot were ultimately excluded; notably 'Patrick Bateman', the scabrous six-and-a-half-minute homage to Brett Easton Ellis's *American Psycho* (sample lyric – 'I fucked God in the ass') that featured on the 'La Tristesse Durera (Scream To A Sigh')' single. The final tracklist, had it been chosen by hardcore devotees, would likely have looked very different.

*   *   *

While *Lipstick Traces* may emit the odd cut favoured by the typical Manics' connoisseur, it also contains some of the most vital compositions in the band's entire canon; starting with the two previously unreleased numbers, '4Ever Delayed' and 'Judge Yrself'. Both have attained cult status in the hearts of many fans, and both are often cited as great, lost singles that should have been. The former shares its title with the previous year's greatest hits package, which was itself named after a lyric from the outro of 1993's 'Roses In The Hospital'. Nicky Wire himself has often said that '4Ever Delayed' should have been released as a single in its own right, a bridge between 2001's *Know Your Enemy* and 2004's *Lifeblood*, in place of the somewhat misunderstood 'There By The Grace Of God,' the 45 ultimately charged with that job. Sweepingly anthemic, with an electronic, Bowie-esque overtone, '4Ever Delayed' is an ode to *'lost vigilantes'* which also references obscure West Country band The Family Cat's 'From The City To The Sea' (*'From the city to the sea, will you all come follow me'*) in its lyrics, further cementing the Manics' appreciation of the late eighties indie scene. It's arguably the most grandiose statement the band had made since 'If You Tolerate This Your Children Will Be Next'. The song's occasional return to the live set during 2018's *Resistance Is Futile* tour was appreciated by fans old and new.

'Judge Yr'self' remains the last completed song left by Richey Edwards. Written and demoed in the same period as *The Holy Bible* and initially intended for inclusion on the soundtrack to the 1995 *Judge Dredd* movie, it was shelved by the band and seemingly archived forever in the wake of Edwards' departure. The song returned to the fore eight years later and stands alongside the band's finest and most revered works. Aided by Dave Eringa's powerful production, 'Judge Yr'self' is a brutal slice of incendiary post-punk that finds James Dean Bradfield in fine form, giving Edwards' lyrics the fanfare they deserve. Musically, it serves as a reminder of how indebted the Manics were to *In Utero* and US underground bands like Shellac at this point. Not played live since 2003 (and only a handful of times then), 'Judge Yr'self' remains a firm favourite and arguably the stand-out moment of the whole collection.

The previously available tracks that make up the rest of disc one can be roughly divided into two eras: the Richey era, and the one that followed the release of 1996's *Everything Must Go*, which brought with it a whole new legion of fans, something Nicky Wire alludes to on 'Close My Eyes' (*It's not about us any more*). Opener 'Prologue To History' is regarded by many fans, not least the band themselves, as one of the strongest songs of the *This Is My Truth, Tell Me Yours* period, and its omission from the parent album had been a source of regret ever since – a point finally addressed on 2018's twentieth-anniversary reissue, where it triggered a thousand online arguments by replacing 'Nobody Loved You'. Originally on the flip side of 'If You Tolerate This Your Children Will Be Next', 'Prologue To History' continues the band's occasional dalliance with baggy, its lolloping piano groove closely resembling that of The Charlatans' 'One To Another'.

Perhaps surprisingly, the other bonus track from 'If You Tolerate This…' ('Montana/Autumn/78') is overlooked here. Instead, 'Socialist Serenade' and 'Valley Boy', originally backing 'You Stole The Sun From My Heart' and 'The Everlasting' respectively, got the nod as representatives from the band's most commercially successful era. The former as an attack on Tony Blair and the New Labour government (*Change your name to New, forget the fucking Labour*) being quite apt for the time. It still stands up as one of the band's finest political diatribes. 'Valley Boy', on the other hand, doesn't hold the same reverence. Clocking in at just over five minutes, it finds the Manics, at least for that stage of the career, at their most experimental. It could almost be three separate songs condensed into one, which disrupts its flow somewhat. Perhaps best remembered as a slogan on one of the band's most popular late 90s t-shirts, it's difficult to envisage 'Valley Boy' featuring highly among many fans 'Best Of' lists.

One of the strengths of *Lipstick Traces* is a tracklist that doesn't follow any chronological pattern, which means that it makes for an engrossing listen. One of the band's oldest compositions, 'Sorrow 16', for instance, finds itself sandwiched invitingly between the two previously unreleased, radically different, numbers. Taken from the b-side of 'Motown Junk' and later reissued as a bonus track on 'Slash 'N' Burn' (as was 'We, Her Majesty's Prisoners', here chosen to close disc one), 'Sorrow 16' was a standout of the band's earliest live shows throughout 1991 and 1992. Its reintroduction to the live set as part of the *Journal For Plague Lovers* tour in 2009 was met with levels of enthusiasm generally reserved for celebrating milestone anniversaries or sporting victories.

Staying with the same era, 'Spectators of Suicide' and a live version of 'Strip It Down' are the only inclusions from the original Heavenly Records release of 'You Love Us'. It's probably fair to say the production and recording lets that EP down somewhat, even if the compositions themselves rank among four of the strongest on any Manic Street Preachers single either before or since. Taking its cue (and riff) from The Skids' 1979 post-punk classic 'Into The Valley', 'Spectators of Suicide' is a song the Manics struggled with in the studio. The cleaner *Generation Terrorists* version lacks the raw sentimentality of this one, and as a result slips into the background, usurped by the fanfaronade of its more radio-friendly compatriots, while the version included here is hampered by its scrappy production. A 2020 re-recording, commemorating Heavenly's 30th birthday and featuring Welsh songwriter Gwenno Saunders, finally does it justice.

'Strip It Down' is a throwback to the band's embryonic phase and was originally included on 1990's *New Art Riot* EP, their only release for the Damaged Goods label. 'Strip It Down' was always considered to be the best song on that record, far superior to the title track, and regularly featured throughout the *Generation Terrorists* tour. This live recording captures the intensity of those early shows and acts as a timely reminder of why they were courted by independents and major labels alike.

'Democracy Coma' was another live staple from the *Generation Terrorists* era which, again, could count itself extremely unfortunate not to make that album's final cut, something curiously reversed on the record's US release. Stuck away on the twelve-inch and CD formats of the 'Love's Sweet Exile' single, many fans and critics have said they prefer the song to its A-side. It's another exercise in the band wearing their influences on their sleeve, nodding to both Guns n' Roses (musically) and Allen Ginsberg, whose poem 'Howl' forms part of the outro.

The only other song from the *Generation Terrorists* era to feature on *Lipstick Traces* is 'Bored Out of My Mind', a semi-acoustic ballad tucked away on the b-side of 'Motorcycle Emptiness'. Tipping a hat once again to Axl, Slash and co, though this time the unplugged, reflective sound of the *G'N'R Lies* mini-album. It's one of that period's more forgettable moments but does, at least, highlight a different side to the band than their punk rock roots. With 'Dead Yankee Drawl', 'Vision Of Dead Desire' and everything on debut single 'Suicide Alley' overlooked, it can consider itself honoured to have leapfrogged in the pecking order.

The *Gold Against The Soul* era saw a sea change in the Manics approach to songwriting, which is more than ably demonstrated by the inclusion of 'Donkeys' and 'Comfort Comes'. Taken from the 'Roses In The Hospital' single, the former finds the band in a more refined state than much of their previous material. It could arguably be cast as a blueprint for the more complete musical visions of both *The Holy Bible* and *Everything Must Go*. In the case of *The Holy Bible*, that is unequivocally the case with 'Comfort Comes'. Formed around a similar guitar riff to the one that would go on to power 'Faster', this flipside to 'Life Becoming A Landslide' suggests the next phase in the band's development would be far more brutal than what had gone before. Given the formative nature of these songs, it does feel as if *Gold Against The Soul* is a little under-represented here. It wasn't until 2020's deluxe reissue that the era was finally afforded some long-overdue recognition.

Perhaps surprisingly, that's also true of the band's much-vaunted *Holy Bible* era. Only one Manics-original from the period, 'Sculpture Of Man', is featured on *Lipstick Traces*. One of only three non-album compositions released during that period ('Too Cold Here' and 'Love Torn Us Under' being the others), 'Sculpture Of Man' mirrors 'Revol' in its structure; the intros are both strikingly similar. Clocking in at under two minutes, it stands up as one of the most ferocious slices of vitriolic post-punk in the band's entire canon. *Everything Must Go* was the album that introduced the band to a wider and more mainstream audience, so it's no surprise to see four songs from that era represented here. The b-sides for 'A Design For Life' alone are responsible for twice as many tracks on *Lipstick Traces'* as *The Holy Bible's* three singles combined. Said to be an autobiographical self-caricature, 'Mr Carbohydrate' finds Nicky Wire at his most amusing lyrically, laughing at himself for being a 'boring fuckhead' who may as well be working in a bank. 'Mr Carbohydrate' has become a cult favourite over the years, despite the Manics only playing it live once, in 2003 at the HMV on London's Oxford Street during an instore for this very compilation. Meanwhile, 'Dead Trees And Traffic Islands' finds the band on an experimental journey that takes in northern soul, woodwind instruments and a pseudo-psychedelic melancholy that brings to mind bands like The Boo Radleys. Taken from the same single, it's another example of the band broadening their musical horizons whilst providing a pleasant, if not necessarily memorable, listening experience.

'Sepia' and 'Horses Under Starlight', the two songs lifted from the 'Kevin Carter' single also display the Manics various talents for arrangement, composition and musical virtuosity. Not least on the latter, where Sean

Moore swaps his drumsticks for the cornet. Leading the band into lounge music territory, this short but sweet, easy listening instrumental remains one of the band's greatest curiosities. Better still is 'Sepia', a song that references *Butch Cassidy & The Sundance Kid* while musically bridging the gap between *Everything Must Go* and *This Is My Truth Tell Me Yours*. While its lyrics suggest an inner turmoil (*'Bleeding inside I manage to keep it all in'*), the arrangement itself is up-tempo and sprightly.

Prior to putting out *Lipstick Traces*, the band's most recent album was *Know Your Enemy*. While that record sacrificed quality control in favour of quantity, its singles did produce several favourable bonus tracks, two of which are included here. 'Just A Kid', a reflective summary of childhood that's both charming and eloquent in its execution sits on disc one, while a cover of McCarthy's 'We Are All Bourgeois Now' kicks off the second disc. If the former once again hinted at another evolution, the latter could easily have been written for the Manics. It wasn't the first time they'd covered McCarthy – a band that first came to prominence on the *NME* 'C86' cassette – nor would it be the last. Hidden away at the end of *Know Your Enemy*, this stands out as one of the finest covers the band has ever done and fully deserves its place here.

*   *   *

With both The Clash and Guns 'N' Roses being prominent figures in Manic Street Preachers' development as a band, the three songs on disc two covering those artists will come as no surprise. Both 'What's My Name' (The Clash) and 'It's So Easy' (Guns 'N' Roses) were regular staples of the band's live set between 1992 and 1994 and the live recordings here are as dynamic and exhilarant as any that exist. A second Clash cover, 'Train In Vain', came later, during the *This Is My Truth, Tell Me Yours* tour, mirroring its creators' career juxtaposition. Often played towards the end of the set, it's a faithful run-through of the original and one that suggests The Clash will always be a huge influence on the Manics. A point that was reinforced two years ago when the band's 'Garageland' briefly appeared in the *Resistance Is Futile* tour set.

While it's difficult to pull out any one show as being a personal favourite from the dozens I've seen, 1999's Manic Millennium New Year's Eve event in Cardiff probably stands out the most. Fans old and new had descended from across the UK and beyond, and the camaraderie was something I've rarely experienced before, or since. The Manics played two sets that evening. A highlight of the first half was a cover of Chuck Berry's 'Rock'N'Roll

Music', and for that purely selfish reason and the memories evoked of that evening, its place on *Lipstick Traces* is fully deserved.

The band's fascination with obscure 1980s music rears its head again here. While McCarthy have already been covered elsewhere, the Manics' take on Primal Scream's 'Velocity Girl' – an early b-side that was featured on the NME's C86 cassette – sits side-by-side with their version of Camper Van Beethoven's 1985 cult classic 'Take The Skinheads Bowling'. Both released initially as extra tracks on the 'Australia' single. Some creative fatigue may well have set in by this point – 'Australia' being the fourth and final 45 to be taken from *Everything Must Go* – and both covers stick true to the original versions.

Far more adventurous is their cover of Happy Monday's 'Wrote For Luck', which gives a glam-metal makeover to the original's indie/dance schtick. It works surprisingly well. Initially released as a bonus track on the 'Roses In The Hospital' CD, 'Wrote For Luck' is another example of the band transitioning musically in the *Gold Against The Soul* era – as well as paying homage to one of their perhaps lesser feted influences.

James Dean Bradfield's mid-set acoustic slot has been a regular feature of Manic Street Preachers live shows for a number of years, and three of the songs here – one a live recording of Art Garfunkel's 'Bright Eyes' – reflect the tradition. Both 'Can't Take My Eyes Off You' and 'Raindrops Keep Fallin' On My Head' might be simplistic in melody and structure[24], but Bradfield's flawless renditions make them worthy inclusions here. Likewise, his intimate run through Wham's 'Last Christmas'. Manic Street Preachers were regulars on Channel 4's *TFI Friday* between 1996 (when this was originally broadcasted) and 1998 and this version fully encapsulates why their covers resonate in a way very few other artists manage to do.

The rest of the album is a bit of a mixed bag. A faithful but instantly forgettable take on The Rolling Stones 'Out Of Time' – initially released as part of the 2002 War Child compilation *1 Love* – is pleasant enough, but lacks the intimacy or comforting melody of the aforementioned 'Raindrops Keep Fallin' On My Head', which the Manics contributed to the first War Child compilation seven years earlier.[25]

Nirvana had made a huge impact on the band, particularly on *The Holy Bible*, and they regularly covered 'Pennyroyal Tea' in their live sets until as

---

24. Burt Bacharach and Frankie Valli are going to be rightly livid when they read this. - MB
25. Adding Jagger and Richards to the list of people affronted by this chapter. - MB

recently as 2008. However, it's a rarely heard version of 'Been A Son' that's included on *Lipstick Traces*. Taken from a 1999 BBC Radio One session, it's a stripped-down, almost country-style arrangement thanks to Bradfield's slide guitar.

Perhaps the most intriguing moment on the second disc belongs to 'Didn't My Lord Deliver Daniel', which was originally recorded by Paul Robeson. The band's fascination with the American civil rights activist culminated in 2001's 'Let Robeson Sing', arguably one of the highlights from *Know Your Enemy*. This poignant and undeniably heartwarming rendition from that single's b-side doesn't veer too far from the original's rootsiness while encapsulating the inspiration Robeson had on the band during this period.

Initial reviews of *Lipstick Traces* were fairly positive. The odd lukewarm reaction was usually due to individual reviewers having their own personal variant of *Lipstick Traces* assembled in their heads already; surely a testament to the band's collective output over this period. Sure, there are some notable omissions and as a complete archived history, *Lipstick Traces* doesn't tell the full story. Nevertheless, what it does do is provide a summary of their development as a band while selecting individual artefacts from those first fifteen years for posterity. When drawn in a format such as this, it makes for a compelling and perpetually evocative listen.

Furthermore, *Lipstick Traces* stands proudly alongside each of the band's studio albums. A musical diary of sorts, charting each stage in the band's career, which, much like like the band's output in general, is flawed in places but still ranks as essential listening experience for both hardcore and casual fans alike.

*   *   *

Part Eight

2003–2004

2003 (continued)

July 14
- The band celebrate the release of *Lipstick Traces* with an in-store gig at HMV on London's Oxford Street, playing a set consisting entirely of b-sides.

July 21
- *Lipstick Traces* charts at number 11.

November
- The band begins sessions for their seventh album, provisionally titled 'Litany', with Tony Visconti at Looking Glass Studios in New York. Lyrics have come from sessions Nicky has held with his brother, the poet and playwright Patrick Jones. Four songs are finished, including 'Solitude Sometimes Is', 'Emily' and 'Cardiff Afterlife'.

November 20
- Visconti reports on the sessions' progress on his blog, praising Nicky's bass playing ('he has the chops of a Motown session bass player' – high praise coming from Visconti, who played bass on two classic Bowie records including *The Man Who Sold The World*), and saying that James has the loudest voice he has ever recorded (again, high praise for the man that produced *"Heroes"*). James will later say that Visconti lifted the band 'out of a hole we dug for ourselves'.

2004

Spring
- Having recorded four songs with Visconti the band decide against returning to Looking Glass, and instead work with Greg Haver at Cardiff's Stir Studios, and Tom Elmhirst at Grouse Lodge in Ireland.

June 12
- The Manics headline the Isle of Wight Festival, their first live performance in over a year. They debut two new songs, 'Empty Souls' and 'Solitude Sometimes Is'.

July
- James Dean Bradfield, the last unmarried Manic, marries his girlfriend, Mylene Halsall, a public relations officer.

August 9
- Indie duo Johnny Boy release their single 'You Are The Generation That Bought Too Many Shoes And You Get What You Deserve', produced by James Dean Bradfield and Dave Eringa.

September 30
- An arena tour is announced for December, with support from currently-massive indie band Razorlight. The band also announce that a tenth anniversary edition of *The Holy Bible* will be out later in the year. Most notably, the band say that they will be joined for the tour by a second guitarist for the first time since Richey's disappearance in order to better represent their records and free James up on stage.

October 18
- *The Love Of Richard Nixon* (Sony/Epic)
  Tracklisting:
  1. 'The Love Of Richard Nixon'
  2. 'Everyone Knows/Nobody Cares'*
  3. 'Askew Road'**
  4. 'Everything Will Be' **
  5. 'The Love Of Richard Nixon (video)'***
  6. *Quarantine (in My Place Of)* - Short film by Patrick Jones°
  7. 'Voodoo Polaroids'°
  * CD1 only, ** CD2 only, *** CD2 and DVD, °DVD Only
  Formats:
  CD1, CD2, DVD, Download

October 24
- 'The Love Of Richard Nixon' charts at number 2

October 27
- *NME* reviews *Lifeblood*, calling it 'possibly their best album since Everything Must Go'. *Q*, meanwhile, calls it 'miserable and insipid'.

November 1
- *Lifeblood* (Sony/Epic)
  Tracklisting:
  1. '1985'
  2. 'The Love of Richard Nixon'
  3. 'Empty Souls'
  4. 'A Song For A Departure'

5. 'I Live To Fall Asleep'
6. 'To Repel Ghosts'
7. 'Emily'
8. 'Glasnost'
9. 'Always/Never'
10. 'Solitude Sometimes Is'
11. 'Fragments'
12. 'Cardiff Afterlife'
Formats
CD, LP, download

Lifeblood

by Adam Scott Glasspool

'A lost soul can live wherever a person who remembers it wishes.'

In September 2013, James Dean Bradfield and Nicky Wire were interviewed on BBC Breakfast as part of the promotional duties for their eleventh album *Rewind the Film*. Whilst answering a question on their legacy, Bradfield alluded to having released some bad albums. Initially coy, when pressed, he named names; and that name was 2004's *Lifeblood*, the Manics' divisive, oft-maligned seventh LP.

Since its release, *Lifeblood* has dragged with it a reputation as the band's weakest, least essential album. A misstep in the direction of soft rock, a maudlin, navel-gazing attempt at pathos, or as *Q* magazine put it in their review at the time, 'miserable and insipid.' Now, seventeen years after its release, *Lifeblood* sits differently in the band's back catalogue. A strange, beguiling album that rests between watershed moments for the band. That finds them at their most soul-searching and unsure. That scared them into a subsequent decade of attempts to recapture something once lost. The initial detractors have slowly disappeared, replaced by those whose patience paid off, having now been won over by the album's blend of deceptive delicacy and understated grandeur.

In late 2003 the Manics were coming to the end of a period in which they were taking stock of their career and thinking about where to go from there. 2001's *Know Your Enemy* had been met with a mixed critical and commercial reception; quite the turnaround from the million-selling juggernaut that was 1998's *This Is My Truth Tell Me Yours*, a suspected deliberate move from the band to blow up their own career, but perhaps one that had worked too well. Having performed something of a commercial re-set, the trio took the opportunity to stop for a second and look back (and also try to shift some units) with 2002's greatest hits compilation, *Forever Delayed*, and 2003's *Lipstick Traces (A Secret History of Manic Street Preachers)*, a b-sides and rarities collection. Whilst the disjointed, energetic *Know Your Enemy* seems more in keeping with the spirit of the band than the following two-year-long victory lap, that rest from perpetual creativity afforded them the time to consider the future. If the compilations were drawing a line under what the band had been, what would they be now? Wire called the process of looking back 'essential,' adding that after the retrospectives, the band had to either split up or reinvent themselves.

One of the more interesting aspects of the Manics' career is their ability to consistently self-analyze, examining their position in culture, and how it ties in with their history. Looking back on a decade in which one of their primary creative forces and best friends disappeared with little explanation cannot have been easy. It felt like a past with which the band had yet to truly reckon. *Everything Must Go* stands in defiance of the context in which it was released. *This Is My Truth, Tell Me Yours* has a resigned, melancholy air; a world-weariness and sterile isolation. *Know Your Enemy* is purposefully obtuse and jagged, dealing with art, America, and a scathing attack on that timeless enemy – disco. It makes sense then that, given time to reflect, their next record would emerge from a more personal place of ghosts and memories. *Lifeblood* is, rather than merely 'miserable' or 'insipid', the point at which the band come to terms with their past and the events that haunt it, and finally lay some of those ghosts to rest.

Trauma is a funny thing. Victims experience its fallout in many different ways; some react immediately, others are prone to bury its effects, only to have them re-emerge later in life. Symptoms of lasting trauma can be negligible or severe, permanent or temporary. Without a doubt, the trauma of the band losing their best friend and a quarter of their tight, creative unit will have been immeasurable. The effects will have resonated deeply through every era of their career. I am not one to diagnose strangers from my poorly constructed Ikea office chair, but this is also something worth bearing in mind when examining an album released a decade after a life-altering traumatic event – the themes dealt with on *Lifeblood* may have been rattling around for quite a while.

*   *   *

Lifeblood began its gestation in early 2003 after a purely cerebral search for a new direction. Wire eventually landed on the sound bite 'elegiac pop,' drawing upon influences such as Springsteen's *Nebraska*, Berlin-era Bowie and Goldfrapp and incorporating aspects of synth-pop and soft rock. Walls of distorted guitars would be replaced by more subtle, serene, and delicate touches. The guitar remained, but processed and warped into unrecognisable soundscapes of texture and colour. Riffs were played with heavy amounts of reverb and delay, or on the piano. Wire's lyrics also underwent a transformation, featuring less overt political references, relentless cultural touchstones, and intellectually informed anger. They were, instead, personal, emotional, and cryptic. 'The main themes are death and solitude and ghosts,' said Nicky in an interview with *The Scotsman* in October 2004, 'being haunted by history and being haunted by your own past.' This is a big statement from a band who, three albums earlier, wanted nothing more than to *escape* from that history.

It's appropriate, then, that the album begins in the past. Opening track '1985' starts quietly, unassuming. Strummed electric guitar chords play second fiddle to a wash of electronic sounds and synthetic pads. '*In 1985*,' begins James Dean Bradfield, referencing the year before the Manics were officially formed. The lyrics take the listener through the world surrounding a Welsh teenager in the mid-80s, referencing figure skaters Torville and Dean, the potential for a civil war brought about by the Conservative government's treatment of coal miners, the influence of The Smiths, and lifelong friendships being founded. The song lifts partway through the first verse as a second drum track fills space, but doesn't expand truly until the chorus: a synth line ripped straight out of the 1980s accompanies references to the German philosopher Friedrich Nietzsche and his claim that the age of enlightenment had killed the concept of a God. Leave it to the Manics to draw parallels between their own coming-of-age and a civilisation rejecting the idea of a deity. It is, on the surface, a triumphant opener, albeit one tinged with classic Manics melancholy as they realise there is '*no going back*' to the band or the people they once were. It also magnificently sets the tone for the rest of the album, foreshadowing a sort-of upbeat melancholia, furnished with synths, a prominent bass, and manipulated, electronic-sounding drums, with Bradfield's voice positioned front and centre, crystal clear, rising above all else.

Although opening the album, '1985' was not where the recording journey began. After deciding on a direction for the songs, they approached one of their production heroes, Tony Visconti (with whom they had almost collaborated on *Gold Against the Soul*,) to helm an album provisionally titled *Litanies*. Having worked with many key Manics influences over the years – the glam rock of T-Rex, the shape-shifting pop of David Bowie, the anarchic spirit of The Alarm – they felt Visconti would bring some of the retro-futuristic sheen that marked his most iconic work. The Manics spent four weeks in Visconti's Looking Glass Studio in New York. 'The sessions were very productive and enthusiastic,' Visconti wrote on his blog at the time, 'I think fans of the band will be pleasantly surprised with the outcome.' Ultimately, five songs were recorded, though only three would find their way onto the album – 'Emily,' 'Solitude Sometimes Is,' and 'Cardiff Afterlife,' and of those 'Emily' would receive some tinkering further down the line.

Sometimes working with a legendary producer is not right for a project. Sometimes the chemistry doesn't work, or the creative juices refuse to flow. The logical assumption that, if one is looking for a Tony Visconti-style sound, one should hire Tony Visconti, had a flaw: the Visconti of *"Heroes"* and *Scary Monsters* had moved on and grown, and his production style had followed suit. Eventually, the band turned to frequent collaborator Greg Haver, who rather self-deprecatingly quipped that he had been 'ripping off Visconti for years.' Haver is very much the unsung hero of the record, and his work with the likes of Bart Simpson will no doubt have prepared him for any antics Nicky Wire could have possibly thrown his way.[26]

Having worked with Haver on *This Is My Truth, Tell Me Yours*, *Know Your Enemy*, and their most recent single, 'There by the Grace of God,' the Manics ensconced themselves in the familiar surroundings of Cardiff's Stir Studios (which would become the band's own Faster Studios in 2005) and set about working on the rest of the album in earnest. Of all of their records, it is perhaps the one that benefits most from the concept of the 'studio as an instrument'. The band was disconnected from one another, both spiritually and physically, with more of the songs being laid down piecemeal than any of their previous albums. Layers of processed guitar were built up to create woozy, tumbling soundscapes. Songs were 'found' in the mixing stage. Some were written in-studio as responses to gaps in the album. Bradfield eschewed the stereotypical image of a vocalist standing in front of a large diaphragm microphone, headphones only covering one ear; instead he sat on the sofa at the far end of the studio's control room, smoking a cigarette, and belting the vocal tracks into a handheld Shure SM58. He didn't even wear headphones, leaving Haver to measure the distance between James and the studio monitors, calculate that distance into milliseconds of travelling sound, and set a delay on the track to ensure everything was in sync, whilst also setting the speakers out of phase to minimise bleed onto the vocal track. The sessions were, to put it mildly, a little more exploratory than usual. The sound of the album morphed and transformed and was 'discovered' as the recording went on. Further sessions at Grouse Lodge in Ireland enabled a third production name, Tom Elmhirst, to add some additional production and mixing, adding the 'sheen' he had honed producing Goldfrapp.

* * *

---

26. Haver wrote and produced 'The Ten Commandments of Bart' from the largely-forgotten 1998 Simpsons tie-in record, The Yellow Album.

After opener '1985' comes the lead single, 'The Love of Richard Nixon,' which started life as what Wire called a 'college rock' infused tribute to R.E.M. In the studio it shifted and changed shape into a jagged electro-pop banger that evoked the spirit of New Order and Depeche Mode. Shifting the narrative of the album further back in time, 'The Love of Richard Nixon' attempts to rehabilitate the image of the disgraced American President, positioning him as a sympathetic character; a hard-working, misunderstood historical figure. As musical statements go, this one was... a little odd. Members of the band have since speculated that humanising the widely despised Nixon, and especially doing so on the lead single from your new album was perhaps a misstep. Subject matter aside, however, 'The Love of ...' is arguably the song on *Lifeblood* best-suited to the task of priming audiences for the stranger sounds the band had been concocting. It lurches forward, propelled by a steady, electronic beat and stabs of synth, with a fantastic solo that straddles the line between guitar and synth, threatening to collapse into either at any second. Even the vocals here are more rhythmic than melodic. This is blended with lyrical references to Vietnam, Nixon's diplomatic efforts in China and the money he poured into medical research in the so-called 'War On Cancer', as well as allusions to a sickly king shutting himself in from the outside world.

Talking to the *R*e*p*e*a*t* fanzine in 2004, Wire compared Nixon and Kennedy to the Manics and Radiohead. 'If Radiohead are Kennedy,' he said, 'then Manic Street Preachers are Nixon; the ugly duckling who had to try ten times harder than anyone else. Paranoid megalomaniacs.' Wire is once again using historical events within his own lifetime (Nixon would have been president when the Manics were all in their early childhood) to parallel the development of his band. Despite its unconventional (even for the Manics) subject matter and oddball musical direction, the single was a moderate success. Released on October 18, 2004, two weeks prior to the album, it charted at number two on the UK Top 40; not bad for an electro-pop song by a band famous for their anthemic rock, about a US President from thirty years prior and with artwork featuring three men in translucent white boiler suits wearing caricature masks of said President and playing with a red ball. The sheer madness of it all is delicious.

Ultimately *Lifeblood* would spawn just one more single, the elegiac 'Empty Souls', released on January 10, 2005, and once again charting at number two. The song opens with a glacially shiny piano riff reminiscent of U2's 'New Year's Day', contrasting curiously aggressive drums that set a pounding snare rhythm above which Bradfield's high guitar slides. The lyrics conjure imagery of lost people, wandering souls, and ghosts, all asking the same questions:

where is it we are supposed to be? Where do we go to find a home? The chorus opens up, rather than doubling down, Bradfield bellowing the one modern reference on the record with the line *collapsing like the twin towers* (edited for the single version to *'dying flowers'* – arguably a better lyric) before gracefully employing his falsetto just in time for the chorus to pick up the pounding rhythm of the verses. It's a masterful arrangement, and a deceptively beautiful production. Bradfield sings with a palpable yearning – exactly what is needed for lyrics in which Wire explores the fate of those trapped between the now and the great beyond, and how those they leave behind must deal with it.

Also examining the notion of leaving is 'A Song for a Departure'. It begins with the sound of a chilly wind, lurking behind a prominent, curiously disco bass and steady drum beat. Wire's bassline features a very 1970s walk up the fret board at the end of each rotation, and the subtle flange decorating the hi-hat almost evokes the mood of an early-noughties nu-disco remix. The lyrics are again mournful; a disposition amply matched by Bradfield's vocal delivery, aching yet robust and vaguely dramatic, a counterpoint to the delicately picked guitar. The chorus is more dramatic still; staccato piano stabs appearing from nowhere as the energy lifts along with the swirling synth and backing vocals (a rare appearance of Sean's voice, and quite beautiful it is too, suggesting perhaps they should give Sean more[27]), the second appearance of which gives way to a particularly great guitar solo. This was another track that was 'found' in the studio, with the band experimenting with layering the piano part fifty times, as ABBA supposedly did. They ended up reverting to just two, as fifty 'sounded shit.'

It's with 'Song for a Departure' that the narrative of the album begins to reveal itself. Here Wire takes inspiration (and his main refrain) from Elizabeth Jennings' poem of the same name, which explores the nature of souls – how they influence our lives and how they move on. The song seems to take those empty and lost souls from the previous track and seek to house or beckon them. It's a song about a song, and that song is *'for a departure... for broken lovers... to take you homewards.'* The Manics began the album by reckoning with their own past in order to surmise how they arrived at the present; a piece of them now missing. 'Empty Souls' is the first track on the record to contend with something more spiritual, asking the question of where a lost soul goes, a question 'A Song for Departure' attempts to nullify, if not answer. A lost soul can live wherever a person who remembers it wishes.

---

27. This pun is absolutely unforgivable, and I can only apologize to you, the reader. – MB

That question answered, the band move on to an adjacent one; why do these souls wander in the first place? 'I Live to Fall Asleep' has dual themes, with Nicky wrestling with two interpretations of 'sleep.' One refers to literal sleep, something Wire is incredibly fond of: 'Sleep is beautiful to me,' he has said, 'I hate dreaming because it ruins ten hours of bliss.' The other theme here is suicide, with Wire examining what it is to reach total and unfathomable despair, to the point where someone might decide that 'sleep' would be a preferable alternative to living. Bradfield, meanwhile, interpreted the song as an exploration of someone finding ending their own life 'heroic.' Usually he would ask Wire (or, earlier, Richey) to de-code some of the denser references or themes in a lyric. For this record, Bradfield chose to write music based on his own interpretations and avoid 'over thinking' the words presented to him.

If any example were ever needed for the descriptor 'elegiac pop,' this would be it. Rippling piano and subtle guitar create a gorgeous foil for Wire's sighing bassline. The song ebbs and flows throughout, its bridge part growing from a sort of spatial minimalism that ascends and grows and builds before dissipating again as Bradfield's beautiful, aching falsetto guides the chorus into a waterfall of gently churning synths, reverb-heavy guitar and lush piano, led by a melodic, New Order-ish bass. It is a highlight not just of the album, but arguably, of the band's career. A calming oasis between the high-strung drama of 'A Song for Departure' and the next song, 'To Repel Ghosts,' a delay-heavy, up-tempo meditation on survivor's guilt.

Another title and theme borrowed from a non-musical artist – the American painter Jean-Michel Basquiat – '...Ghosts' is the closest thing to an all-out rock song on *Lifeblood*. Riffs intertwine with one another through layers of delay, feedback and some particularly clever arrangement, while Bradfield delivers some of the best vocals on the album. '*A soul in pain has no image to reclaim,*' he sings, amongst other references to ghosts of the past, the spectres within, and building a bridge between them and one's self. Once again, Wire is reckoning with his own ghosts and haunted past.

Bridges are also built between the past and present, most prominently on 'Emily,' the first track to feature production by Tony Visconti. The song itself is perhaps the least remarkable on the record; its heavily accented rhythm adorned with chimes and synth strings before a low-key version of one of those big, Manicsy choruses that on an earlier album may well have provided a moment of explosion. Thematically, this is Wire at his most politically minded and least personal. The lyrics deal with Emmeline Pankhurst, the British activist that organised the UK Women's Suffrage movement and played a huge part in gaining women's right to the vote. Wire felt Pankhurst was being forgotten, replaced instead by more modern icons – chiefly Princess Diana – that in his opinion had done very little to further the feminist cause. Below the surface the song wrestles once again with the idea of memory and ghosts, '*it's what you forget that kills you,*' sings Bradfield, '*it's what you remember that makes you.*' And again, it is our memories of departed people that ultimately keep them alive.

Another key to the album's themes is 'Glasnost'. Written toward the end of production, after a disappointing record company playback revealed the need for more singles (alas, its destiny was to languish unloved – ultimately *Lifeblood* would birth just two singles), this finds the Manics searching; looking within for answers to impossible questions and finding a need to slow down time and return to a simpler life. In a period where the band were unsure what they wanted to be, it's as though they are referring to their need to fall back in love with music itself. In order to do so they must embrace 'glasnost,' a Russian word meaning transparency and openness, employed as a buzzword policy by Mikhail Gorbachev in the dying days of the Soviet Union. It's a typical, perhaps almost cliched reference for the band (see 'Revol' and its cries of '*Lebensraum*' and '*Kulturkampf*'), doubling as a shorthand for an album in which the band are employing their most emotional, personal, open, and transparent lyrics. In order to continue making music, the band were indeed making their own glasnost.

If 'Glasnost' stands out as being somewhat 'designed' in reaction to feedback, then 'Always/Never' stands out for being unlike anything the Manics had previously attempted – and this is on an album stuffed *full* of things the Manics had not previously attempted. One of the shiniest slices of pop on the record, 'Always/Never' is unique not just for featuring some rather good 'Ashes to Ashes' slap bass, as yet unheard of on any MSP record, but for being a rare Manics song in which the music came first. Conceived primarily as a compositional experiment, James recorded a gibberish melody to which Nicky wrote lyrics. Alas, they're the weakest words on the record; an afterthought to the arrangement rather than form-meeting-function, to elevate a notion or idea. Still, the song earns its place for the synth line in the chorus alone.

Lifeblood's second Visconti number, 'Solitude Sometimes Is', opens with a sort of ghostly, rhythmic static and builds from there. Unusually for a band that can occasionally be formulaic when it comes to song structure, it continues to build and build, eschewing solidity for tone and texture, a glockenspiel ringing out its melody against a backdrop of picked, clean, and later, struck, distorted guitar. Bradfield's voice begins fragile and becomes more and more robust as the song becomes grander; his emotive delivery furnishing Wire's lyrical meditation on the joys of one's own company. Inspired by the Irish poet, Louis MacNeice and his writings on solitude, Wire voices frustration at forced social interactions and the contrived sharing of ideas. He uses his solitude to block out the world and spend time with himself and his demons, perhaps also longing for a simpler world, in which everything was less nuanced and confusing. It echoes the thrust of the record as a whole. James has likened their return from New York to Cardiff as the band 'creating their own world.' It is here that Nicky explores that world, allowing demons, ghosts, and memories to visit him.

That narrative continues into 'Fragments', with Wire and his brother, poet Patrick Jones, writing around the theme of fragmented memories and finding peace with them. Initially easy to cast off as lightweight or simple, 'Fragments', has a deceptively sweet and subtle arrangement; a serene, gentle lullaby that takes great pains to cement the themes of the album as a whole. A melancholy melodica provides a soothing counterpart to some of the darkest lyrics on the record, *'two minutes silence in a century of screams'* being a highlight. Wire turned to his brother after deciding the lyric needed more 'blood-soaked misery,' and Jones provided in spades. A darkness rages in the verses and is calmed in the chorus, where both the darkness and the narrator find a place of peace … only to stubbornly resist it, the music tumbling back down the rabbit hole with them. It is the sound of someone struggling to reconcile different states: to reckon with trauma, to make sense of only fragments of ideas and memories, to find relief.

That relief finally comes on the album's final track, 'Cardiff Afterlife.' Instantly something feels different; lighter, and more organic. An acoustic guitar and harmonica work together to provide a brighter, almost-soaring quality, as though breaking free from restrictions. This is one of the few songs that the band have been happy to say is about Richey Edwards, or rather about dealing with his legacy and the space he left behind. It's about the reclamation of memory, about not letting things become apocryphal or a part of some mythology defined by others. Ultimately the band remember Richey as a friend, a collaborator, a son to his parents, and a brother to his sister. He is not able to be distilled down into a rock 'n' roll myth, try as some might. In this song the Manics seem to come to terms with the trauma they have been through, the ghosts, the memories, the haunted past, and instead remember the person, the splendour and evil, the kindness and vanity. *'Your memory is still mine'*, sings James. You realise that Richey, his memory, and his legacy and the gap in the world he left behind – or at least the idea of those things as they relate to anyone – has been at the heart of *Lifeblood* from the very beginning. These were, all of them, songs for a departure.

'Cardiff Afterlife' is the oldest song to appear on the record, a refugee from Wire's unfinished *Cities* project – ten songs about cities with titles like 'Tokyo Hole' and 'Leeches Over Havana,' the lyrics all written on large painted canvases so Bradfield would not be able to lose them. Produced by Tony Visconti in those initial sessions, the Manics knew that this was always *Lifeblood's* ultimate destination. They just needed to work out how to get there. The album is the result of that journey, the band figuring out who they were and what their past meant as they recorded it. In New York they knew they wanted the chorus of this song to sound reminiscent of the score to Martin Scorsese's *Taxi Driver*, disorienting with shuffling drums and backwards trumpets. It makes the return of the verses from this fog feel all the more freeing. James sees this song as mirroring the band's state of mind, emerging from the mist of other people's perceptions and into real acceptance. The album ends with that emergence, a final, peaceful bell ringing out. The perfect ending to the narrative they had been building, ghosts and memories recognised and accepted.

* * *

The clearest indication of their frame of mind at the time comes from a song not even featured on the album. 'Askew Road', a *Lifeblood* era b-side, finds the band looking back on their time living with Phillip Hall, their first manager who died in 1993, and his wife, Terri. It includes a voice clip of Richey. When Terri heard it for the first time she broke into tears. The band were truly laying things to rest.

Lifeblood was released on November 1, 2004, its artwork stark and white, a nude female figure revealed only by the blood pouring down her body – a photograph taken by John Ross. The album sold relatively poorly in Manic Street Preachers terms, entering the charts at number thirteen with 23,990 copies sold in its first week. Even now it has yet to sell more than 100,000 units, a rarity in the band's career. Upon release it was met with generally favourable reviews (*Q* magazine aside), but caused a distinct division amongst fans. Both of those factors ultimately scared the band into a hiatus followed by, arguably, a decade of looking back; featuring attempts to either reconnect with their past or recapture the glory of it.

Looking back on *Lifeblood* now, Greg Haver wonders if they 'went too far in some places.' The prevailing opinion for many years was that this was their one truly 'bad' album, too soft and too maudlin. With hindsight we can see Manic Street Preachers as a band constantly wanting to grow, change, confound, challenge, and surprise. The biggest surprise here is that people seemed to be blindsided by this album. It's the sound of a band doing exactly what they want, unafraid to challenge not just the audience but themselves – that's very Manic Street Preachers. Does it have the youthful joy of *Generation Terrorists*, the spiteful anger of *The Holy Bible*, or the grandiosity of *Everything Must Go*? No, but then it was never supposed to. It's a quiet meditation on the band as people, and potentially the most revealing album they have released. Sadly, the legacy of its reception is a band slightly less willing to push their own limits, a band that would find themselves in a relatively safe mode until 2014's *Futurology*. Having said that, the tide of popular opinion seems to be shifting somewhat, and the album reassessed.

I once spent a year hosting a podcast devoted to Manic Street Preachers and their discography. I was joined by somebody who knew a handful of the band's songs and somebody else who knew nothing about them. I have always liked *Lifeblood*, so it was a joy to see my co-hosts respond very positively to it. Outsiders, unfamiliar with the band and their lore rated this album amongst their best pieces of work. The interaction with listeners too, was overwhelmingly positive and filled with comments such as 'I didn't like it at first, but now it's one of my favourites.' Some detractors remain, of course, but there is a lot of love for *Lifeblood* out there. It remains a fascinating insight into the band and how they became comfortable with who they are. Viewing it from a distance, with all the context we now have, makes it an all the more rewarding listen.

A strange, beguiling, warm, sterile, bleak, open, honest, catchy, shiny, brave, experimental, heartfelt album that encompasses everything worth loving about Manic Street Preachers.

Part Nine

2004–2008

2004 (continued)

November 7
- *Lifeblood* charts at number 13, the lowest showing for any Manic Street Preachers album since *Generation Terrorists* in 1992. It will drop out of the top 40 entirely by the end of the month.

December 4
- The *Lifeblood* UK arena tour begins in Brighton and will end on December 17 in Manchester. Many venues don't sell out. It is the last time the band will play a whole tour of venues of this size for some years. The stage set and amplifiers are an austere white to match the album artwork, and for the first time since Richey's final show at the Astoria in 1994, the band are joined by a second guitarist, Guy Massey.

December 6
- A 10th Anniversary reissue of *The Holy Bible* is released as a box set, containing the unreleased US mix of the album, b-sides, live tracks and a DVD documentary. It charts at number 99.

December 13
- A show at Cardiff International Arena, and another the next day at Glasgow SECC are cancelled at the last minute after James is struck down with 'severe flu'. The shows are rescheduled for the beginning of January.

2005

January 10
- *Empty Souls* (Sony/Epic)
  Tracklisting:
  1. 'Empty Souls'
  2. 'All Here Alone'*
  3. 'No Jubilees'**
  4. 'Litany'**
  5. 'Empty Souls (video)*°
  6. 'Dying Breeds (video)***
  7. 'Failure Bound'***
  * CD1 only, ** CD2 Only, *°CD2 & DVD, ***DVD only
  Formats:
  CD1, CD2, DVD, download

January 11/12
- The Manics play rescheduled shows in Cardiff and Glasgow

January 16
- Thwarting claims that the band are in commercial decline, 'Empty Souls' charts at number two. It is the band's 30th consecutive top-30 hit (and third number two), and narrowly misses out on being the 1,000th UK number one single (held off the top spot by an Elvis re-release). However, plans to release a third single from *Lifeblood* (probably 'Glasnost') are abandoned.

January 22
- Cardiff's Millennium Stadium plays host to the Manics for a third occasion, this time headlining a benefit show for victims of the devastating tsunami that hit Indonesia at Christmas. The band appear alongside Snow Patrol, Goldie Lookin' Chain (a band Nicky loves), Charlotte Church, Craig David and Keane amongst others.

Feb 1
- The tenth anniversary of Richey's disappearance brings the usual clutch of ghoulish media stories re-examining the details of his last known days. The band largely keep their head down, though do lend interviews to *Mojo* and *The Word* for pieces looking more specifically at their friend's legacy.

Feb 8
- The tenth-anniversary edition of *The Holy Bible* is released in the US, meaning American audiences can finally access the US mix of the record, the release of which was abandoned ten years earlier.

February 10
- The Manics embark on a short Japanese tour.

April 3
- A tour of English and Welsh theatres, known as the 'Past/Present/Future' tour, kicks off at Southampton's Guildhall. It will conclude two weeks later with two sold-out nights at London's Hammersmith Apollo.
- The band announce that a new three-track EP, *God Save The Manics*, recorded at Stir Studios with Dave Eringa, will be available for free at shows. One song, 'Picturesque', is especially notable, as it contains the first 'new' Richey Edwards lyrics in ten years – the words are a composite of two songs from the folder he left the band before his disappearance, 'Doors Closing Slowly' and 'All Is Vanity', with Nicky adding his own

words to them. Unfortunately, as the CDs were left out on the merch stall for fans to help themselves to, supplies run short.

April 8
- Nicky is given an Honorary Fellowship by the University of Swansea, which is awarded in person during the band's show at Brangwyn Hall. Nicky is delighted – he had missed his own graduation at the same venue in 1990 to support the Levellers on tour.

April 19
- During the final show of the tour at Hammersmith Apollo, James announces that the band will be taking a break from performing for two years.

April 20
- *God Save The Manics* is made available for free on the band's website.
- *God Save The Manics* (Sony/Columbia)
  1. 'A Secret Society'
  2. 'Picturesque'
  3. 'Firefight'
  Formats:
  CD, download

September 9
- A third War Child compilation album is released, *Help! A Day In The Life*, featuring songs all recorded in 24 hours between midday on September 8 and midday on September 9, and available to download later that day. The Manics record a new song, 'Leviathan'.

September 18
- Nicky announces that both he and James will be releasing solo albums in 2006.

December 23
- Despite claiming to have gone into temporary retirement, the Manics are announced as headliners for a charity concert called One Earth, to be held at the Millenium Stadium on January 28, alongside Embrace, Elbow and The Strokes among others, to raise awareness of Climate Change.

December 25
- The first fruits of Nicky's solo labours, a song called 'I Killed The Zeitgeist', is made available to download for free from *manics.co.uk*

2006

January 11
- The One Earth concert is cancelled so as to allow for the participation of 'further bands of significant stature whose current commitments did not allow them to perform this month'. It is never rescheduled.

February 27
- The band contribute a cover of 'The Instrumental' to *Still Unravished*, a tribute to 80s indie pop band The June Brides.

March
- Recording begins for the eighth Manics album at Grouse Lodge Studio, Ireland, with Greg Havers and Dave Eringa as co-producers.

May 22–24
- James Dean Bradfield plays a trio of solo shows at small clubs in Manchester, Glasgow and London

June 4
- Nicky Wire makes his solo live debut at the Hay-On-Wye festival.

July 1
- Nicky plays his first and only London solo show, performing a set at Stay Beautiful, the club night run by journalist and Manics biographer Simon Price, held at the Purple Turtle in Camden.

July 7
- James tells the BBC that the band are working on their next record at Stir Studios in Cardiff, which they recently acquired the lease for. They will later rename it 'Faster Studios' and describe it as 'a bit of a clubhouse'.

July 10
- James Dean Bradfield's debut solo single, 'That's No Way To Tell A Lie', is released. It peaks at a respectable 18 in the charts.

July 16
- Nicky performs a solo set at the Latitude Festival.

July 24
- James's solo album, *The Great Western* is released by Sony/Columbia. One reviewer calls it 'his best since *Everything Must Go*'. It peaks on the album chart at number 22.

August 19/20
• James plays the V2006 festival.

August 29
• Nicky tells *NME* that the next Manics album will sound like '*The White Album* played by Guns N' Roses'.

September 4
• Nicky's debut solo single, 'Break My Heart Slowly', is released by Red Ink records.

September 14
• A planned joint solo tour of Japan by Nicky Wire and James Dean Bradfield is cancelled.

September 24
• Nicky's album *I Killed The Zeitgeist* is released on the Red Ink label, which he describes as 'a conscious decision to be as nihilistic as possible'. It gets favourable reviews, but charts outside the top 100. *NME* says it's the best record any of the Manics have made since *Everything Must Go*.

September 25
• The second single from James' *The Great Western*, 'An English Gentlemen' is released. The b-side features a cover of Frank Sinatra's 'Summer Wind'.

October 4
• James embarks on a lengthy UK club tour beginning in Dundee. He will be on the road until October 23.

November 6
• A tenth anniversary box set edition of *Everything Must Go* is released, including b-sides, demos, alternative takes (including Steven Hague's versions of 'Australia' and 'The Girl Who Wanted To Be God') live tracks and a DVD.

December 8
• Breaking their self-imposed live exile, the band return to action to headline XFM's Winter Wonderland event at Manchester Apollo. They premier two new songs, 'I'm Just A Patsy' and 'Autumnsong'.

December 9
• Nicky tells *Music Week* that the next Manics album will be called *Send Away The Tigers*.

2007

January
- *Q* Magazine award the band the 2006 'Merit Award'.
- The band reconvenes at Grouse Lodge to finish work on *Send Away The Tigers*. Mixing is done in LA with Chris Lord-Alge, who produced hit records for Green Day and My Chemical Romance.

January 1
- James tells the *South Wales Echo* that their new album will be their 'best since *Everything Must Go*'.

March 5
- Nicky writes a blog for *MySpace* saying that the band are in the process of 'destroying what we are', and goes track-by-track through the new album.

March 19
- A new song, 'Underdogs', is given away for free via the band's website.
- The new Manics single, 'Your Love Alone Is Not Enough', a duet with the Cardigans' Nina Persson, gets its radio premier on the XFM breakfast show.

March 30
- The band perform 'Your Love Alone Is Not Enough' on the Charlotte Church Show, with the host singing Persson's parts.

April 2
- The Manics play their first London show since 2005, a warm-up at the tiny Hospital Club.

April 14
- The first 'official' Manics show (according to Nicky, who for some reason doesn't count the show at the Hospital Club) of the *Send Away The Tigers* promotional campaign takes place at a small club in Cologne.

April 17
- Writing on the band's official website, Nicky announces that *Send Away The Tigers* is being released in the US by Red Ink, the label that handled his *I Killed The Zeitgeist* album ('Nicky Wire's f**cking solo career pays dividends again!', he says).

April 23
- 'Your Love Alone Is Not Enough' is released for download via iTunes.

April 29
• 'Your Love Alone ...' charts at number 26 on downloads alone.

April 30
• ***Your Love Alone Is Not Enough*** (Sony/Columbia)
  Tracklisting:
  1. 'Your Love Alone Is Not Enough'
  2. 'Boxes & Lists' *
  3. 'Love Letter To The Future'**
  4. 'Welcome To The Dead Zone'**
  5. 'Little Girl Lost'**
  6. 'Fearless Punk Ballad'***
  7. 'Your Love Alone Is Not Enough (James solo acoustic)'°
  8. 'Your Love Alone Is Not Enough (Nina solo acoustic)'°
  * CD only, **Maxi CD only, *** 7″ only, °Download only
  Notes:
  The song is written entirely, words, chords, melody and all, by Nicky Wire.

May 1
• *Music Week* reports that the Manics are on track to hit number one in the
  singles chart.

May 6
• 'Your Love Alone Is Not Enough' charts at number two (the band's fourth
  number two single) behind Beyoncé and Shakira's 'Beautiful Liar'.

May 7
• ***Send Away The Tigers*** (Sony/Columbia)
  Tracklist
  1. 'Send Away The Tigers'
  2. 'Underdogs'
  3. 'Your Love Alone Is Not Enough'
  4. 'Indian Summer'
  5. 'The Second Great Depression'
  6. 'Rendition'
  7. 'Autumnsong'
  8. 'I'm Just A Patsy'
  9. 'Imperial Bodybags'
  10. 'Winterlovers'
  11. 'Working Class Hero' (unlisted)
  Formats:
  CD, 12″, Download.

Send Away The Tigers

By Mayer Nissim

'The return to form is a rock 'n' roll myth'

Manic Street Preachers are British pop's ultimate survivors. Over 35 years they've powered through every obstacle. They've battled indifference, mockery, depression, disappearance and death. They've also overcome the challenges brought by success and the sort of stadium superstardom they'd always dreamed of but surely never actually expected.

The only time they've ever really felt close to breaking up was in the hazy three-year gap between *Lifeblood* and *Send Away The Tigers*. Having grown old gracefully if awkwardly, the Manics suddenly risked drifting out of existence. Nicky later spoke of a 'general malaise' and the very real threat of the band fading away, if not exactly burning out. For all its audience-splitting quiet grandeur and glossy sheen, *Lifeblood* felt like a dead end. Not just a full stop but a coda. It seemed impossible to see where the band could go next.

Something had to change. In April 2005, there was the immediately energising but almost-forgotten limited edition freebie *God Save The Manics* EP. Its three tracks haven't been bundled anywhere else on a B-side or reissue. It's not (at present) available to stream (legally, anyway). It's as though it's been written out of official Manics history. Nodding at the near future for the band it featured a suitably punky sleeve and sharp sub-four minute songs. Opener 'A Secret Society' set things alight. 'Firefight' was only the second James Dean Bradfield Manics lyric after 'Ocean Spray', hinting at his brief upcoming independence. And while it was all-but ignored at the time, closer 'Picturesque' featured lyrics from the scrapbook of ideas left behind by Richey Edwards that would eventually become *Journal For Plague Lovers*. Taking breath, James Dean Bradfield and Nicky Wire both released solo albums within a few months of each other in 2006. James's *The Great Western* clocked in at a respectable 22 in the charts while Nicky's indie-released *I Killed the Zeitgeist* slipped off page three at 130. They worked a lot out of their respective systems.

On the heels of *God Save The Manics* and just eight months after 'Empty Souls' had limped out as *Lifeblood*'s almost apologetic second and final single, there was an even more striking sign of life. Rush-recorded for charity album *Help!: A Day in the Life*, 'Leviathan' was neither poor nor nasty, but suitably brutish and short. It showed that the band were again ready to make an album with big guitars, big sounds and big themes. Put plainly, a *Manic Street Preachers album*.

A couple of years later it came. *Send Away The Tigers* was a high-energy defibrillator shock to the heart of the Manics that has kept them going ever since. Nicky Wire called the band a 'hopeless mass of contradictions' at their outset and in truth that's never really changed. *Send Away The Tigers* is the perfect distillation of that. The complete opposite of a traditional Manics album at the same time as being a neat synthesis of all that came before. A procession of repetitive choruses that sound focus-grouped for radio but also layered, lyrical depth. A shameless grab for the charts and a stranger, more jagged album than its legacy would have you believe.

*   *   *

The return to form is a rock 'n' roll myth. Any once-successful band that dares to continue releasing records after a poorly-received album or one that sells naff-all is doomed to have 'return to form' dangled over them by critics until the end of their career. You can file it alongside 'their best album since...' as meaningless rock review blather. It betrays a failed attempt to force the swirling mess of pop into a neat biographical narrative. By *Send Away The Tigers*, the Manics had by some counts already had a couple of returns to form, anyway. *The Holy Bible* and 'Masses Against The Classes' were both clear rebounds against a looming threat of decay.

With all that said, after *Lifeblood* the band made a startlingly conscious decision to jettison the cynicism that had been weighing them down since the turn of the century and instead reconnect with the giddy, hopeful euphoria that got them going on *Generation Terrorists* and gave them their previous, necessary rebirth on *Everything Must Go*. On that first post-Richey album they attempted to escape from their history. Here, instead, they made a definite embrace of it.

In pop you should always judge a book by its cover, and *Send Away The Tigers* is no exception. Every previous Manics album had a distinct visual direction that set it apart from what came before. This time the band took a deliberate look back and tried to recapture the glories of the past by either magick or sheer force of will. In a steal from *The Holy Bible*, they swapped out their Rs for faux crillic 'Я'. The lettering positively screams 'Manic Street Preachers' (or rather, 'MANIC STЯEET PЯEACHERS'), but there are no photos of the band anywhere in the liner. Instead, the sleeve features a whopping six different images from Valerie Phillips's 2005 photobook *Monika Monster Future First*

Woman on Mars, and still more would be used on the album's singles. Phillips had shot the band in the early 1990s, with her pictures being used on the cover of 'Motorcycle Emptiness', itself a sepia-tinted exercise in premature nostalgia. It was another look back in order to push forward. On the front of *Send Away The Tigers*, Phillips' Polish-American muse Monika and her cousin Kate strut across the Verrazano-Narrows Bridge from Brooklyn to Staten Island. They weren't at all connected to the band, but in their Halloween getup they look every bit the die-hard fans, fluffy-handcuffed to the barrier at every Manics show from 1988 to today. The definition of confident outsiderdom. The epitome of youth, rather than an epilogue of it.

There was also a classic Manics quotegrab for the inner sleeve. *'When a man is young, he is usually a revolutionary of some kind. So here I am, speaking of my revolution.'* At first glance, the words from Vorticist and *BLAST* editor Wyndham Lewis feel almost like a call to arms. In fact, the line originally kicked off an essay to promote a career-spanning Lewis exhibition at the Tate, just six months before his death at the age of 74. A reflection on past revolutions rather than a suggestion of impending ones. James, Nicky and Sean were only inching towards 40 when they recorded *Send Away The Tigers*, but you can at least double that in rock 'n' roll years. Manics songs had long-obsessed over reflection and memory ('La Tristesse Durera', 'This Is Yesterday' 'No Surface All Feeling' etc. etc. etc.). On *Send Away The Tigers* the nostalgia is for the band itself, sonically as well as lyrically. Like the Vorticists, the Manics were trying to (re)capture activity, significance and movement, set up in opposition to tasteful passivity, dull anecdote, and hysterical fuss. These were attributes they had to spare from *Generation Terrorists* through to *Everything Must Go* but lost somewhere along the way after that.

Send Away The Tigers is the shortest Manics album, clocking in at under 35 minutes and just ten songs and whereas previously the band were frequently happy to have plenty of loose threads flapping all over the place. *Generation Terrorists* rambled its manifesto for 73 minutes over 18 songs. *This is My Truth, Tell Me Yours* stretched out its 13 tracks for over an hour. *Know Your Enemy* was a hit and miss 16 songs and 65 minutes. It's abundantly clear that the scaled-back *Send Away The Tigers* was a choice. They'd written around 30 tracks for the album and the endless formats of its four singles were littered with original B-sides. At least a handful of those could have rounded things out without letting the side down. 'Boxes and Lists' and 'Anorexic Rodin' would have improved it.[28] Even when they slipped 'Welcome to the Dead

---

28. I'm going to go to bat here for the lost Manics masterpiece 'Fearless Punk Ballad', one of Nicky Wire's most perfect lyrics and completely wasted on the 70 of 'You Love Alone'. - MB

Zone' on the main running order for the 10th anniversary reissue they felt the need to shunt off a song to keep it trim.

After the only intermittently successful sonic experiments of *Lifeblood*, the band reunited with producer Dave Eringa, and the sound of the album deliberately picked up where 'Leviathan' left off. Obvious guitar riffs, obnoxiously Slashy solos, machine-gun drums, big multi-tracked vocals and soaring Britpop strings are all designed to hammer home the point that this is a Manic Street Preachers record. The often-repetitive singalong choruses led some to dismiss the lyrics as throwaway, and sure, some of them are. But like any Manic Street Preachers album the words are the key to everything. When they hit, they intertwine the personal and political, the autobiographical and historical. There's oblique allegory and allusion rubbing up against almost comically straight rock references. All those contradictions once again.

Nicky Wire has suggested that on *Know Your Enemy* in general and 'Freedom Of Speech Won't Feed My Children' in particular the band had already pre-empted the seismic political shifts at the turn of the century. But aside from a clumsy reference to the falling Twin Towers on 'Empty Souls', the Manics had in truth sidestepped the post-9/11 world for half a decade. While the end of the end of history was being proclaimed, the Manics were writing about Richard Nixon and Emily Pankhurst. On *Send Away The Tigers* the band finally got a real grip on the 21st century, and on themselves too.

The album is *explicitly* about the war in Iraq. It's about the slowly unfolding economic, social and cultural crisis in America that was soon to spread across the West. It's about torture and suicide. About death and drinking. More than anything, it's about depression and decline, and hope-filled and hopeful attempts to banish those ultimately fatal beasts. It's often knowingly daft and ridiculous in a way that rock 'n' roll should be. Like the very best pop music it takes absolutely everything deathly seriously except itself. *Send Away The Tigers* is a self-realising act of rebirth, or at least revitalisation, that pointedly leaves out spring as it sequentially weaves in the seasons ('Indian Summer','Autumnsong', 'Winterlovers') to avoid jinxing its own resurrection spell.

'Underdogs' was the first song heard from the album. Released as a free download back when that meant anything, it's a swaggering, sweary, celebration of Manics fans; a direct mirror of the snarling 'You Love Us', which had reflected back the widespread antipathy that existed towards the band 15 years earlier. Once they were out on their own. Now they belonged among their tribe of outcasts. The lost and weak beautiful freaks who finally found and fucked each other. Yet even here, the band acknowledge their status as 'fading stars'. The disappeared, or at the very least, disappearing. Its earnestness is almost embarrassing. That's probably why it was destined for the chopping block when 'Welcome to the Dead Zone' was plonked on the reissue.

* * *

When they started the Manics had promised an all-out assault on the pop charts. They eventually achieved that success several times over, clocking up unlikely number ones with 'If You Tolerate This Your Children Will Be Next' and 'Masses Against The Classes'. They had it in a more enduring sense with modern standards like 'A Design For Life'. But they'd never before pulled off as pure a distillation of powerpop as 'Your Love Alone Is Not Enough'. For the album's proper lead single, the group roped in The Cardigans' Nina Persson for a call-and-response, while Nicky even got to roll out his strangled drawl for the knowing *I could have written all your lines* towards the end. The Manics had always juggled supposed iconoclasm with veneration of their accepted rock heroes (The Clash, Guns 'N' Roses, Public Enemy), but they always protested too much. 'Your Love Alone' is sprinkled with references to perhaps the least underground bands in the rock 'n' roll cannon, all the way from The Beatles to the ultimate punk *bête noir* Pink Floyd. They even throw in a nod to 'You Stole The Sun From My Heart', one of their own least combative, most radio-friendly moments. Again, it's all about contradictions. A hookup with a Proper Pop Star, albeit an indie one. A love song (of sorts). A verse bigger than most band's choruses and a chorus bigger than anything the band had done since *Everything Must Go*. But it's about suicide, regret and the knowledge that no matter how strong it feels, love can't save the world. If 'Leviathan' and then 'Underdogs' had nudged ajar the door to the Manics reborn, 'Your Love Alone' kicked it wide open. The first vocal duet to make it to a Manics album since they teamed up with Traci Lords for 'Little Baby Nothing', its artistic and commercial success also paved the way for the collaborations that would be scattered across Manics albums in the years to come.

'Send Away The Tigers itself' was a phrase borrowed from actor/comedian/alcoholic/icon Tony Hancock, who used it to describe drinking away his demons. The first title track to open a Manics album, its lyrics explore Hancock's self-imposed end-of-life exile in Australia and riffs on the devastating line in his suicide note that 'things just seemed to go too wrong too many times'. It lays down the album's mashup of personal and political by threading Hancock's decline through the fall of Baghdad Zoo after the invasion of Iraq. When the zoo infrastructure was destroyed during the 2003 Battle of Baghdad, most of the animals died or were killed, leaving only some of the largest predators. Many of the lions who escaped the enclosure were later shot dead by American soldiers. It's a companion piece to both 'Black Dog on My Shoulder' and 'Small Black Flowers That Grow in the Sky' with its play around the literal/allegorical animal representations of depression, captivity and freedom. 'A misguided idea of liberation' is what Nicky called the doomed lions' flight and Hancock's career-ending, (life-ending?) split from his writers and move abroad. The open question is if or how that phrase applied to the Manics themselves. Did it mean the band trying to escape themselves on *Lifeblood*? Or did it refer to their then-current attempt to shock themselves out of their stupor with a self-conscious return to their classic rock influences and own back catalogue?

The rest of the album doesn't entirely succeed in answering that question. It flits back and forth between straight-as-an-arrow rock stomps borrowing heavily from *Generation Terrorists*, and the sort of string-laden anthems they'd mastered on *Everything Must Go* and *This Is My Truth Tell Me Yours*, taken to an extreme of radio friendliness. In that first column, 'Rendition' and 'Imperial Bodybags' are both about victims of the wars in Iraq and Afghanistan. The US had been using extraordinary rendition since the 1980s, but stepped it up under Bill Clinton and took it into overdrive with George W. Bush, aided and abetted by the British security services. After the Manics' cool detachment of the previous few years, 'Rendition' is a full-throated scream of righteous anger, albeit one lightened by a nod to Jack Lemmon in 1982's *Missing* and the self-mocking concern that the band might be slipping into, ugh, liberalism.

'Imperial Bodybags' is more nuanced. Here those being mourned are the soldiers of the invading forces. Instead of pure indignation, there's a juddering mix of sympathy, pity and scorn. It's a more ambiguous if no less-heartfelt lament for the rule-keeping disposable Prom Queens coming back from foreign lands full of holes. It's not clear from the lyrics beyond the title, but Nicky was also concerned with the bloody execution of Tsar Nicholas II. Not only was the Empress Alexandra killed with the Tsar, the couple's children Olga, Tatiana, Maria, Anastasia, and 13-year-old Alexei were also shot and bayoneted to death in a locked basement alongside them. Wire admitted to having spent half his life thinking the killings were ultimately righteous, before later being of the mind that that the massacre was perhaps 'just one evil replacing another'. It was a circumspect approach from a band who started off relatively black and white but had long refused to stick to the party line. *The Holy Bible* featured the pro-gun sloganeering of 'Ifwhiteamericatoldthetruthforonedayit'sworldwouldfallapart', death penalty advocacy of 'Archives of Pain' and anti-political correctness rant of 'PCP'. 'The Love of Richard Nixon' was a rare sympathetic artistic appraisal of the disgraced former president. Both of *Send Away The Tigers'* War Songs have distinct echoes of 'La Tristesse Durera', with one sniping at liberals and the other empathising with soldiers betrayed by hypocrisy. Again, the band were drawing on their past.

Almost as stomping but with much less clarity is 'I'm Just A Pasty'. Is it really about JFK assassin Lee Harvey Oswald? Is Oswald's raging conspiracy theorism being used as a quirky analogy for a romantic crush? Being brutally honest, it feels like filler needlessly shunted on to the record despite that oh-so-short running time. Some of the potentially best lines on the album are just tossed out here and there, being buried by horrors like the plainly absurd opening couplet (*'the Oswald in Lee Harvey'*) and a rhyming-for-rhyme's sake chorus (*'love/above'*).

Meanwhile, 'The Second Great Depression' and 'Winterlovers' skirt around ideas of economic and cultural collapse (*'the beauty of dead industry'*) but are actually about the swirl of personal depression and interpersonal breakdown. Both songs are a much more successful melding of the early Manics guitar sound with the consciously soaring anthems of their middle period than they managed on their previous two albums. 'Winterlovers' is *Tigers'* finest moment, pulling off the remarkable trick of being alternately quietly understated and dizzyingly overblown, *'nah nah nah nahs'*, pounding drums, bolshy guitar solo and all.

Tying it together are those two seasonally-minded singles. Like the album as a whole, 'Indian Summer' feels like an attempt to will the band's renaissance into being by incantation. The band acknowledge that they've had to look back and remember why they formed in the first place, and that act of introspection has once more given them a reason to be. Musically it's a surely-intentional 'Design For Life' knock-off, albeit with less conviction as a result of trying too hard. 'Autumnsong' goes a step further than settling for continued existence, instead boldly promising that the best is yet to come. Wearing those early influences on a ripped denim sleeve, the opening riff is just a few notes off 'Sweet Child O' Mine', while the vocal hooks steal from early Aerosmith power ballad 'I See You Crying' and the group's own 'If You Tolerate This Your Children Will Be Next'. It's more MOR than AOR in places and the lyrics are maybe the most empty ever recorded by the band, but it was consciously made to recapture the euphoria of youth and conquer the charts, which it just about succeeded in doing.

Perhaps the biggest surprise comes after the bell on a so-called secret track, that relic of the CD era no-one really misses. To say the Manics had catholic tastes in covers would be an understatement. They never restricted themselves to punk/rawk covers in their live sets or on their B-sides. They've done songs by The Rolling Stones, McCarthy, Chuck Berry, Frankie Valli,

Sleez Sisters, Camper Van Beethoven and Art Garfunkel. They've even covered Primal Scream at their jangliest and the Happy Mondays at their most lairy. Despite that, for the band who burst on the scene with their breakthrough single claiming *'I laughed when Lennon got shot'* to cover John Lennon's pompous/brilliant 'Working Class Hero' was still a real shock. There's not the tiniest shred of irony, either, with the band instead taking a lead from Tin Machine and amping up Lennon's sparse post-Beatles class conscious anthem as the very straightest of rock songs.

*   *   *

The legacy of *Send Away The Tigers* has been confused and undercut by what happened next. Before the year was out, the band looked poised to build on the album's populism and popularity with a Proper Christmas Single. They prepped the gloriously gauche glam of 'Ghost of Christmas', sleigh bells and all, but wimped out at the last minute and chucked it out as a free download at the start of December. A few months later they released a cover of Rihanna's recent mega-smash 'Umbrella' as a digital-only single. A bombastic celebration, it showed that the band could appreciate the very biggest pop melodies and might be inclined to try to match them in the near future. Instead, they took a typically Manics turn and returned to the journal of lyrics left behind by Richey that they'd only glanced at for *God Save The Manics*. *Journal for Plague Lovers* wouldn't have happened without *Send Away The Tigers*, and unarguably surpassed it. There's the lingering temptation to see *Tigers* as a gateway rather than a significant Manics album in its own right.

Send Away The Tigers had an overflowing 50-track reissue just ten years after the original release, and there plainly won't be another. That compares to similarly comprehensive versions of *Generation Terrorists* (20 years), *Gold Against The Soul* (27 years), *The Holy Bible* (ten years and 20 years), *Everything Must Go* (ten years and 20 Years) and *This is My Truth Tell Me Yours* (20 years). The retrospectives that accompanied the *Tigers* reissue felt premature. It was too soon to really know what the album meant for the band in themselves and the wider pop landscape. The promise of artistic reinvigoration was borne out by the albums that followed, but 'Autumnsong' remains the last Manic Street Preachers single to go into the top ten. Given how the charts work in the streaming era, you could easily imagine it will be the last top ten single they ever have. But where the failed sprawl of *Know Your Enemy* and lukewarm reception to *Lifeblood* narrowed the paths available to the Manics, the admittedly qualified success of *Send Away The Tigers* gave the band a real choice of where they could go next.

Part Ten

2007–2009

2007 (continued)

May 8
- The 26-date *Send Away The Tigers* UK tour begins at Cambridge Corn Exchange, having sold out in two hours. The tour will roll straight into festival season; this will be the busiest the band has been since the burnout-inducing campaign that followed *This Is My Truth, Tell Me Yours* in 1998. They will be on the road almost non-stop until the end of June.
- Wayne Murray, recently of James' solo band, joins the touring line-up on second guitar, a position he will occupy on a semi-permanent basis for the next decade and beyond.

May 9
- *NME*'s review of *Send Away The Tigers* says it's their best album since *Everything Must Go*.

May 13
- *Send Away The Tigers* charts at number two in the UK album charts, having sold 38,769 copies in its first week. It is deprived the number one by just 690 copies of Arctic Monkeys' *Favourite Worst Nightmare*. *Tigers* will pass the 100,000 sales mark by the end of the year.

June 1
- Recording work resumes at Stir Studios, where b-sides are tracked for the next single, 'Autumnsong'.

June 6
- A Christmas tour is announced, seeing the band return to bigger venues, including arenas in Manchester, Cardiff and Birmingham, plus two nights at Brixton Academy.

June 24
- The band return to Glastonbury Festival's Pyramid Stage.

July 23
- *Autumnsong* (Sony/Columbia)
  Tracklisting:
  1. 'Autumnsong'
  2. 'Red Sleeping Beauty'*
  3. 'The Long Goodbye'**
  4. 'Morning Comrades'**
  5. 'The Vorticists'***

6. 'La Tristesse Durera (Scream To A Sigh)'°
7. 'Autumnsong (Acoustic version)'°
* CD only, **Maxi CD only,***7" only, °download only
Formats:
2-track CD, Maxi CD, 7", digital download

July 29
• 'Autumnsong' charts at 10.

August 11/12
• The band return to the V Festival, (V2007), at Cheltenham and Stafford.

September 7
• Nicky tells *NME* that the Manics are recording a Christmas single, saying they're going 'The full Slade and Wizzard', and that it's something they'd always wanted to do.

October 1
• **Indian Summer** (Sony/Columbia)
  Tracklisting:
  1. 'Indian Summer'
  2. 'Anorexic Rodin'*
  3. 'Heyday of the Blood'**
  4. 'Foggy Eyes'**
  5. 'Lady Lazarus'**
  6. 'You Know It's Going To Hurt'***
  7. 'Indian Summer (demo)'°
  * CD only, **Maxi CD only, ***7" only, °download only
  Formats
  2-track CD, Maxi CD, 7", digital download

October 6
• 'Indian Summer' charts at 22, the first Manic Street Preachers single to miss out on the top 20 since 1994.

October 9
• The annual *Q* Awards take place. The Manics take home a gong for 'Best Single' for 'Your Love Alone Is Not Enough'.

October 10
• According to the *Daily Star*'s James Cabooter, who cornered Sean in a pub after the *Q* Awards, the band are bailing on the idea of releasing a Christmas single, as the final result is 'too cheesy' and might 'make us look like dickheads'.

They expect to release the song as a free download instead. Nicky will later tell *Planet Sound* (the music section of Nicky's beloved Channel 4 Teletext) that he wanted to give the song a 'proper release' but 'got outvoted.'

December
- Nicky and James interview Canadian prog legends Rush, a favourite of both, for *Classic Rock* magazine.

December 1
- The Manics' much-touted Christmas song, 'The Ghost of Christmas', is released as a free download via the band's website and newsletter. Though they shy away from actually playing it live, the track is blasted through the PA after every gig on the December UK tour.

December 2
- A nine-date, sold-out UK tour begins in Aberdeen.

December 7
- Nicky is quoted in the *Daily Star* as saying that Radiohead have 'demeaned music' by allowing fans to download their latest album on a pay-what-you-like basis. Sean says that the band have made more money touring in 2007 than they have in the last seven of releasing albums.

December 18
- *NME* names the Manics as the recipients of 2008's 'Godlike Genius' award, the 'Lifetime Achievement' nod given to a legendary figure at the annual ceremony, previously awarded to New Order, Mark E Smith, Ozzy Osbourne, The Clash and John Peel. The band will also headline a post-Awards 'Big Gig' at the O2 Arena, featuring Bloc Party, Kaiser Chiefs and The Cribs on February 28.

December 25
- Nicky tells *Planet Sound* that the band plan to record with noise-nic extraordinaire and founder member of Big Black, Steve Albini in the new year.

2008

February 28
- The Manics are crowned 'Godlike Geniuses' at the Shockwaves *NME* Awards. They play a short set during the ceremony itself, held at the IndigO2 theatre in the former-Millenium Dome in London, and then a

longer headline set at the O2 Arena next door. Cerys Matthews, formerly of Catatonia, duets on 'Your Love Alone Is Not Enough' at both gigs.

March
- Work on the ninth Manics album begins in earnest at the now-renamed Faster Studios in Cardiff with Dave Eringa. Nicky says he needs a break from writing lyrics (he jokes on the band's website that Sean will be writing the next record), and claims that James is leaning musically back into the direction of *The Holy Bible*.

March 6
- *Umbrella EP* (Sony/Columbia)
  Tracklisting:
  1. 'Umbrella'
  2. 'Umbrella (acoustic)'
  3. 'Umbrella (Gran Slam Mix)'
  Formats:
  Digital download only.
  Notes:
  The band's cover of Rihanna's instant classic 'Umbrella' is released as a digital single, having previously appeared on an *NME* covermount CD. An acoustic version and a remix are also included as a bundle, though the band don't see it as a 'real' single. Much to the trio's surprise the download is enough to push the cover into the UK charts, at number 47 with a bullet.

June 2
- The Manics open for Foo Fighters at the City of Manchester stadium.

June 5
- The band kick off a busy festival season at Caribana in Switzerland. The summer's schedule will take them across Europe, including – for the first time – gigs in Eastern Europe and Russia.

July 8
- Patrick Jones' new play, *Revelation*, tackling the under-reported subject of male victims of domestic violence, opens in Cardiff. The soundtrack is composed by James Dean Bradfield and includes a new song, 'Shut That Door'.

August 23/24
- The Manics headline the *NME*/Radio 1 stage at the Reading and Leeds Festivals, eleven years after headlining the mainstage for the first time. Interviewed on the band's official website, Nicky says he sees the shows

as capping off the *Send Away The Tigers* era, and again reiterates that their next record will have more of the feel of *The Holy Bible*.

September 12
• Heavenly Records host an evening celebrating the label at London's Royal Festival Hall. The Manics play a set consisting only of the songs they had recorded for Heavenly in 1990/91: 'Motown Junk', 'Sorrow 16', 'We Her Majesty's Prisoners', 'Starlover', 'Spectators of Suicide' and 'You Love Us'. A new mix of 'Motown Junk', titled the 'Johnny Boy Anniversary Mix' is streamed on *manics.co.uk*

September/October
• The Manics de-camp to Rockfield, Wales, to work on their ninth album with legendary US studio engineer Steve Albini, who recorded (amongst many other classic albums) perennial Manics favourite *In Utero* by Nirvana. The band will record directly to tape with no computer editing or overdubs.

October 11
• James appears at a tribute to the singer Nico, organised by her Velvet Underground comrade John Cale, at the Royal Festival Hall.

November 4
• The band update fans on the progress of their new album via their website, revealing for the first time that the new music will be comprised entirely of lyrics by Richey Edwards, taken from the folder of work he left them before his disappearance. They speculate that the record might be called 'Journal for Plague Lovers' or 'I Know I Believe In Nothing But It Is My Nothing'. The announcement is met with excitement and astonishment from fans. The band had always said that they didn't intend to use Richey's final works, though anyone looking closely at the *God Save The Manics* EP a few years earlier, will have noticed that attitude was softening.

November 8
• A 'work in progress' cut of *No Manifesto*, an independent documentary dedicated to the Manics, is screened at the Sheffield Documentary Film Festival.

November 23
• News breaks via several outlets that Richey Edwards' family have successfully petitioned to have him presumed dead, officially closing his missing person's case. The family's lawyer, David Ellis, stressed that the decision had come from 'an acceptance that his affairs have got to be sorted' rather than 'an acceptance that he is dead.' The Grant of Probate

had been issued on October 13 and named Graham and Sherry Edwards as the executors of Richey's estate, officially declaring that he had 'died on or since February 1, 1995'. His estate, totalling £455,990 (barely a third of the figure the tabloids had estimated a decade earlier), is released to his family. Several newspapers print obituaries. The band keep a dignified silence on the issue, though will later confirm that the legal issues had no bearing on their decision to use Richey's lyrics.

November 24–26
- The Manics play their last shows of the year at festivals in Hong Kong and Singapore. A final event, which would have seen the band return to Bangkok for the first time since 1994, is cancelled by organisers.

2009

January 20
- Nicky Wire turns 40. Two London-based fans called Sam and Amanda create a 'Birthday Book' containing messages from fans and celebrities, including members of The Clash, Feeder and Echo and the Bunnymen, cricketer Matthew Maynard (immortalised in the 1996 b-side 'Mr Carbohydrate'), Welsh rugby international Johnathan Davies, golfing legend Ian Woosnam, MP Peter Hain and more. Nicky says he is 'blown away' by the gesture.

February
- Work finishes on the album now confirmed to be called *Journal For Plague Lovers*. The record is completed with Dave Eringa, as Steve Albini has to leave the country earlier than expected after his wife has a health scare.

March 24
- The band announce that they will play *Journal For Plague Lovers* in its entirety during a nine-date UK tour, which will include three nights at London's Roundhouse.

March 25
- Fans get their first taste of the new album when Zane Lowe premiers a new song, 'Peeled Apples', on his Radio 1 show.

March 28
- Nicky tells *NME* that artwork for the new album will be provided by Jenny Saville, whose painting 'Strategy (South Face/Front Face/North Face)' was used on *The Holy Bible*.

March 30
- Another new song, 'Jackie Collins Existential Question Time', is premiered simultaneously on XFM and *Kerrang!* Radio.

April
- Reviews of *Journal For Plague Lovers* start to appear. *Q* awards it five stars, *The Guardian, Observer, Uncut* and *Mojo* four, and *NME* 8/10. *Clash* says it is the Manics' 'best since *Everything Must Go*'.

May 14
- Several UK supermarkets say they will only display the new album in plain slip-cases, calling Jenny Saville's artwork 'inappropriate' as it appears to show a child with a blooded face. James calls the decision 'utterly bizarre', pointing out that the 'bloodied' effect is simply Saville's trademark muted colours and brush style. Nicky tells *Attitude* that he's 'a bit soul-destroyed' by the reaction.

May 15
- The first live action of the year as James Dean Bradfield plays an in-store acoustic show at the legendary Spillers record store in Cardiff.

May 16
- Channel 4 screen a documentary, *Shadows and Words*, featuring the band talking to the writer John Niven.

May 18
- **Journal For Plague Lovers** (Sony/Columbia)
  Tracklisting
  1. 'Peeled Apples'
  2. 'Jackie Collins Existential Question Time'
  3. 'Me and Stephen Hawking'
  4. 'This Joke Sport Severed'
  5. 'Journal For Plague Lovers'
  6. 'She Bathed Herself In a Bath of Bleach'
  7. 'Facing Page: Top Left'
  8. 'Marlon JD'
  9. 'Doors Closing Slowly'
  10. 'All Is Vanity'
  11. 'Pretension/Repulsion'
  12. 'Virginia State Epileptic Colony'
  13. 'William's Last Words'
  14. 'Bag Lady' (unlisted)
  Formats:
  CD, deluxe CD/book with a second disc of demos, 12″ LP

Journal for Plague Lovers

By Erica Viola

'It's easier to be hung as a martyr than to live as a peasant'

In 2009, I was four years out of one bad relationship and four years into another. Without realising it, I'd been slowly letting go, becoming aimless, settling into the hopeless passivity that I'd once convinced myself I would always resist. This was the year *Journal for Plague Lovers* was released. As with their other albums, I read it like a book and let it fill me – the old impassioned Manics sound, loud and bright and sharp as a bruise, jolted me out of the stupor. In late summer, the Metro Chicago announced that the band were bringing the album to the States. I'd purchased tickets two minutes after reading the announcement, and was already ringing a hotel. Manic Street Preachers were coming to us.

* * *

Journal for Plague Lovers is an album no one expected to happen – least of all, I think, Manic Street Preachers themselves.

Shortly before Richey Edwards' disappearance in early 1995, he handed to Nicky Wire a journal of sorts: a loose collection of haiku, couplets, and uneven poetry. Initially, Edwards' bandmates were reluctant to use what they would eventually come to accept as his last words: his fractured thoughts, observations made through the one-way mirror of mental illness, and disgust with a world that grew colder even as Edwards' star was rising. His would-be lyrics seemed impossible, even to a band used to working with a writer whose lines had been consistently bleak and irregular from the very start.

In the beginning, at least, James Dean Bradfield, Wire, and Sean Moore were hoping that Edwards would return to help them make sense of what he'd left behind. The wait – for friends, family, and fans – was fat with speculation, and grew bleaker by the year. However, in 2008, Edwards' family petitioned successfully to have him declared legally dead. The band began recording *Journal for Plague Lovers* in the weeks before that declaration, at last putting those seemingly impossible words to use.

Edwards was resurrected, made accessible once more, with an album that stitched together the contents of his surviving notebook with the musical compositions of his bandmates – his childhood brothers-in-arms.

For one album, Richey Edwards lived again, and the Manic Street Preachers were beautifully whole.

Ravenous for the old Manics sound, fans and critics embraced the album. Not quite a companion to *The Holy Bible* and not quite a sequel, it still evokes the passion, the hopeless existentialism, and the anguished self-reflection of its predecessor.

The first impression of *Journal for Plague Lovers* is of a fragmented collection of horror, despair, and unanswerable questions, all tailored to fit fervent, sometimes fierce music reminiscent of the band's earlier records. Crafted exclusively from lyrics written by Edwards – the only Manics album to do so – with composition duties shared by Bradfield, Wire, and Moore; *Journal...* is an explosion of nostalgia. That timeless, heavy post-punk Manic Street Preachers sound is heavily laced with ageless relevance and iconic imagery.

*   *   *

The vibe in the Metro Chicago was utterly unlike my first Manics gig, which had been in the UK. Fans mingled, handing out zines, trading anecdotes, comparing tattoos and vintage t-shirts. The taller members of the crowd moved back to give everyone a clear view of the stage. People held each other's spots as drinkers circled to the bar and back. It felt like a neighbourhood celebration. Gratitude and wonder and suspense were palpable.

When the band took the stage, shouts of 'thank you!' filled the auditorium. Waves of applause melted into music. *Journal for Plague Lovers*, performed live, had even more intensity, more vibrancy, more grit than the recorded album. On the stage and amongst the congregation of the faithful, Richey Edwards existed again: eloquent, vivid, and aching with new life.

The gig began with crowd favourites. Some of my fellow audience had waited half a young lifetime to hear 'Motorcycle Emptiness' live. Frenzied and hoarse from shouting along, we waited, tensely. As the last notes of 'No Surface All Feeling' faded, 'Peeled Apples' – *Journal's* opening track - began to blaze. At once mournful and frenzied, it's an extraordinary mashup of Edwards' own torments. It left the crowd breathless. Visceral descriptions of self-inflicted bruises punctuate references to the never-ending loop – the infinity – of modern warfare. Vietnam explodes in denim as conflict shouts down peace in the White House; Edwards struggles against the barbarism that flows from the headlines onto his doorstep, clenching his fists to keep from disintegrating. These lyrics are a stark reminder that history is on repeat, no matter how well we numb ourselves to the cycle of inhumanity. 'Peeled Apples' is an ode to civilian shellshock: it is a cry from a young man who has been wounded by a strife-torn world as much as he has been by his own inner demons. The song stops almost as abruptly as it begins, leaving the listener dizzy, with guts full of agony, yet hungry for more.

* * *

It wasn't easy to find British music in the United States. As a teenaged girl on the cusp of adulthood, I spent hours with my glasses pressed against shelves of CDs, searching for used Manic Street Preachers singles, EPs, and LPs. Before the era of online shopping, I counted myself lucky to find a battered copy of *Generation Terrorists* in a second-hand shop. I made friends with the cute guy at my local record store, who'd save posters and Japanese versions of Manics albums for me in return for showing him my tattoos. I joined UK Yahoo groups dedicated to Manics music, begging bootlegs from online friends, dissecting songs with acquaintances in Newcastle and Israel until my parents disconnected the internet at 3 am. My best friend from high school and I went 'halfsies' on editions of *Gold Against the Soul* and 'The Masses Against the Classes' culled from the bargain bins at Chicago's Virgin Megastore. We'd each take one and burn the other a copy. I'd transfer my treasures to cassette, turn up the volume on the tape deck of my rickety old car, and race through conservative Omaha neighbourhoods, foot glued to the gas pedal, veins tingling with an angst I didn't understand.

The Manics didn't have much of an audience in the States; in the mid-sized Midwestern city where I grew up in the late 1990s, it was Nickelback or nothing. To me, though, Manic Street Preachers were a lifeline: a window to culture, subversion, rebellion, freedom. They were a world my parents and my schoolteachers had never permitted me to enter. I filled my ears with Bradfield's brutal vocals, but not until I'd read the liner notes; it was like reading poetry. As a teen, I'd lie on my bedroom floor, memorising segments, scrawling choruses on my arms. (As an adult, I still flipped surreptitiously through the booklet of each new release, after my partners went to bed, silently straining to make out the stanzas near moonlit windows.)

I talked about my new favourite band until my high school best friend was as Manics-mad as I was. When the *Forever Delayed* tour was announced in the UK we pooled our dollars, begged our professors for mercy, then bought flights and gig tickets. In December of 2002, we landed at Heathrow, blew through London like champagne-drunk leopard-print hurricanes, and found ourselves with an online friend in a queue in front of the Birmingham NEC arena. We waited for 10 freezing hours, drinking vodka straight from the bottle, our eyeliner melting in the intense winter sunlight[29]. This would be our *NME* dream, our mini-Glastonbury, a shot of musical adrenaline.

'When they open the doors – RUN,' our new friend, an older veteran of many Manics gigs, told us wisely. But why?

'You'll see.'

When evening fell and the venue did open the doors, it was as if a dam had burst; hundreds of people howled like feral animals and rushed towards the stage like a blitz, everyone simultaneously trying to form a front row that could only fit a fraction. I clung to the metal barrier with my hands and knees, fending off claws, kicks – and once, I swear, a bite.

I barely had my breath back when the Manics materialised onto the stage. 'Motorcycle Emptiness'. I began to radiate. Joy felt like a drug; every bassline of every song shook my nerves. I was both distinctly present and disassociated. The music was, of course, over too soon, and our motley little group stumbled outside, giggling, weeping, hyperventilating. I can no longer remember how I got into the after-show party. My ears still ringing, I slid around on my high heels, clutching a handful of albums and a just-in-case Sharpie. I met the band, I behaved politely, they signed my albums; I was twenty-one years old and breathless with my first love affair.

When I stumbled through the door, Sean Moore took my singles covers politely and scrawled his name across them. 'I haven't seen this one in a while.' I stuttered that I'd gotten it in America, and he commented on my accent. 'We'd like to play there again, but Sony won't fund it.'

The night ended, the holiday ended, and my friend and I returned to the dirty slush of snow-banked Nebraska, feeling a little more alienated from our peers, crashing from the ebbing euphoria of a realised dream.

*　　*　　*

On stage, in 2009, the flirtation of 'Your Love Alone is Not Enough' and the upbeat/desolate conundrum of 'La Tristesse Durera' gave way to 'Jackie Collins Existential Question Time'. The second track from *Journal for Plague Lovers* is inscrutable, peppered with cultural references and sarcasm. It begins with cheery euphony and tosses a question directly to the listener:

---

29. This is the most Manic Street Preachers thing I have ever read. - MB

if you sin and don't get caught, is it a sin? The chorus poses a sardonic query; it is a childish, childlike refrain, an acerbic reference to Sex Pistols (and their inflammatory merchandise). Bradfield's voice is thick with sarcasm. The song is enigmatic, incomprehensible, as though glued together from random scraps of Edwards' diary. Part pop, part punk, and all snark, it leaves the listener with an absurd mental picture of Joan and Jackie Collins, queening it over a vintage panel show, cluelessly holding forth on avant garde political issues.

'Enola/Alone' gave us a chance to breathe after a stinging, snarling rendition of 'Faster'. When 'Marlon JD' – *Journal's* eighth track – began, we all strained to listen, and to understand. Conceivably a reference to Marlon Brando's brutish, macho films and James Dean's rebellious, sensitive persona, the song is an elegant image. We see a vulnerable young hero, battered, whip-lashed across the face, scarred inside and out. Is Marlon JD allegorical – was Edwards stepping outside himself and into a late-night television screen? Marlon JD is a portrait, a vision of Richey Edwards in a dingy room, huddled beneath blankets on a bare mattress, blankly watching grainy old films on a sputtering television screen as he clutches a warm bottle of Jack Daniels. It is, perhaps, a love song to the *idea* of a Hollywood hero; Edwards mentally dresses up in an impenetrable, gorgeous-tough-guy costume, dreaming of conquered battles and victorious confrontations, until this splintered poem dissolves into the next page of his notebook.

'You Stole the Sun From My Heart': it's a crowd favourite, a singalong, palatable for the most casual listener. The shouty, lovelorn lyrics dim when the guitars crack into 'Motown Junk', and we shouted along to lines we couldn't keep up with and didn't fully know. The song ended; the mood did not.

'Me and Stephen Hawking' is incongruous. It began before we were ready to let 'Motown Junk' go; the last discordant notes rallied and became a tangle of lines that left us lightheaded. Without prologue, the song stabs into meaning: eugenics and an imagined bond of frailty. Lamenting genetic imperfection but smirking at science, 'Me and Stephen Hawking' creates a strange brotherhood between the writer and the subject. On another plane of existence, Edwards and Stephen Hawking laugh mockingly at the idea of simplicity. They share a strange connection. One member of this imaginary and unlikely pairing sits in a failing body that contains the world's brightest mind; the other, a gifted young man ravaged by dysmorphia, anorexia, and disillusionment, rages against the idea of engineered perfection. In Edwards' world, he and Hawking are spectators watching the world burn as it attempts to polish itself to an impossible finish. Even if we couldn't make out the rapid-fire words, we became the mood: our cigarette-filled lungs exploded with outrage and kinship; we heard the word 'sex', so we screamed.

And that was all.

On the *Journal for Plague Lovers* tour, Manic Street Preachers pacified a hungry foreign crowd; only four songs from their newest album were played. It was a sensible enough decision; after a US absence of 10 years, audiences wanted to hear the hits. 'Little Baby Nothing' made us stroke our hair gently; 'You Love Us' was an anthem dedicated informally to the aging indie kids of Chicago. The shuddering silence after 'A Design for Life' sent us slouching out onto the pavement in front of the Metro; we stood shivering in the autumn air, struggling to maintain the camaraderie we'd built before the set began. My dress was thin; at 27, I hadn't yet learned to dress myself sensibly. Nicky Wire appeared from a mysterious door, signed autographs, posed for photos, chatted politely; it began to rain. James Dean Bradfield gave me a smeared autograph on a Navy Pier postcard while looking longingly at the tour bus. It sounds like a let-down, but it wasn't. The gig and the afterglow were the kick I needed to become myself again; like *Journal for Plague Lovers*, my life became a slow burn that flamed; I started an excruciating climb into a reality of love and adventure and creativity.

When I listen to the album now, over a decade later, I marvel at the songs that *didn't* make it onto the Chicago setlist in 2009.

'This Joke Sport Severed' is loneliness itself; it's a strange ballad of self-hatred and the longing for happiness and stability. The word 'bruised' resurfaces; Edwards now speaks in past tense of his attempts to find peace. Some lines seem to refer to both critical acclaim and, conversely, journalistic opinion about his disturbing lifestyle[30] of self-injury and drugs. The music-fan public were witnesses to the drunken red demons Richey Edwards wore on his sleeve. As with 'Me and Stephen Hawking', sterility is referred to; in context, it's ambiguous – is Edwards referring to physical dysfunction or a hardening creative block? 'This Joke Sport Severed' is a still-life of disillusionment; there is silk and amputation and jealousy and a search for a grim, maybe tragic, liberation.

The title track sounds like a rant against God – the 'higher power' of Alcoholics Anonymous, the higher power of self-entitled Christians, the

---

30. It's worth noting here that both Gorbachev's attempt to save the Soviet Union and the Manics' bid to reinvent themselves as tasteful art-pop were ultimately rejected by their intended audiences. In the end, for both, Glasnost was a distraction rather than a destination. Still, Wire will probably be happy with the comparison. - MB

higher power of the broken – perhaps, the God that Richey Edwards wanted to believe in, and couldn't. It is a rant about what only a god can do – punish, reward, forgive, kiss, kill. 'Journal for Plague Lovers', the song, is Edwards battering his fists against the idea of omnipresence, and a hate-note to those that pretended to believe and continued to judge regardless. He takes on the role of God, himself: if only a god can bruise, then Edwards is his own god, controlling – and punishing – his own body, his own mind, his own end. If only a god has the divine power to punish and placate, to provide peace – every negative being in Edwards' life is inconsequential. He stands alone, wishing for his own Presence.

Perhaps every victimised, hopeless, marginalised woman has fantasised about lowering herself into a steaming bath of toxic chemicals. It sounds like both a passive and a luxurious way to end. 'She Bathed Herself in a Bath of Bleach' is apocryphally about a woman Richey Edwards met while recovering in the Priory. Evoking a victim of domestic violence, the subject walks on metaphorical glass. Her wet skin burns pink as she imagines a sweet picnic. Edwards is furious – whoever this is, don't hurt her anymore. She's got empty arms – the abuser is gone, perhaps taken away from her in a flurry of blue lights. Perhaps the abuser is waiting at home for her, to set a nice dinner table once she returns and promises to behave. This song is unique in that Edwards steps outside himself and advocates for an individual, one battered, hopeful, hopeless woman. Here, Richey Edwards is a voice for one single broken human, instead of a scream for the miasma of brutality.

'Facing Page Top Left' is delicate and disjointed – Edwards is surreptitiously gasping with – and for – existence. He deplores beauty standards, basic prettiness, cosmetic regimens; he gives us a bath again; this time, a bath of acid. Rather than a whole piece, 'Facing Page Top Left' is a collection of words and phrases in Edwards' discarded diary, lovingly pasted together by the remaining Manics into a serenade. It is a delicate anthem to skin-surface failure – sugar pills, calories, facial care, cancer – if the body is broken, charisma dies. Everything Edwards' psychiatrists have told him to abandon is scrawled across this song; he rejects it all. He is announced, in all his self-perceived insufficiency, by his cologne. The sunlight scours the thin skin, initial perceptions mean nothing, getting better means more credibility and, at the same time, less.

'Doors Closing Slowly' is a funeral dirge, and the victim is hope. This song opens, like others, upon Edwards' internal struggle with an imaginary higher power. He is lonely; isolated even though fandom and acclaim attempt to pierce his apathy. It's easier to be hung as a martyr than to live as a peasant; Edwards abhors both religious iconography and those who seek to gain from it. 'Doors Closing Slowly' – the title recalls Edwards' own struggle with survival. The final lines are a bitter growl at the believers who selfishly suck up unearned justice.

Cymbals tapping give way to a dark rhythm; 'All is Vanity' could be inserted into *The Holy Bible* seamlessly. This is a to-do list gone wrong. Edwards cannot make himself understood. Wrong, right, neutrality – he wakes to what he should do and spends the day writhing in sarcasm and sickness and confusion. It's the facts of life – but he's screaming them into a void. It's the void of his tattered posthumous pages, but we hear it here, on this track. He'd rather have a regimen. He'd rather have everything neat and tidy and be told what to do; but he's languishing, unshaven, hesitating - knowing that if he heads out into the sunlight, too many choices and the honesty of a world rife with options and opinions would destroy his fragility.

'Pretention/Repulsion' is another confused outcry. This/that, yes/no, cartoon/porn – the song is a nest of insecurity and fury. Edwards is shut down, started up, a broken piece, a whole entity, a sex symbol, a cartoon. Toiling intelligence is shaven off by shards of his own insecurity. He fetishises himself just as the gig girls and the music journalists did: he's a one-dimensional doll, an iconic soft-sex graphic. This is another song that seems pieced together; it's as if a scrapbook collapsed upon itself and erupted into a ferocious hurt. It may be album-filler, but it's also a small screening of the words that ripped through Richey Edwards' brain.

'Virginia State Epileptic Colony' is like a film; it blends scenes from an archaic sanatorium with Edwards' own experience in psychiatric hospitals. The deceptively poppy chorus mocks hospital staples such as lifestyle skill courses – cooking, decorating, cleaning. The song is rooted in history: The Virginia State Colony for the Epileptics and Feeble Minded was an Edwardian-era American institution commissioned by faux-humanitarians and real-life eugenicists. In this lilting, almost carelessly-sung track, Edwards returns to his mockery of idealised mental and physical perfectionism; his deep, fraternal sympathy for the broken and the disadvantaged gilds Bradfield's caustic, nasal vocals.

And, finally, 'William's Last Words' is a Manics anomaly: a wistful, loving sigh. This not goodbye; it is goodnight, a thank you, a love letter to the casualty of a shared childhood. It sounds like dawn, though it was penned in the dusk of a painful youth. It features rare vocals by Nicky Wire, Edwards' 'glamour twin': his more stable second self. Wire's charmingly off-key vocals are tender with grief and with acceptance. Richey Edwards, in the flesh, will not return, but he is still the core of a band who still salute him from the stage. He is part of their DNA; Manic Street Preachers are a three-piece now but there is still a space for Richey's shadow. He is watching.

Fans and fan-adjacent cynics still speculate. Perhaps Edwards is wandering the streets of Goa, barefoot, clad in burlap. Is he hiding in Paris, writing poetry in a damp basement flat? Was he spotted in the mud-spattered crowds of Glastonbury Festival, shielded by sunglasses and a blond dye job? Kurt Cobain aside, Richey Edwards is the 'It' boy of the 27 Club, the question mark that ended an era of rock in general and of his own band in particular. His singularity as a Manic Street Preacher – the poet in residence, but rarely a musician – adds to the fascination with his life and with his uncertain death. Credited with rhythm guitar he could scarcely play, Edwards was nonetheless the soul of a band that no longer exists. After *Everything Must Go*, on which the last of Edwards' intended songs appeared, the band was effectively a trio. We've gotten used to it; they were a new band, with a link to an old dream. But when *Journal for Plague Lovers* was released, Manic Street Preachers were a whole unit again, the bad boys of Blackwood, the liberation of spirit and fire and furious consciousness we all needed. If not a full stop, the album is, at least, a curtain call.

Expertly produced, beautifully scored, *Journal for Plague Lovers* is Edwards' last hallelujah. Bradfield's voice, when not pulsing with fury, glows with a rare gentleness. If Edwards' last lyrics were his swan song – a final gift to his bandmates – *Journal for Plague Lovers* was the remaining Manics' gift to Richey Edwards. Whatever it is, and whatever it is not, it is, at least, beautifully imperfect, and entirely complete.

Part Eleven

2009–2010

2009 (continued)

May 18
- *NME.com* offers fans free downloads of two Manics songs, 'Doors Closing Slowly' – taken from the new album – and a cover of The Horrors' 'Vision Blurred'.

May 24
- Surfing a wave of good press and good will, *Journal For Plague Lovers* charts at number three, alleviating fears from Nicky Wire that such an uncommercial record could nullify the renewed popularity the band had gained from *Send Away The Tigers*.

May 25
- The *Journal For Plague Lovers* tour begins at Glasgow Barrowlands, with the band playing the album in its entirety in the first half of the show, then after the interval coming back to play a second set of hits (plus a rare resurfacing of 1990 b-side and fan favourite 'Sorrow 16'). The set will stay more-or-less the same throughout the tour, which ends on June 6 in Belfast.

May 26
- At a gig in Llandudno, Wales, a prolapsed disc in Nicky's spine goes into spasm, meaning he is virtually rooted to the spot throughout the show. He vows to continue the tour, but warns fans it will involve 'a combination of standing still, sitting down on stage, back braces and pain killers'.

June 4
- 'Bag Lady', the album's hidden track, is offered as a free download on the band's website, alongside a remix by Jonathan Crisp.

June 8
- The first conventional show of the year comes courtesy of the *Mojo* 'honours list' series of gigs, and takes place at London's HMV Forum (previously the Kentish Town Forum), with support from New Young Pony Club.

June 11
- James, Sean and Nicky are presented with *Mojo* magazine's 'Maverick' award at a ceremony in London. The award is presented by Guns N' Roses bass player (and Manics hero) Duff McKagan.

June 13
- The summer festival season starts at Denmark's Rock Under Broen. The band will play a comparatively light eight European Festivals across the summer.

June 15
- An EP of *Journal For Plague Lovers* remixes is released on iTunes, including takes by Patrick Wolfe, Saint Etienne, The Horrors, Andrew Weatherall and more.

June 18
- *Drowned In Sound* pairs Nicky with emerging singer/songwriter Catherine Anne Davies for an 'Artist on Artist' feature. He tells her that playing their old albums all the way through on tour is something the band would only do when they're 'finished and need the money', saying that 'it's a sign that you don't matter anymore'.
- Nicky begins to talk up the tenth Manics album in several interviews, which he describes as 'Heavy Metal Tamla Motown' (noting that James hates it when he makes statements like this). For his part, James tells the *South Wales Echo* that the next record needs to 'lighten the mood'.

July 9
- Patrick Jones' second album *Tongues For Stammering* is released, featuring four tracks with music by James Dean Bradfield.

July 11
- The band headline the King Tuts Wah Wah Hut stage at T In The Park.

July 20
- The Manics cancel appearances at a trio of Japanese festivals after Nicky comes down with gastroenteritis and is declared unfit to fly.

September 15
- *Journal For Plague Lovers* is released in the US.

September 18
- The Manics begin a 13-date tour of the US and Canada, playing clubs including San Francisco's Fillmore and Chicago's Metro. Aside from the 1,500-capacity Webster Hall in New York, average attendance is still numbered in the low-hundreds rather than thousands.

October 23
- James appears at Dame Shirley Bassey's show at The Roundhouse to play guitar on 'The Girl From Tiger Bay', a song he and Nicky have contributed to her upcoming album *The Performance*.

November 2
- James performs a short acoustic set at Brixton Academy to raise money and awareness for poverty relief charity CARE International.

November 7
- Nicky tells *NME* the next Manics album will be called 'It's Not War Just The End of Love', and that work on it is starting that month.

November 9
- Dame Shirley's album, *The Performance*, is released.

2010

February 18
- A brief escape from the studio to play a show celebrating the 20th anniversary of the legendary King Tut's Wah Wah Hut in Glasgow. For the first time in many years the band performs as a three-piece with no keyboard player or extra guitarist. They open the set with 1990 b-side 'Strip It Down'. Nicky calls Radiohead's Ed O'Brian a 'cunt' from the stage.

May 28
- Details of the tenth Manics album, now titled *Postcards From A Young Man*, are announced. Nicky says that the album will be 'one last shot at mass communication.' The release will be supported by a 23-date UK tour; the longest the band has ever undertaken. *Postcards* was recorded entirely at Faster Studios, produced by Dave Eringa and Loz Williams, and features guest spots by John Cale, Ian McCulloch and Duff McKagan. The band also confirm that they have re-signed with Columbia Records, having fulfilled their original ten-album deal.

June 26
- The band open for Paul McCartney at the Millenium Stadium.

June 30
- The Manics join Twitter, initially with the handle @ManicsPostcards, though they will later shorten it to @Manics. Nicky says that he does the

words and Sean does the technology. When asked who they're following he says 'Sean wrote them all down for me, but I can't remember. It's a lot of Formula One.'.

July
• James travels to New York to finish tracking on the album.

July 21
• Nicky says he's attempting to write an episode of *Doctor Who* about Dylan Thomas called 'Do Not Go Gentle'.

July 26
• The new Manics single, '(It's Not War) Just The End Of Love' gets its radio premiere simultaneously on the Radio 2, XFM, 6Music and Absolute breakfast shows. The band announce that Welsh actor Michael Sheen (*The Queen*, *Twilight*) will star in the video.

August 5
• The Manics play a secret show at Hammersmith Working Mens Club in London for an audience of competition winners selected through Twitter. They premier '(It's Not War) Just The End of Love', 'The Descent Parts 1 & 2', 'Postcards From A Young Man' and 'Some Kind of Nothingness'.

August 15
• James appears on BBC 6Music's 'The First Time With', a show dedicated to his favourite music.

August 26
• The video for '(It's Not War) Just The End Of Love' is premiered on the *GMTV* website.

September 8
• A live version of 'Faster' recorded at the Hammersmith Working Mens Club show is released as a free download from the Amazon website.

September 12
• Nicky tells the *News of the World* that the band plan to follow *Postcards From a Young Man* with 'a vast, sprawling triple album' inspired by Magnetic Fields' classic *69 Love Songs* provisionally titled '70 Songs of Hatred and Failure'.

September 13
- *(It's Not War) Just The End Of Love* (Sony/Columbia)
  Tracklisting:
  1. '(It's Not War) Just The End of Love'
  2. 'I'm Leaving You For Solitude'*
  3. 'Distractions'*
  4. 'Ostpolitik'*
  5. 'Lost Voices'**
  6. 'I Know The Numbers'**
  Formats:
  CD1, CD2 (available only through manics.co.uk), 7"

September 17
- Nicky interviews left-wing political heavyweight Tony Benn for *The Quietus.*
- *The Independent On Sunday* says the new Manics is album is 'surely their best since *Everything Must Go'.*

September 19
- '(It's Not War) Just The End of Love' charts at 28, their lowest chart placement since 'Life Becoming A Landslide' in early 1994, and the first 'lead' Manics single to miss out on the top 20 in 17 years.

September 20
- *Postcards From A Young Man* (Sony/Columbia)
  Tracklisting:
  1. '(It's Not War) Just The End of Love'
  2. 'Postcards From A Young Man'
  3. 'Some Kind Of Nothingness'
  4. 'The Descent (Parts 1 & 2)'
  5. 'Hazleton Avenue'
  6. 'Auto-Intoxication'
  7. 'Golden Platitudes'
  8. 'I Think I Found It'
  9. 'A Billion Balconies Facing The Sun'
  10. 'All We Make Is Entertainment'
  11. 'The Future Has Been Here 4Ever'
  12. 'Don't Be Evil'
  Formats:
  CD, deluxe 2-CD book with demos, ltd edition box set, LP

Postcards from a Young Man

By Tracey Wise

'It's not easy when it matters'

It's a sunny day in September 2010, and for reasons long since forgotten, I am walking down Oxford Street, passing HMV. A large, external display has been constructed for a new album, the new release from *My Boys*. Suddenly, I am 15 again. My stomach is doing cartwheels and I'm smiling. 'My Boys' being the name I have long used in affection and adoration for the band that means everything to me and more – and has done for the last 25 years. They are the band that made me realise that it is okay to be proud of your own intelligence, your love of books, your politics and your decidedly working-class background. The band I have followed across Britain and Ireland, that has made strangers into friends, formed reading lists, and found me other bands and albums to love. The band that I have often been accused of being an 'obsessive' about (I wear that as a badge of honour).

Manic Street Preachers.

Except, it's 2010, and I am no longer a shy, awkward GCSE student with bad skin, bad hair and no idea yet of what eyeliner is and what it can do for you. It's 2010, I'm a part-time barmaid, just over six months from qualifying as a nurse; the country has not-long elected a Conservative-lead coalition (not great news for an almost-nurse.) It's 2010, and my Dad is terminally ill. A new album from My Boys may seem a small reason to smile, but we must take the small victories where we find them. And in 2010, damn, I needed a reason to smile.

* * *

Postcards from a Young Man makes you smile. After the wilfully difficult, Albini-recorded-Richey-penned *Journal for Plague Lovers*, it heralded a return to a more 'classic' Manic Street Preachers; to the use of sweeping strings first embraced on *Everything Must Go*, to those big choruses that brought them back to the charts with *Send Away the Tigers*, and that still-present trait of fitting in as many words as possible, whether they should work together or not. In their earlier years you could argue that this was employed in order to flaunt their intelligence; a signal that 'we're better than you in ways you'll never understand'. What felt like a superiority complex has softened as the Manics have grown older. Those wordy, barely scannable lines are about urgency, a need to get across the whole jumble of ideas and feelings in Wire's head. The band have become masters of welding the awkward and the populist: Opening track '(It's Not War) Just the End of Love' hardly trips off the tongue as a title – but makes up for this by being a statement of big sounds and big ideas. The Manics are having their cake and eating it. *'We're so post-modern'* says Wire on 'All we Make is Entertainment', *'we're so post everything'*.

One of Nicky Wire's strengths as a lyricist has always been his introspection – his ability to pull apart his own vulnerabilities. It's not always the case, and as much as I love the man there are times when he has, on occasion, appeared a tad arrogant. His motormouth mode may be entertaining, but he is arguably at his best when examining his own insecurities, for example the pervading notions of manhood and masculinity on *This is My Truth, Tell Me Yours'* beautiful 'Born a Girl'. Having kept his silence on the Richey-penned *Journal*, *Postcards from a Young Man* allows Wire to once again direct his gaze inward. The album's title track being just one instance in which he admits that he might not always have been right in his beliefs ... a statement completely at odds with the cocksure early Manics. Likewise, on 'The Descent (Parts 1 & 2)', Wire again admits to being less than confident in his own abilities.

That said, amongst the politics and introspection, *Postcards* also errs towards hopefulness. The post-Richey Manics can feel, quite understandably, like they're trying to make sense of the past, processing what the hell has just happened. *Postcards from a Young Man* feels like a band telling their story of surviving shock without forgetting; a band trying to ... not move on exactly, but not let the grief and sadness continue to define them. On 'I Think I Found It' occasional lyricist James Dean Bradfield ponders on chance meetings and his own love of music, while 'The Future Has Been Here 4 Ever' remembers that, whilst we cannot always look to rewrite our past, sometimes having had someone, or something, in your life is enough.

*   *   *

Like many my age, my love of music came from being a teenager in the mid 90's – just about old enough to catch the end of Nirvana and the emergence of Britpop, when chart battles were talked about on the Six O'clock news and *Top of the Pops* was still a must-watch. We had the *Evening Session* on Radio One, *Select* magazine, *NME* and *Melody Maker*. I had never known anything like it – and hell, the teenage me needed this! The impact of the music I found at this time is still enough, even now in 2021, to knock the wind out of me. I am still known to cry at albums from that era, ruminating on times long gone; stuck in a sweaty, hot gig venue with the best people. Still in love with the music and culture from those times. Crying at a certain band, or that one album or song that said *everything* just as it was needed. This is very much my relationship with Manic Street Preachers.

I can still tell you exactly which show Nicky Wire wore a tiara that I had thrown on stage. I still remember seeing in the Millennium with them, or the show in which my skirt fell off in the mosh pit and my adorable, very good, very brave friend Sarah saved me by diving on the floor to find it whilst her fiancé, Will, tried to maintain my dignity (true story). I still remember the weirdness of seeing them the day after the 9/11 attacks; the time my best mate David drove us from Hampshire to Essex after work for me to see them play their first show in over a year, the pilgrimages to see them in Wales and Ireland. I even got audience tickets to see them on *CD:UK*. Heck, I got engaged at one of their biggest gigs. As such, it is more than fair to say that my love for My Boys has seen me through many days and life events, both good and bad. And outlasted the engagement.

*   *   *

There is always a bit of a routine that comes with a new Manic Street Preachers release. It usually starts with the announcement of a long, wordy album or lead single title. Nicky Wire will inevitably start talking up the sound – and he did not disappoint when it came to *Postcards from a Young Man*, announcing it as 'heavy metal Tamala Motown'. Then working out which formats you can afford/justify in pre orders. And of course, then there is the planning of which tour dates you can catch, the travel, and the (then inevitable) Manics-fan wardrobe decisions. For someone for whom music is everything, this should all be hugely exciting. But this is *Postcards for a Young Man* I'm talking about. It's 2010, I'm no longer 15 and everything, from politics to personal issues, feels like one gigantic mess.

I have never been one for the 'New Year, New Me' or 'this is gonna be MY year' phenomena that accompanies every January 1. But 2010, on paper, looked for many reasons to be amazing. I had moved back to my home city two years previously and now had an incredible circle of friends around me. I was becoming an auntie. I had found my career – not just a career but a *vocation*. And to get through my poorly state-financed training, I had a flexible bar job at a gig venue, meaning I got to see many of my music idols – and discover new ones – in exchange for pulling pints. But spring that year would present a blow. My Dad would be diagnosed with terminal, inoperable lung cancer, on top of an already existing serious respiratory condition, and a congenital defect meaning chemotherapy was not an option. It is fair to say that my Dad and I had not shared the best of relationships, especially since I had left home for university at 18, due to him not understanding my music, clothes, dyed hair, piercings, and books, and me disliking his anachronistic, old-fashioned ways and views. Incredible, given how he had worked for Stiff records, enjoyed a bit of Bowie and had grown up working class in London.

Nothing is black and white. It's not easy when it matters. If you haven't gone through the illness and death of a parent, especially when many things remain unsaid and undone, you can't know that it challenges you and changes you in ways you cannot predict. Combine this with physically and emotionally demanding study and training, often working more than forty hours a week, at all hours, and all else life likes to throw at us all – and well, yeah. 2010 was hard. Bloody hard.

In the midst of this, a new album from My Boys was just confusing. How can you get excited about something as trivial as an album release at a time like this? And for this music loving, almost 30-something – how could everything that was happening not tarnish it? The album that will, more than likely, become important, that will always be associated with a life changing, traumatic event? Whilst music had long been my refuge, something that I turn to when I am in need of solace, I had never experienced anything like this in my life – nothing so complex, painful or challenging. And it was terrifying. For the first time since I had discovered music, there seemed to be very little I could find that felt appropriate or could be a go-to as a panacea for this.

It was not just one of these elements: the fear of listening, and potentially marring the new album or the meaning I had found in my love and devotion of Manic Street Preachers, or even (crassly, but unintentionally) soundtracking the most difficult period imaginable – it was the whole package.

How do you plan to go to gigs in far off towns and cities when you have degree studies and work and emergency trips to Accident and Emergency with your Dad in an ambulance, and calls to district nurses for help and hunting around for prescriptions; when you could get the call from your family, or a health professional telling you to 'come, come NOW!' How do you respond to your friend, Cat, in Sheffield inviting you to come and stay, to see the gig, without seeming callous or indifferent to your family, your seriously ill father, and others around him? How do you see your friends – some that you have not seen in a while – and pretend that this is okay, that this is normal? And how do you stop this incessant, but justifiable overthinking and likely burnout?

I didn't recognise it then, but if you asked me now what I learnt most from this period, it is that you *have* to do the things that allow you to function during these times. Very clearly, you *have to*. Otherwise, it will become all too hard, and you *will* burn out. Never, ever second guess your friends and choose to hide your current norm from them. Because they would not, and should not, be your friends if they choose not to support you in that kind of situation. They are your friends for a reason. Similarly, My Boys are My Boys for a reason.

*   *   *

So, *Postcards from a Young* Man. I hate to break it to you, but *Postcards from a Young Man* doesn't sound like 'heavy metal Tamla Motown' (sorry Nicky, but it just doesn't). It *is*, however, the sound of band that is still creative, still has lots to say, and trying to claim back the universality they had made their own when, heartbreakingly, they found themselves without Richey Edwards. 'One last shot at mass communication', as Wire said at the time, having delivered anything but 'mass communication' on their previous album. This followed an established pattern for the band: Just as *Everything Must Go* rightly couldn't be *The Holy Bible* take two, *Postcards from a Young Man* couldn't be a continuation of its predecessor, *Journal for Plague Lovers*. This was a return to the Everyman Street Preachers, and contained much that both translated their strengths for the mainstream, while emphasising their credentials as national-treasure-status British heavyweights.

2007's *Send Away the Tigers* had begun a tradition of guest vocalists and musicians, each adding something of themselves to their nominated tracks, and while that had been skipped on the intensely personal *Journal* (where the guest was very much Richey himself), the tradition is picked up on *Postcards* and has been maintained on every album since. Sharing vocal duties with James Dean Bradfield on 'Some Kind of Nothingness', Echo and the Bunnymen's Ian McCulloch brings his familiar baritone to the subject of Nicky Wire's beloved pet dog's last days, while the inclusion of Duff McKagan on bass for 'A Billion Balconies Facing the Sun' is a nod to the early Manics' much-discussed ambition to give Guns N' Roses a run for their money, and must have made even the most cynical of fans smile. 'Auto-Intoxication', meanwhile, welcomes Welsh avant-garde royalty in the form of John Cale on keyboards. All three are confirmation, if needed, of the respect the band had built over the years as a musical and ideological force.

The Manics' political agenda is another trademark very much at the fore here. Nicky Wire's frustration with modern politics and the perceived failure of liberalism is laid clear. *Postcards* was released in the wake of the 2010 General Election, which saw in the country's first Conservative government of the century, and the political climate of the era runs through the album. 'Golden Platitudes' reflects on the niceties of the New Labour project and its seeming inability to focus on substance over style. 'Don't Be Evil' now reads like a premonition for everything that has happened in politics, both domestic and international, in the last six or seven years – *'the sickos and bullies praise your name'* could lift easily from a critique of Trump, Farage, Johnson and a whole heap of other bile born in the 'post-truth' world.

*   *   *

I let myself listen to the album. I listened, and I bought the gig tickets for Sheffield and Brixton. I even dug my favourite feather boa out and bought one for my friend and gig buddy, much to the confusion of a more casual observer in the crowd at Sheffield. And once I did, once I stopped fixating on some misinformed belief in the 'rights and wrongs' of dealing with an incoming death and carrying the weight of the supposed expectations I believed others to have of me, there was one hell of a release waiting. Music, of course, was the thing I needed.

In my own burgeoning grief, that was an important realisation; even if, back in 2010, I could not always see it. And, when in the midst of a crisis, when you can't always see the obvious staring you in the face, music can be a great way to soften the edges of those times. Whilst *Postcards from a Young Man* isn't Motown meets Metal, and is not seen by many as one of the band's classics, it remains a solid Manic Street Preachers record, adding to the depth and directions they have taken along their career. For me, it will always be a massively important album by My Boys – how could it not? Just as they had to find a way to deal with the emotions, and not let their grief swallow them whole in the wake of Richey's disappearance, I now had to do the same. Ten years on, I've learned that although grief feels in that moment like it will consume you completely, we do have an enormous capacity to deal with the emotions and come through the other side. Manic Street Preachers – forever and always *My Boys* – might not return to the glory days of spray paint, camo chic and furiousness, but I'm forever grateful for those days, and always will be. They taught me so much about myself and helped me discover so many amazing things – history, literature, pop culture, and mostly, that eyeliner is always your friend. Through *Postcards from a Young Man*, they taught me how to grieve. And for that, I will always be thankful.

So, I went to the show, I hugged my friends hard, I cried, I wore the animal print, the eyeliner, the glitter. I listened to Nicky Wire compare the *Lifeblood* era Manics to them 'looking like Westlife'. I laughed as a newly acquired friend, Dave, nearly deafened me, shrieking in my ear at the Brixton gig, taking place in the interim between my Dad's death and funeral – something we still laugh about to this day. And I had nights I will always remember, despite all else that was happening. For more years now than I'd like to admit to, music has been my comfort, the thing that I cling to, the thing that makes me thrive. For that moment in time, *Postcards from a Young Man* was perfect.

Part Twelve

2010–2013

2010 (continued)

September 22
• Channel 4 screens a special dedicated to the band entitled *One Last Shot At Mass Communication*.

September 26
• *Postcards From A Young Man* charts at a respectable number three.

September 27
• The mammoth *Postcards* tour kicks off in Newcastle. The band will be on the road pretty much constantly until mid January. 54,000 tickets are sold in advance.

October 10
• *Richard*, a novel by Ben Myers that fictionalises Richey's final days, is published by Picador to reasonable acclaim. The band are far from thrilled about this, but stop short of actually condemning it, saying that though they're not happy, such rock mythologising is inevitable and something they've indulged in themselves with their own idols.

October 23
• Nicky places at number 30 in *NME's* annual 'Cool List'.

October 26
• True to form, three shows on the Manics tour (one in Birmingham and two in London) are postponed after James is diagnosed with acute laryngitis.

October 31
• The tour resumes at Leicester's De Montfort Hall.

November 1
• *The Guardian* premieres the video to the next Manics single, 'Some Kind of Nothingness', featuring Echo and the Bunnymen's Ian McCulloch, on its website.

November 13
• The Manics begin their first Australian tour since 1999.

November 26
• The tour moves on to Japan for two shows, with support from The Libertines' Carl Barat.

December 5
- The band perform 'Some Kind of Nothingness' with Ian McCulloch on BBC One's *Strictly Come Dancing*, much to the horror of some fans and satisfaction of others. *The Guardian* runs a piece entitled 'Will The Manics' Appearance On *Strictly Come Dancing* Be Subversive Or Just Submissive?'

December 6
- *Some Kind of Nothingness* (Sony/Columbia)
  Tracklisting:
  1. 'Some Kind of Nothingness'
  2. 'Broken Up Again'*
  3. 'Red Rubber'*
  4. 'Evidence Against Myself'*
  5. 'Slow Reflections/Strange Delays'**
  6. 'Time Aint Nothing'***
  7. 'Some Kind of Nothingness (BBC Live version)'°
  8. 'Masses Against The Classes (live)'°
  9. 'Sleepflower (live)'°
  10. 'Yes (live)'°
  * CD1 only, ** CD2 only, *** 7″ only, °digital only
  Formats
  CD1, CD2 (manics website exclusive), 7″, digital download.

December 12
- Despite the band and their team's best efforts (and a very high profile TV performance on the heavily-rated *Strictly*) 'Some Kind of Nothingness' has the dubious honour of being the first proper Manic Street Preachers single not to chart in the top 40 since the band signed to Sony in 1991. It's their lowest placing since the original Heavenly release of 'You Love Us' charted at 62. Nicky will later say that he is 'devastated' by this, saying 'I was on the floor'. At the time of writing (May 2021) the Manics have yet to have another true top 40 single.

December 15
- Undeterred, the band headline XFM's annual 'Winter Wonderland' at Brixton Academy.

December 16
- Nicky tells *NME* that all he wants for Christmas is 'world peace, the Orange Juice box set and for my *Doctor Who* script to be accepted'.

2011

January 21/22
• The two cancelled Brixton Academy tour shows take place in London.

January 27
• The Manics return to their home town of Blackwood for a Radio 2 special at the Miners Institute. The gig is broadcast live on air, with video streamed on the BBC's website. The band spend the day of the show wandering around old haunts, with Nicky keen to see if his and Richey's names are still on a board at Oakdale Comprehensive commemorating their A-Level results.

February 7
• Nicky writes a guest blog for *The Guardian* railing at the Conservation/Lib Dem coalition government's cutting of funding for libraries in England and Wales.

February 28
• *Postcards From A Young Man* (Sony/Columbia)
  Tracklist
  1. 'Postcards From A Young Man'
  2. 'Inky Fingers'*
  3. 'Engage With Your Shadow'*
  4. 'Kiss My Eyes For Eternity'*
  5. 'Midnight Sun'**
  6. 'The Passing Show'***
  7. 'This Joke Sport Severed (live)'°
  8. 'Peeled Apples (live)'°
  9. 'Marlon JD (live)'°
  * CD1 only, ** CD2 only, ***7" only, ° digital download only
  Formats
  CD1, CD2 (manics website exclusive), 7", digital download.

March 6
• Despite an encouraging midweek showing, the 'Postcards From A Young Man' single charts at 54.

March 15
• Nicky signs a two-book deal with Faber & Faber, the first fruits of which will be a coffee table book of polaroids taken over two decades of touring and recording with the band.

April 22
- Michael Sheen puts on a 72-hour immersive theatre production, *The Port Talbot Passion*. As part of the performance the band plays a short set at a local social club, modifying the words to 'A Design For Life'. They are led away by armed police (hopefully as part of the story).

June 11
- The 2011 festival season – increasingly the band's bread and butter – begins with Pinkpop in the Netherlands. The Manics will play 13 festivals across the summer, including T In the Park, Ireland's Oxygen and V2011 as well as events in Switzerland, Germany, Finland, Turkey, Hungary and Japan.

July 3
- The band headline a show at Apple's iTunes Festival, held at the Roundhouse in London. The gig is streamed live online, released as a download and broadcast on ITV2 the following weekend.

August 30
- Following performances at V2011 the band announce the release of a new collection entitled *National Treasures – The Complete Singles*, coming in October. The double-disc will feature all 37 Manic Street Preachers singles starting with 1990's 'Motown Junk' and stretching to 2011's 'Postcards From A Young Man', plus a new cover of The The's classic 'This Is The Day'. They will play all 38 singles at a one-off gig at the O2 in London at Christmas, after which they will be taking time off to regroup.

September 2
- *This Is The Day* (Sony/Columbia)
  Tracklisting
  1. 'This Is The Day'
  2. 'We Were Never Told'*
  3. 'Rock 'N' Roll Genius'**
  *Digital download only ** HMV exclusive CD
  Formats:
  Download, streaming platforms, HMV exclusive CD

October 4
- James embarks on a four-date acoustic tour to promote the new release, with audiences composed of competition winners.

October 10
- A specially re-recorded version of 'Loves Sweet Exile', rendered as a countrified acoustic slowie called 'The Blue Acoustic Version', is given away for free via Amazon.

October 31
- *National Treasures – The Complete Singles* (Sony/Columbia)
  Tracklisting:
  DISC ONE
  1. 'Motown Junk'
  2. 'Stay Beautiful'
  3. 'Loves Sweet Exile'
  4. 'Slash 'N' Burn'
  5. 'You Love Us'
  6. 'Motorcycle Emptiness'
  7. 'Theme from M*A*S*H (Suicide Is Painless)'
  8. 'Little Baby Nothing'
  9. 'From Despair To Where'
  10. 'La Tristesse Durera (Scream To A Sigh)'
  11. 'Roses In The Hospital'
  12. 'Life Becoming A Landslide'
  13. 'Faster'
  14. 'Revol'
  15. 'She Is Suffering'
  16. 'A Design For Life'
  17. 'Everything Must Go'
  18. 'Kevin Carter'
  19. 'Australia'
  DISC TWO
  1. 'If You Tolerate This Your Children Will Be Next'
  2. 'The Everlasting'
  3. 'You Stole The Sun From My Heart'
  4. 'Tsunami'
  5. 'Masses Against The Classes'
  6. 'So Why So Sad'
  7. 'Found That Soul'
  8. 'Ocean Spray'
  9. 'Let Robeson Sing'
  10. 'There By The Grace Of God'
  11. 'The Love Of Richard Nixon'

12. 'Empty Souls'
13. 'Your Love Alone Is Not Enough'
14. 'Autumnsong'
15. 'Indian Summer'
16. '(It's Not War) Just The End Of Love'
17. 'Some Kind of Nothingness'
18. 'Postcards From A Young Man'
19. 'This Is The Day'
20. 'The Endless Plain Of Fortune'*
*LP only
Formats:
2CD, Deluxe edition (including DVD disc), Super Deluxe Edition box set,
DVD, *Selected Singles* vinyl LP.
Notes:
This compilation plays relatively fast and loose with the definition of 'single'. Technically 'Umbrella' is a single (it had b-sides and everything) but is omitted, while 'Life Becoming a Landslide' is included despite being the first track on an EP rather than a true radio single, which means we should also be getting 'New Art Riot' and *God Save The Manics'* 'A Secret Society'. 'Loves Sweet Exile' and 'Faster' are both double a-sides, which makes 'Repeat (UK)' and 'PCP' singles as well. 'Suicide Alley' is technically a demo, rather than a single, so we'll let them off that one, but arguably 'UK Channel Boredom', sold with copies of the fanzines *Hopelessly Devoted* and *Goldmining*, should be counted, all of which would boost the tracklisting up to 44 songs.

November 9
• *Classic Rock* magazine awards the Manics the 'Classic Rock Songwriters' award at their annual awards ceremony.

November 11
• Nicky's first book, *The Death of the Polaroid – A Manics Family Album* is published.

November 26
• Nicky appears at number 42 in *NME*'s annual 'Cool List'.

December 17
• The final Manics gig of the year (and final UK show for nearly two years) sees the band play a sold-out O2 Arena in London, performing all 37 of

their Sony singles (plus 'Motown Junk'), with Super Furry Animal's Gruff Rhys providing a guest voice on 'Let Robeson Sing' and Nina Persson reprising her vocal for 'Your Love Alone Is Not Enough'.

2012

April 15
• The band embark on their 'International Treasures' tour, taking a greatest-hits show around Europe.

February
• The 20th anniversary of *Generation Terrorists* generates various think-pieces and much nostalgia in the music press.

May 17/18
• The 'International Treasures' tour heads to Japan for two shows, with Super Furry Animals supporting.

July 2
• The Manics contribute a cover of Amy Winehouse's 'Wake Up Alone' to a tribute CD given away with *Q* Magazine.

August 12
• The band performs at the Incheon Pentaport Festival in South Korea. It's the Manics' first time playing the country.

September 12
• A 20th Anniversary edition of *Generation Terrorists* is announced. A limited edition, triple-disc-plus-DVD-and-vinyl 'Special Collector's Edition' sells out almost immediately in pre-sales.

October 6
• Nicky updates *NME* on the progress of new material being demoed at Faster Studios, saying it has a delicate acoustic half and a more electronic, European side.

October 18/20
• *Culture, Alienation, Boredom and Despair,* a new documentary about the making of *Generation Terrorists* by acclaimed Welsh filmmaker Kieran Evans, is screened at the SWN film festival in Wales. An edited version of the film will be included in the *Generation Terrorists* reissue.

October 23
- *Generation Terrorists* is given the 'Classic Album' award at the *Q Awards*.

November 5
- The *Generation Terrorists* 20th Anniversary editions hit shelves, garnering rave reviews and prompting a second burst of appraisals and nostalgia pieces.

November 6
- James plays an acoustic set and does a Q&A at London's Rough Trade records to promote the new box set.

2013

February
- James and Sean head to Hansa Studios, the legendary studio used by Bowie, Depeche Mode, Iggy Pop and more, with Alex Silva – the producer of *The Holy Bible* – in the production chair to work on their eleventh album. Nicky misses the sessions after an outbreak of norovirus in his house, but does send new lyrics via text.

February 22
- Nicky reveals on Twitter that the band are working on a cinematic, seven-minute song called 'Rewind The Film'.

March
- Work on the album moves to occasional Manics haunt, Rockfield Studios, Monmouthshire.

March 28
- Welsh singer Cate Le Bon records vocals for a new Manics song called 'Four Lonely Roads'.

April 30
- In possibly the most Manic Street Preachers move ever, the band announces that they will be touring Australia and New Zealand to coincide with the British and Irish Lions rugby tour in June.

May 2
- Sheffield's Richard Hawley, once a member of the Longpigs and now an acclaimed solo artist, is in the studio with the band adding vocals to 'Rewind The Film'.

May 3
• James creates an ambient soundtrack for award-winning Welsh filmmaker Gideon Koppel's new film *Borth*.

May 6
• Recording at Rockfield finishes. The band will complete the album(s) at their own Faster Studios.

May 29
• *NME* reports that the Manics have abandoned the occasionally touted plan of '70 Songs Of Hatred And Despair' in favour of two separate records, one largely acoustic and the other krautrock influenced.

June 28
• The 'Send Away The Lions' tour begins, shadowing the British and Irish Lions rugby tour of New Zealand and Australia. The band will spend a happy month watching rugby between playing shows. James and Nicky will occasionally busk on the streets.

July 1
• The Manics appear on the New Zealand's version of *The X-Factor* to perform 'If You Tolerate This Your Children Will Be Next'.

July 2
• The Manics play their first ever full show in New Zealand, at Auckland's Vector Arena.
• 'If You Tolerate This' makes an unexpected appearance in the New Zealand charts.

July 8
• Details of the eleventh Manics album, *Rewind The Film*, are announced, set for release in September. Fans pre-ordering on iTunes are given an instant download of the title track, featuring Richard Hawley. The song receives its premiere on BBC 6Music.

July 11
• Kieran Evans' melancholic video for 'Rewind The Film' drops on YouTube and quickly hits 100,000 views

July 30
The video for a new Manics track, 'Show Me The Wonder', again directed by Kieran Evans, is added to YouTube. Nicky and James both say that 70s Elvis is an influence on the song. The video, an entertaining nod to

1970s teenagerdom, stars Craig Roberts, recently seen in *Skins* and Richard Ayoade's movie, *Submarine*.

September
- Reviews begin coming in for *Rewind The Film*, which receives five stars from *The Independent*, four from *The Guardian* and *Q* and 7/10 from *NME*. Regrettably, for the first time since 2004, no-one says that the new Manics album is 'their best since *Everything Must Go*.'

September 1
- James tries his hand at radio presenting, covering for Stuart Maconie as the host of 6Music's left-field and outsider music programme, *Freakzone*.

September 4
- Nicky reveals that the next Manics album, much of which is already recorded, will be called *Futurology*.

September 8
- The first Manic Street Preachers UK performance in nearly two years takes place, with the band playing at BBC Radio 2's massive 'Festival In A Day' in London's Hyde Park.

September 9
- ***Show Me The Wonder*** (Sony/Columbia)
  Tracklisting
  1. 'Show Me The Wonder'
  2. 'Melancholyme'*
  3. 'Tsunami (live)'*
  4. 'T.E. Lawrence on a Bike'**
  *Digital download only, ** 7"1 only, **7"2 only
  Formats:
  Digital download, streaming, two 7"s

September 10
- The Manics play a tiny show for Absolute Radio at London's iconic 100 Club on Oxford Street.
- *Rewind The Film* is Album of the Day on BBC 6Music, with each show playing a new song from the record.

September 15
- The band headline BBC 6Music's Festival No.6 in Portmeirion, Wales. Richard Hawley guests on 'Rewind The Film' live for the first time.

September 16
- *Rewind The Film* (Sony/Columbia)
  Tracklisting:
  1. 'This Sullen Welsh Heart'
  2. 'Show Me The Wonder'
  3. 'Rewind The Film'
  4. 'Builder of Routines'
  5. '4 Lonely Roads'
  6. 'I Miss The Tokyo Skyline'
  7. 'Anthem For A Lost Cause'
  8. 'As Holy As The Soil (That Buries Your Skin)'
  9. '3 Ways To See Despair'
  10. 'Running Out Of Fantasy'
  11. 'Manobier'
  12. '30-Year War'
  Formats:
  CD, Deluxe 2–Disc CD, LP, download, streaming

Rewind The Film

By Marc Burrows

'We don't push real buttons enough these days'

It took me ages to get the VHS player up and running and I could feel you looking over my shoulder the whole time. You're smiling quietly to yourself. Not impatient, just amused. The back of the TV is now a tangled snakepit of cables; coaxial to SCAAT adaptors, SCAAT to HDMI convertors, each with their own annoyingly long leads to get inexplicably knotted and tangled like goth spaghetti. That, I am well aware, is the thing that will annoy you most. Your cables were always neat. You bought special little loops of velcro and plastic tubes for them. I think I've done it though, finally, after much swearing, hammering buttons, and same-day-delivering the right connections at prohibitive expense just because once I've made my mind up, I've made my mind up. You know what I'm like. Kelly endured my grunting and swearing for a while, sped through her sarcastic phase, and eventually went for a run. She doesn't understand. I don't think she can. She wasn't *there*.

I found the tapes in Mum's attic. We were going through her things, cleaning out the house. One of those things you just have to do. You could pay someone else, but who can afford that? And, really, would you want to? Some jobs are for the family; scrabbling around in the attic is one of them. Indulging in the insignificance of the memories: the day Dad put the TV aerial up there, running the cables down the side of the house and into the living room. He was exceptionally proud of himself for that. Or the time he and my brother spent a weekend nailing in floor boards so we could move around more easily. They're odd spaces, attics, even in new houses. Non-rooms. Places where things get put, but no-one spends time. No personality has been imprinted. Somehow, they still have some sort of weird power – the Christmas decorations, the knackered guitar amp, the suitcases, the two bags of summer clothes to be swapped with Mum's jumpers and thick coats, currently hanging in the bedroom wardrobe, when winter ends. Except now they're probably off to the Age Concern shop. The piles and piles of board games, all in ratty, torn and sellotaped cardboard boxes, likely for the bin.

I have no idea what made her keep a box of video tapes. It's not like I'm going to need my *X-Files* feature-length-mythology-episode collection (limited edition, in genuine mock evidence boxes). All the seasons are on streaming for a start, and besides, I've lost 'Tunguska'. I can't see my sister wanting her copy of *Free Willy*, either. If the charity shop want them I'll be amazed, although I might try CeX for the *X-Files* ones. You never know. Fuck, I saved for those for *months*. You get a brief kick out of seeing this stuff, and then it's best to move on. These aren't little treasures of nostalgia. It's just … stuff.

And then I found them. Three VHS tapes, two official ones, bought new, one a trusty Scotch 120-minute, taped off the telly. A few words have been written in biro on the label of the latter and then crossed out ('*Alien 3*, *Deep Space Nine tape one*', if you must know). Over these someone – me, obviously – has written the word 'MANICS' in inch-high letters using a thick, black felt tip. Five point stars and hammer-and-sickles cover the rest of the flimsy sleeve in pink highlighter. I was nothing if not subtle. The other two are professional jobs, officially released: *Everything Live* and *Leaving The Twentieth Century*, the Manic' first two video releases. I just stared at them, turning them over in my hands, reading the blurred tracklisting through the plastic sleeve, opening them to examine the cassettes inside. The labels on the tapes are completely familiar. Two minutes ago I couldn't have told you what they looked like, now it's like looking into the face of an old friend.

It is two days later, and I'm kneeling in front of the machine on knees that are far from happy about it, still grumpy from a morning of trying to get the fucking thing to work. 'What is the point?' an exasperated Kelly had said, 'It's all on YouTube. I'm pretty sure we've got one of them on DVD anyway'.

'I lost the disc' I said, absently

'Then why the fuck is the case still there?'

I can't tell her that the answer is that if you've got a Manic Street Preachers DVD then you damn well display your Manic Street Preachers DVD, in case people come round and look at your DVDs. She's not going to understand. She doesn't understand any of this. I only half-do myself. You would have got it though.

I try the home-recorded one first. This tape was several years of work. There's no track listing but even with twenty years' distance I know pretty much what's on it. Every performance of the band on TV, no matter what time, no matter when, was taped. There's *Top of the Pops* and *TFI Friday*, the *Jools Holland* when Nicky sprained his wrist 'answering the phone' and Pete Townsend's bass player stood in for 'Everything Must Go' and 'Australia', the Hillsborough concert, Phoenix Festival, everything. More exciting for me is the older stuff, an old late-night Channel 4 show called *Butt Naked* with a full set from the *Holy Bible* era, my boys all camo and cheekbones. There's a bit in 'You Love Us' where you can actually hear Richey's guitar. There's edited highlights from Glastonbury 94 too. It's a treasure trove. Come to think of it, I'm amazed it all fits onto one tape. The machine pulls it into the slot. Clunk-click. Satisfying. Obviously I hadn't wound the tape back to the beginning last time I watched it, whenever that was, so I rewind the film (and this is the point where you can do a shot if you're playing the 'crowbar in the album title' drinking game), and let it rattle backward. I honestly don't think I've heard this sound for over a decade. It sounds oddly like The Bullet Train. I'd never made that connection before. We got it once, from Osaka, when we saw them in Japan. The Summer Sonic festival. Tokyo. 2007. Remember? I'd cried during 'Ocean Spray', because of Dad, and we couldn't afford the beer so had shared one between us. Click, whir, stop. Here we go. I genuinely get a kick from the resistance against my finger and the tactile click of the play button. We don't push real buttons enough these days.

Immediately it's clear that something is wrong. This is our boys, the impossibly young lads that, at the time, had seemed like an older version of themselves. I think this is 'A Design For Life' on *Top of the Pops*. Except there's no audio and the video is playing as if in fast forward. Stop. Start. No difference. Rewind. Again. Nothing. Eject, inspect tape, blow on it. I'm not sure why. It's just something we do. Back in. Click. Play. Same. Speedy silence. I sit back and think about this, because there's a faint bell ringing somewhere. Wasn't there a mode or something? Where you could make a tape last twice as long by recording at twice the speed? I do a quick Google on my phone, trying to remember the terminology – 'Long Play Mode', I discover. Scanning the front of the VCR I found on eBay pulls an 'oh for fucks sake' out of me that startles the poor, long suffering cat. This machine doesn't have long play mode. I watch the band sweep comically in double time for a few minutes, but it's not the same. Eject. I don't really feel anything.

We used to watch this together, you and me. After your or my parents had gone to sleep. If we were at yours I'd be in a made-up bed on the living room floor, by the gas fire with the fake coal made from brightly coloured glass. If we were at mine we just slept in my bed. My parents honestly didn't care. I suspect they were just happy someone was paying attention to me. My Dad enjoyed getting us drunk. Your folks would be horrified if they knew what mine were fine with. Of course, eventually, they were exactly that. And then some. We'd turn out the lights and put the video on, holding hands and discussing this or that detail. The evolution of Nicky's hair. The gap stage-right. The way Richey's interviews burned on the page when you read them, but those same quotes spoken aloud sounded soft and contemplative. Seeing those old interviews on telly, having read the quotes so often, was a genuine surprise. We loved the way Richey called the *NME* 'Noo Moosikul Express' in his lovely, quiet voice. We'd rewind it to hear it again. There's another bit, where Richey does this little pogo on stage, that we'd watched so often that bit of tape had developed a line of static. I was desperate to see that crackle again. It represented a groove, worn down by ritual. The ritual of us.

Still. This one's a bust. I reach around for the next. *Everything Live* has a blushing red cover. I always thought it would taste like cheap strawberry cider if I licked it. People often talk about the smell of old books, but no-one ever mentions the smell of old plastic VHS tape cases. They smell like toffee. This one's a recording of the Manics' gig at the Nynex, the then-current name for Manchester Arena. Radio 1 had broadcast it live and we'd listened to it as it had happened, 200 miles south, lying on the floor of my room on those big, ridiculous dark-blue floor cushions with gold stars and suns on them. Everyone in the 90s had those. We'd closed the curtains, turned the light off and the stereo up, just the stereo display to see by, and the glow-in-the-dark stars on the ceiling that Mum had glued there when I was little, and I couldn't bear to ever take down. They were still there when we cleaned the house out, despite that room being a place to stash the unused exercise bike and the laundry for the best part of a decade. Mum loved them. So did you. It occurs to me that the two people I associate most with those stars are lost. No plastic constellations to guide them home.

I have more luck with *Everything Live*. The concert had been a surprise when we'd first watched it together – for some reason, without discussing it, we'd both assumed it had been an open-air stadium show. I have no idea why. At fourteen you don't really understand how this stuff works. Nor that the Manics weren't quite at Wembley-levels yet. Manchester may as well have been like Las Vegas for all we knew. I only had the picture in my head. We watched it together, obviously, round mine, Mum popping in and out, asking about Nicky's tiara, giving us an oddly suggestive look, as if vaguely cross-dressing rockstars were a built in component of what *your* parents called our 'almost like brothers' friendship. We'd talked a lot about how this gig seemed to lose some of what we'd loved about the broadcast, although I maintain it's a substantially better audio mix. The keyboards were way too high before. You told me I was being 'finickity'. I love that word. Still, I miss Steve Lamacq popping up at the end.

I stay where I am for the first song, crouched in front of the video, convinced it's going to chew the tape up any second, but it seems to be fine so when the band roll into 'Enola/Alone' I get up, my knees clicking painfully, an unconscious grunt. Kelly *hates* the noises I make when I stand up and sit down. 'You're like a fucking old man', she says. 'It's so unattractive'. It's my fortieth next year. I *am* a fucking old man. My knees hurt. On the screen the crowd are jumping as one to the song. Fuck, I loved that about gigs. We'd hold hands and let the whole, bouncing, sweating brownian motion of the sway move us around, trying not to lose each other. I'd seen the Manics last year, and it was nothing like this. I'd won tickets off the radio. No-one jumped. No-one danced. A small, redheaded woman in leopard print and lavish eyeliner near the front and the inevitable presence of Simon Price is all that made this feel like a Manics gig. They were doing songs from *Rewind The Film*, but the intimacy was strangely lost in what should have been an appropriately intimate location. I should have been so excited, but I just hung at the back. I watched, and I enjoyed, but the all-of-us-together-what-do-you-think-of-this-one vibe felt too warm, too cosy. I felt like I was watching a friend's band do a reunion gig down the local. All I could think about was what it wasn't. The inconceivable notion of listening to *these* songs leaning against a pillar with a beer. You'd have hated it, I know that much. You were pissed off enough at the Oasis t-shirts on the Nynex video, let alone a bordering-middle-aged crowd of perfectly pleasant Absolute Radio listeners.

On the video James is doing an acoustic version of 'This Is Yesterday'. A song about losing yourself in the past that was hard enough to watch back in the 90s. Watching this pion to painful nostalgia, twenty-something years later … that's sadness squared. Too rich for my blood, I eject the tape. I don't bother to rewind it.

The next one is going to be the hardest to watch. Kelly is right, I do have this on DVD, though ever since I lost you, I haven't been able to watch it. I'm not sure what happened to the disc. It seems appropriate that it's missing. Miraculously this video is already rewound. I must have lent it to you, because I'm never this fastidious. It occurs to me that this means you were the last person to touch this tape, you and Mum, before she boxed it up, and suddenly the case feels heavier. Clunk. Click. I sit and watch the montage of fans travelling to the Millenium Stadium in Cardiff, set to a Joy Division instrumental; it seems so dated, amateurish. The hair cuts and the clothes and the chilly weather all sync into my memory though. We were there. You and me, and everyone else. I pause, watching a mid-interview Nicky Wire at a press conference wobble slightly on the screen. VHS freeze frame. You know, I'm not sure I'm ready for this.

We'd been almost at the front, right in the feather-bowered vice of the crowd, grasping each other's arms, plastic bangle to plastic bangle, eye-linered boy tethered to eye-linered boy. This was the pinnacle of Manicsdom. It was our Sermon on the Mount. Our Woodstock. At midnight we'd kissed and kissed, and pressed ourselves together and cried and our friends had laughed and clapped and James had played 'Can't Take My Eyes Off Of You' and I couldn't. I never could. In a way, I never have. Everywhere we've been, everywhere we'd seen them, Tokyo, Berlin, Vancouver. Even, weirdest of all, a leisure centre in Kettering. None of them were as special as this one. They were reflections of it really. I can't just sit and watch this video, if I move into the linear flow of the songs then I'm back there, and the fact you're not holding my hand makes that unthinkable. Creaking knees crouch in front of the player and I scan through with the crisp, smooth, satisfying buttons. There is so much joy here. There's something like 60,000 people in that stadium and every one of them knows that this is a special night. We kissed and I felt the millennium turn over. I scan back and forth, jumping from moment to moment, from memory to memory. I remember being younger, thinner, more in love, more in lust, angrier, more energetic, caring more, hating more, smiling more. I don't think I can feel that strongly about anything now. The calluses are too thick. I remember you. I remember loss. I sit up and my back hurts and my knees hurt and I rewind the film and I start again.

Part Thirteen

2013–2014

2013 (continued)

September 20
- A short UK/Ireland tour begins in Dublin. The band play smallish theatres in keeping with the intimate tone of the album, with the traditional 'big' London show taking place on September 24 in the comparatively modest 2,000-capacity Shepherd's Bush Empire.

September 22
- *Rewind The Film* charts at number four, the Manics' tenth top 10, and their fourth consecutive top five album (only *Lifeblood*'s poor showing at 13 and the willfully obscure *Lipstick Traces* b-sides collection going to number 11 breaks up a clean run of top tens going back to *Gold Against The Soul* in 1993).

October 10
- Kieran Evans' video for 'Anthem For A Lost Cause' lands on YouTube, the third part in a narrative trilogy with 'Rewind The Film' and 'Show Me The Wonder'.

October 21
- 'Show Me The Wonder' wins a *Q* Award for 'Best Video'.

November 14
- James wins the 'Musicians Union Maestro' award at the *Classic Rock Awards*.

Nov 12
- The band announce a UK tour for the following Spring. A second date at Brixton Academy is added after the first sells out.

November 25
- *Anthem For A Lost Cause* (Sony/Columbia)
  Tracklisting:
  1. 'Anthem For A Lost Cause'
  2. 'Death of a Digital Ghost'
  3. 'She It Like Sutherland'
  4. 'She Is Suffering (live)'
  Formats:
  Digital download/streaming only
  Notes:
  Only the second Manics single to feature lyrics written by James Dean Bradfield.

December
- The trio head back to their own Faster Studios to add the finishing touches to the band's twelfth album, *Futurology*, much of which was written and recorded at the same time as *Rewind The Film*.

2014

March 28
- An 11-date UK tour kicks off in Leeds, three new songs find their way onto the setlist: 'Europa Geht Durch Mich', 'Futurology' and 'Let's Go To War'.

April 24
- The new Manics single, 'Walk Me To The Bridge' is accidentally released early on some digital platforms. The original release had been moved to later in the year, unfortunately some online stores neglected to remove the track from their schedules. The band issue a statement saying 'This week, new Manic Street Preachers music became available online via legal and illegal download stores. As many have gathered, this wasn't the launch we had in mind for a campaign that we're all incredibly excited about. Originally, the plan had been to issue information on 'Walk Me To The Bridge' and the album 'Futurology' at the start of this week. That date moved due to the album release going back a fortnight – unfortunately several online retailers didn't manage to take the track off their schedules. This has caused horrendous problems for us and a lot of confusion for you.'

April 26
- A free (and this time, intentionally released) live EP, culled from 2011's mammoth O2 show, is made available via the band's website.

April 28
- A new video by Kieran Evans (now the band's videographer de jour) for 'Walk Me To The Bridge' is released on YouTube, shot on location in Berlin. The track is made available on iTunes with pre-orders of the album.

May 7
- The band embark on a 14-date tour of Denmark, Norway, Sweden, Finland, Germany, the Netherlands, Czech Republic, Belgium and France, plus the Manics' first ever show in Luxembourg.

May 12
- 'Europa Geht Durch Mich', a duet with German actress Nina Hoss, is added to digital platforms, with a lyric video released on YouTube. iTunes customers pre-ordering *Futurology* are now also given the title track on top of 'Europa Geht Durch Mich' and the already-released 'Walk Me To The Bridge'.

June 28
- James tells Absolute Radio that, despite Nicky's long opposition to the idea, the band are considering playing *The Holy Bible* in full to mark its 20th Anniversary later in the year.
- The Manics make their fifth appearance at Glastonbury Festival, playing a late-afternoon slot on The Other Stage, the same stage they had headlined 20 years earlier on the eve of the release of *The Holy Bible*. Nina Hoss flys over to sing on 'Europa Geht Durch Mich'

June 29
- *Walk Me To The Bridge* (Sony/Columbia)
  Tracklisting:
  1. 'Walk Me To The Bridge'
  2. 'Walk Me To The Bridge (live)'
  3. 'The Sound of Detachment'
  4. 'Caldey'
  5. 'Europa Geht Durch Mich (Erol Alkan's Mesmerise Eins Rework)'
  6. 'Europa Geht Durch Mich (Erol Alkan's Mesmerise Zwei Rework)'
  Formats:
  Digital download only

July
- *Futurology* becomes one of the best-reviewed Manics albums, garnering five starts from *The Telegraph*, four from *Mojo*, *Q* and *The Guardian*, 9/10 from *Gigwise* and 8/10 from *NME* and *Clash*. *Gigwise* say it is 'their greatest achievement since *Everything Must Go*.'

July 7
- *Futurology* (Sony/Columbia)
  Tracklisting:
  1. 'Futurology'
  2. 'Walk Me To The Bridge'
  3. 'Let's Go To War'
  4. 'The Next Jet To Leave Moscow'

5. 'Europa Geht Durch Mich'
6. 'Divine Youth'
7. 'Sex, Power, Love and Money'
8. 'Dreaming A City (Hughesovka)'
9. 'Black Square'
10. 'Between The Clock And The Bed'
11. 'Misguided Missile'
12. 'The View From Stow Hill'
13. 'Mayakowsky'
Formats:
CD, Deluxe 2-Disc CD, LP, download

Futurology

By Claire Biddles

'This recalibrated form of aspirational glamour'

At the climax of Christian Petzold's 2014 film *Phoenix*, the protagonist Nelly – played by Nina Hoss – stands on the precipice of the unknown. In post-war Germany, the potential for a new kind of European state hangs over the mass of generational trauma, and Nelly is seconds away from making a decision that will allow her to rise anew within it. A concentration camp survivor who has undergone facial reconstruction surgery, she can either choose to continue hiding under layers of adopted identity, or to live as her real, authentic self – stepping forward into a future entirely of her own making.

It feels significant that in 2014, Hoss also appeared as a guest singer on the Manic Street Preachers' twelfth album *Futurology*. Both film and album are pregnant with the utopian possibilities of breaking with the past. They are concerned with recalibration of self rather than a full reimagining – a curious look at a world turned to an unseen angle.

The fresh start of *Futurology* came at a fitting point in the Manics' now well-established trajectory of looking back and forging ahead. Released just ten months after the retrospective restraint of *Rewind the Film*, it was a brisk snap forward; its point of view as crisp and precise as the sun-dappled ice on its cover, and more complex and artful than its on-the-nose title would suggest. The album's conceptual newness came not from what was objectively futuristic in 2014, but from optimistic views of a distinctly European future mined from both personal and universal histories: from the utopian possibilities of the Soviet project, to the first time the band crossed the continent on tour, and what Nicky Wire defined in the album's notes as 'the relief of breathing in a new country'.

When mid-to-late career rock bands start talking of optimism and fresh starts, it often signals the blandness after the brink – think of Suede's post-hedonist *A New Morning*, REM's Beach Boys pastiching *Reveal*, or Pulp's *We Love Life*, a strong album which nonetheless sees the band's sharp edges being sawn off in favour of organic lushness. Conversely, the hope inherent to the Manics' music is hard-won and pronounced – or has been since 1996, at least

– and so their 'positivity album' is something different from the norm, more referential and inventive, and more self-aware of its possibility of failure.

Musically the album is a peculiar version of 'European' music, largely inspired by bands who interpreted the sounds of the continent from their removed positions in British towns and cities. A key influence is Simple Minds' 1980 masterpiece *Empires and Dance,* a Euro-centric post-punk album whose design the Manics had referenced before, in the reversed 'R's that first appeared on the cover of *The Holy Bible.* James Dean Bradfield names *Empires and Dance* as one of his favourite records, citing the tension of a British band trying on European modernism as key to its success. 'I've always liked records which are completely misinformed and displaced,' he told Melody Maker in 1995. '[Simple Minds] were aware that they were Scottish, and trying to shun it. They tried to become really European, this dark, unemotive, industrial band.' For bands like Simple Minds, European aesthetics were aspirational even (or perhaps especially) when they were defined by darkness.

The influence of Simple Minds and their version of European synth music is evident in the anthemic expanse of *Futurology*'s title track, which marries tricksy guitar stabs with miles-wide echoing electronics. The driving verses of 'The Next Jet to Leave Moscow' channel Echo and the Bunnymen, another band whose British origin felt too small to contain their ambition. Even the ill-fitting power-punk of 'Sex, Power, Love and Money' contains a reference to the Bunnymen's 1983 single 'The Back of Love'. Named after an Edvard Munch painting, 'Between the Clock and the Bed' goes one further by featuring additional vocals by Green Gartside of Scritti Politti, whose emphasis on continental sophistication and blue-eyed soul saw them outgrow their Wales-via-Yorkshire roots.

The band also characteristically took ideas from art and culture as prompts. These primarily came from *Die Brucke,* the group of early twentieth century German expressionists whose work was intended as 'a bridge to the future', a mantra which is repurposed as the title of the lead single 'Walk Me to the Bridge'. The influence of Futurist thinking is also referenced in the track 'Black Square', which takes its title from a 1915 painting by Russian artist Kazimir Malevich. A black mass painted over an older, allegorical image, it is widely considered to be the first non-representational painting – a revolutionary step into the unknown, and an invitation for the viewer to 'free yourself from the tyranny of objects'. When asked to define the album's theme, Wire responded with a paraphrase of Malevich's intentions: 'the idea of feeling over seeing'. In 2014, the Futurists were something of an overdone inspiration to call on, having already been referenced by a breadth of musicians from The Human League to Ryuichi Sakamoto since the late

1970s. As is often the case with the Manics, their sincere use of these well-worn, somewhat obvious references is part of their charm.

In the spirit of adopting a European mindset, the Manics recorded parts of *Futurology* (alongside much of *Rewind the Film*) at Berlin's Hansa studios, famous as the setting for a raft of celebrated recordings, most notably parts of David Bowie's late 1970s trilogy of *Low*, *"Heroes"* and *Lodger*. If *Futurology* has a relation in that trilogy it's *Lodger*, which shifts Bowie's insular art-pop to take in the outside world. Its influence can be heard on 'Black Square', which shimmers exquisitely with Eno-esque electronics and mournful counter-melodies, while at the periphery, voices chatter in German – a field recording of Berlin residents courtesy of a voice note from Sean Moore's iPhone. A number of other recordings made in the intimidatingly historied studio also feel significant to *Futurology*: Depeche Mode's *Some Great Reward*, which took inspiration from German industrial band Einstürzende Neubauten, and *Tinderbox* by Siouxsie and the Banshees, which significantly expanded their sound with atmospheric electronics.

In its lyrical references and retro-futurist aesthetic, *Futurology* is rooted in a time of division between East and Western Europe. The album's spirit of utopian optimism – and the Manics' well-established leftist views – appears to align it with the ideals of the Soviet project, a notion which is cannily complicated on 'Next Jet to Leave Moscow'. The lyrics send the Manics up, mocking the idealist lefty Western tourist visiting a failed communist state in an acknowledgement of the complicated contradictions of the Manics' political position. It contains a reference to their 2001 live show in Havana, and the scrutiny they have since received from fans in former Soviet countries. 'You're fucking taking the piss shaking hands with Castro,' Bradfield recounted to Wales Online in 2015 about such an encounter, 'we've just had the worst period of our lives!' The song's gently self-critical quality feels pointedly mature for a band whose political views have always been forthright and uncompromised, if often contradictory.

But *Futurology* isn't just a tourist project, and – as with the majority of their albums since *This is My Truth, Tell Me Yours* – it deliberately traces its roots back to Wales. The evocative instrumental 'Dreaming a City (Hugheskova)' is perhaps the most overtly Eurocentric-sounding track on the record: a Krautrock stomper free of language, indebted to the sonic explorations of Faust and Neu!. The title refers to a mining city in the Ukraine established by Welsh settlers in the late nineteenth century, which represented a chance for prosperity away from economic difficulties back home. Like the reference to Welsh-Argentinian settlement Patagonia in 'Ready for Drowning', the city is emblematic of the ambition and hardship that characterises the Welsh emigrant experience. Like 'If You Tolerate This Your Children Will Be Next', which charts the Welsh volunteer involvement in the Spanish Civil War, the song originates in outward-looking idealism. Of course, this act of situating Welshness in relation to European identity was revealed as its own kind of failed utopian thinking a mere two years later, with the catastrophic result of the 2016 Brexit referendum.

The most on-the-nose distillation of the album's leanings comes on 'Europa Geht Durch Mich' ('Europe Passes Through Me'), the collaboration with Nina Hoss. A bilingual duet originally titled 'European Miracle', the song evokes movement and possibility both in its lyrics and its glam rock stomp. The opening line is stolen from 'I Travel' by Simple Minds, but the rest of the song is an all-out Goldfrapp pastiche, a slowed-down industrial take on Euro-dance. One can almost hear the glitter sparkle on Nicky Wire's bass, and it's the perfect match for Hoss' deadpan dominatrix vocals.

Hoss – who is married to the album's producer Alex Silva – joined the Manics for a number of appearances in 2014, including a performance at Glastonbury which she described to the New York Times as 'like a childhood dream'. The appearance of this striking, Amazonian woman on stage with the band wasn't just a symbol of their present European sensibilities, but a signifier of a more subtle shift in the band's complex relationship to femininity. Taken alongside the album's similarly striking cover image by Catrine Val, here is a more mature, enigmatic and multifaceted image of womanhood than we are used to from a band who have historically used women's voices and images as a mirror image of their own.

Like so many things about them, the Manics' adoption of feminine signifiers, aesthetics and personas is sometimes empathetic, sometimes awkward, but always revelatory. From the outset, the band's adoption of pound-shop glamour aesthetics had more to do with class than gender performance. Wrapped in faux fur and leopard print, they both approximated the working class glamour of soap opera matriarchs, and were a continuation of a well-established lineage of provincial bands who used clothing as a tool to shock, mark themselves as distinct, and ultimately escape the towns they came from. The image of the fur-clad Manics walking the brick-red streets of 1980s Blackwood could be Roxy Music in 1960s Washington, or David Bowie in 1960s Brixton. These intellectual boys with thick eyeliner and artistic ideas above their station don't (necessarily) want to be girls, but understand that the glamour of working class women is a historical signifier of aspiration and difference.

The first time the Manics used a woman's voice rather than just women's clothes and makeup to represent themselves was on 'Little Baby Nothing' in 1992. Although the song's lyric alludes to a woman taken advantage of by men – and hinges on a cringe-worthy idea of female 'innocence' – its female protagonist is positioned as superior. At the time, Richey Edwards described guest singer Traci Lords as emblematic of 'female power', and her contradictory combination of control and victimhood made her a fitting choice for the song's definition of it. One cannot help but think that if made now, the song would prompt eyerolls for its soft-boy male feminism, but taken in the context of the early Manics' earnestness, the song's lauding of the strength in women's vulnerability comes off as awkward but sincere.

After the bombast of *Generation Terrorists*, the Manics' references to womanhood were sparser, and more focused on interiority than outer presentation. 'She is Suffering' falls flat in its attempt to empathise with female pain. Its video is even worse, swapping 'Little Baby Nothing''s clunky but joyous spectrum of womanhood for angsty montages of grimacing girls. As always, these female figures were a reflection of the band's own state of mind, specifically their heel-turn from cartoon punk to self-seriousness around the time of *Gold Against the Soul*.

Richey Edwards often talked about men as incomplete versions of women – literal 'walking abortions' – and saw women (somewhat reductively) as simultaneously untouchable and aspirational. Jenny Saville's cover image for *The Holy Bible* could be read in a number of ways, but its subject's simultaneous vulnerability and superior attitude towards the viewer aligns with both Richey's view of women, and his own mindset at the time. It feels trite and inappropriate to speculate whether his disgust in masculinity and worship of women was reflective of any personal gender dysphoria or queerness in the context of this essay – but there is perhaps another essay to be written about the links between gender and Edwards' lyrics, his eating disorder, and his hero worship of models like Kate Moss.

Nicky Wire, on the other hand, more openly addressed the relationship between gender aspiration and performance in the eloquent, quietly devastating lyrics from 1998's 'Born a Girl'. In the song, Wire's identity is stuck between freedom and disguise, portrayed as complex veneers of gender performance that stack like layers of skin around his body. The chorus expels the pain of this concealment as exasperation. Wire's masculinity has failed – because of his androgyny? Because of his gender? One suspects that he sees masculinity as inherently doomed to – or perhaps synonymous with – failure.

At this point in their career, the Manics' relationship with womanhood was more plainly reflective of a personal sense of unworthiness. Around this time, the band wrote two songs with Kylie Minogue for her 1997 album

Impossible Princess,[31] 'I Don't Need Anyone' and the single 'Some Kind of Bliss'. Recognisable as Manics compositions for their anthemic, guitar-driven style, the tracks ostensibly suited Kylie's 'indie' persona of the time, but were outliers on the album, which leaned towards more trendy, electronic forms of alternative music. Despite Minogue claiming *Impossible Princess* as her most personal album, Wire has stated that he partially blames himself for its failure (it has since, rightly, been critically reassessed). The songs' perception as 'failures' could be blamed on *maleness itself*: the inherently blokey tone of 1990s indie rock cancelling out the effervescent glamour that made Minogue an icon of the Manics in the first place. Perhaps these events were unrelated, but it feels significant that, after a year or so of unadorned sportswear on stage, Wire chose this time of masculine defeat to dig out the boas and see-through dresses again.

The Manics' primary relationship with femininity, encompassing all genders and interpretations, is the one they share with their fans. In the band's early days, it was seen as notable that their fanbase was largely made up of young women. Even after their mainstream breakthrough introduced a cohort of Britpop lads to the band, there remains a strong female presence in each Manics crowd. Although they were initially mocked for this, in the way that all media beloved of young women tends to be, the band wore it as a badge of honour. Their totalising insistence that their pride came from the fact that women are more intelligent than men was half sincere, half targeted trolling of the patriarchal music press – but the way Manics fandom manifests proves, if not that women have superior intelligence, certainly that they are well-matched with their chosen band. The tendency of women to be more 'active' fans than men – turning their fandom into *production* – dovetails with the band's advocacy for autodidacticism and transformation of self through art. For many, Manics fandom is a catalyst – for the creation of zines, artwork, their own bands, and even higher educational choices.

Where some of these connections between the band and fan creation are obtuse, and only clear to those in the know, the most visible way that fans connect with the band is through clothing. The development of a specific fan 'look' is common in pop fandom, but the Manics are outliers in their inspiration of such a multifaceted series of styling symbols. Usually, looks either align fans with a wider movement – goth, grunge, glam rock – and if not, often focus on one item as a signifier of allegiance – The Libertines' military jackets, Bros' Grolsch bottle tops – or a head-to-toe cosplay look: think Slipknot fans in boiler suits and masks, or Madonna fans in rubber bracelets and lace gloves.

---

31. Known at the time officially as Kylie Minogue to avoid any connections to the recently deceased Princess Diana.- MB

Through their eclectic use of imagery, the Manics have created an ever-increasing collage kit of references for fans to mix, twist and adapt in their own looks. Thirty years into their existence, it wouldn't be unusual to see four fans wearing a copy of James' *Holy Bible* sailor suit, a leopard print tracksuit, a Karl Marx t-shirt, and a cobbled-together fairy outfit stood next to each other on the barrier at a gig. The Manics fan look is disparate but recognisable, and – like the band themselves – often plays with ideas of femininity, costume and suggestion. As a band characterised by their outsider, underdog status, the Manics also attract a large number of queer, trans and gender-nonconforming fans, whose adoption and transformation of the Manics' cut-and-paste feminine aesthetic is an act of further expansion.

As the members of Manics have got older, they have become less visually expressive in their styling choices, choosing to largely convey their aesthetic through record sleeves and music videos. By the time of *Send Away the Tigers* in 2007, their aesthetic influence had come full circle, and Manics fans were influencing the look of the band itself. The cover of the album features an image of two young girls dressed in fairy and devil outfits, easily interpreted within this context as Manics fan dress. The image is not a literal representation of Manics fandom – it comes from the book *Monika Monster Future First Woman on Mars* by Valerie Phillips (*see Chapter 9*), which documents the life of a Polish woman in New York – but the selection of the image to represent the band is telling.

The image chosen for the 2013 singles collection, *National Treasures*, also references fandom. For their earlier Greatest Hits compilation, 2002's *Forever Delayed*, Warhol-style images of Wire, Edwards, Bradfield and Moore as young men are stacked against a wall – an artistic, glamorous representation of the band. *National Treasures* goes a step further: this time the history of the band to date is represented by a young woman in a military outfit, an updated version of the band's *Holy Bible*-era look of fatigues mixed with femininity. On the cover of the compilation's lead single 'This is the Day', the woman swaps her soldier's hat for a crown – an even more accurate representation of Manics' fans' tendency to mix signifiers from different eras, and play with combinations of masculine and feminine in their presentation.

One year later, and a woman was again gracing the cover of a Manics album. *Futurology*'s artwork – a self-portrait by German photographer Catrine Val – shares the album's spirit of icy newness, depicting a woman in all-white ski clothing in the midst of an ice-topped field, holding what looks like an old architectural model, tipped in front of her face like a mirror to catch the midday light. The sun is so bright that she glows – a regal alien in an everyday setting.

Val is an intriguing choice of cover artist. Her practice is driven by 'what it means to be a woman now' and often tracks the threat to women in the 'turmoil of the post-capitalist world.' The *Futurology* cover, and the images chosen for its singles, come from her 2013 photobook *Feminist*, a post-Cindy Sherman project in which Val plays with costume, artifice and the tropes of fashion photography to highlight the contradictions of twenty-first century womanhood. The images are bizarre, funny and out of time, mixing the past with the present, the butch with the femme, the decorative with the banal. Val's mission statement aligns with the album's interest in utopian relics of Europe's past: 'It is not that the past is brought back to life, but rather the very fact that it is over.'

Val's interest in the incongruity of womanhood, and her use of mixed visual signals to express it, is very much in the spirit of the Manics' long-established aesthetic, but their choice of cover image represents a significant shift in their relationship with femininity. This image of womanhood is still glamorous and aspirational, but no longer gaudy and cartoon-like – their inspiration is now in the form of a more sophisticated, enigmatic, and grown up woman. It is also significant because it isn't self-referential – nothing about the woman's appearance could be interpreted as a 'Manics thing' – which in itself is a sign of the band stepping into uncharted territory. This is a fresh addition to the visual lexicon; new canonical iconography presented under the familiar banner of inverted 'R's across the top of the album cover.

This recalibrated form of aspirational glamour is represented by all three female voices on the album: Hoss, Welsh folk singer and harpist Georgia Ruth Wiliams, and returning guest vocalist Cate Le Bon, who contributes backing vocals on 'Let's Go To War'. All three are striking, singular women, with distinct personal styles, both visual and artistic. The voice of Green Gartside could also be interpreted as a transgressive version of femininity; an emasculated male voice, synonymous with the prettiness of his 1980s image.

Another even more enigmatic female presence on the album is that of the imagined woman who occupies its suggestive sonic landscapes. The album's instrumentals – 'Dreaming a City (Hughesovka)', and 'Mayakovsky', named for the Russian-Soviet Futurist poet – are evocative of industrial urban spaces, in the midst of which the listener can project any number of fictional or historical figures. 'Dreaming a City (Hughesovka)' especially is almost tailor-made for the soundtrack of a cold war thriller, the theme perhaps for a lone woman who, like Val on the cover, both blends in with her surroundings and stands as the clear protagonist.

These real and fictional women feel spiritually linked in a way that aligns with the album's mantra of 'feeling not seeing'. There's something alchemic in the way they come together as a group, much like the way that a row of women at a Manics show fit together through their disparate aesthetics. It feels like, for perhaps the first time, the band are drawing on women's voices (both literal and figurative) as research, rather than to fill an already existing ideal. In short: they're listening. Of course, the women they're listening *to* still fit into a narrow ideal – it would be encouraging and artistically beneficial for the band to work with women who aren't white, or cis, for example.

So does this adoption of a mature, sophisticated woman as avatar signify the band 'growing up'? As always with the Manics, the answer is not certain. Although *Futurology* was a bold statement of evolution, its appearance in 2014 was unfortunately overshadowed by the concurrent twentieth anniversary celebrations of *The Holy Bible*, the old Manics contradictions in motion. It didn't get its own post-release tour, settling instead for a couple of tracks included during the 'greatest hits' half of *The Holy Bible* anniversary shows. Despite glowing reviews, and positive reception from fans, its appearance in public felt too brief – a failed utopian project made in reaction to failed utopian projects. The pull of nostalgia tours and a string of 1990s reissues continued to stunt the band's progress over the next few years, dragging them back into the past after their tentative step into a complicated future.

Despite this relegation, the influence of *Futurology* is slyly evident in some of what the Manics did next. 2018's *Resistance is Futile* includes a duet with Catherine Anne Davies, known professionally as The Anchoress, an iconoclastic Welsh singer-songwriter who, significantly, was also a touring member of Simple Minds at the time of recording. 'Dylan & Caitlin' saw Bradfield and Davies take on the roles of Dylan and Caitlin Thomas for a complex portrayal of a tempestuous relationship, with equal weight given to the voice of the overshadowed woman as that of the celebrated male poet. On New Year's Day 2021, Wire posted a series of polaroids of his daughter Clara, thanking her for her 'make-up expertise' – this old Urban Decay addict learning new tricks from the women in his life.

The Manics' adaptation – or more accurately, expansion – of their feminine ideal on *Futurology* could also be interpreted as them creating a feminine image not defined by the influence of Richey Edwards. Aside from one possible interpretation of 'Walk Me To The Bridge', his presence is largely absent on the album, in a way that feels respectful and freeing, even – not a letting go, but a natural change that comes with age and distance. Like Nina Hoss' Nelly at the end of *Phoenix*, or the architects of Hughesovka, or just three men in their late 40s still full of longing and curiosity, *Futurology* proposed a question of which it did not know the answer, and – even if just for a moment – dared to imagine a future entirely its own.

Part Fourteen

2014–2018

2014 (continued)

July 8
- The Manics make a rare in-store appearance as a three-piece at London's Rough Trade East. The ten song set is divided 50/50 between songs from *Futurology* in the first half and *The Holy Bible* in the second.

July 12
- The band play second on the bill to the Pixies on the King Tuts Wah Wah stage at T In The Park. After a particularly energetic and vicious show, Nicky smashes one of his favourite basses, cutting his hand in the process.

July 13
- *Futurology* enters the album chart at number two, beating its predecessor by one place. It's the band's fourth number two album.

August 16
- Following a set at Hungary's Sziget Festival, the band's plane back to the UK is delayed then cancelled, meaning the Manics miss their appearance at the first leg of the V2014 festival.

September 19
- James, Sean and Nicky appear on BBC Radio 4's *Mastertapes* programme to discuss *The Holy Bible*, performing acoustic versions of 'Faster', 'PCP', '4st 7lb' and 'This Is Yesterday'.

September 22
- After much speculation, the Manics announce a December tour in which they'll play the now 20-year-old *Holy Bible* in its entirety, including a three night run at London's Roundhouse.

October 29
- *NME* photographer Kevin Cummins publishes *Assassinated Beauty*, a book collecting some of his most memorable images of the Manics. The book is promoted with an exhibition at the Proud Galleries in Camden.

November 10
- The Manics contribute a cover of the Rolling Stones' last great single, 'Start Me Up', to a new album, *Radio 2 Presents the Sound of the 80s*

December 8
- A deluxe 20th Anniversary box set entitled *The Holy Bible 20* is released containing all the material from the 10th anniversary edition (newly

remastered), plus a disc of live performances and sessions, a 12x12" book of images and lyrics and the album on heavyweight vinyl.

- *The Holy Bible* tour begins at Glasgow Barrowlands. James, Sean and Nicky perform the full record alone, with no secondary musicians, following a DJ set by Manics authority Simon Price. A second set sees the band joined by usual sidemen Wayne Murray and Nick Neysmith to play a set of hits, including tracks from *Rewind The Film* and *Futurology*. Therapy?'s Andy Cairns joins on guitar for 'You Love Us' at the London shows.
- A second run of *Holy Bible* gigs is announced for Summer 2015, including a show at Cardiff Castle.

2015

January 22
- A North American *Holy Bible* tour is announced for April and May.

January 30
- After twelve years of work, US Manics fan Elizabeth Marcus' documentary *No Manifesto* is completed and gets its first screening at Cardiff's Chapter Cinema. It will be screened several times over the coming year before being released on DVD and eventually making its way to Amazon Prime.

February 1
- The 20th anniversary of Richey's disappearance inevitably brings a fresh wave of press raking over his case. Rachel Elias *née* Edwards, Richey's sister, gives a handful of interviews campaigning for more attention to be given to the cases of missing young men. The fact the band are promoting *The Holy Bible* reissue and tour means they are inevitably dragged into the conversation. There are no significant new lines in the story, however.

April 20
- The *New York Post* runs an interview with Nicky under the heading 'Inside Rock 'N' Roll's Greatest Mystery.'
- The US tour begins at Washington DC's 9.30 Club.

April 30
- 22 years after they first visited the country, the Manics make their US TV debut, performing 'A Design For Life' on James Corden's *Late Late Show*.

May 21
- The band are given the 'Ivor Inspiration Award' at the annual Ivor Novellos. The award is presented to the band by members of Kasabian.
- Manic Street Preachers re-sign with Columbia Records.

May 30
- The second UK leg of the *Holy Bible* tour kicks off at Edinburgh's Usher Hall.

June 5
- The band play a sold-out show at Cardiff Castle. BBC iPlayer viewers are treated to the strange sight of *The Holy Bible* being performed in broad daylight when highlights from the gig are broadcast a few days later.

June 15
- Nicky guests on 'Nothing Left To Talk About', a new single by Saint Etienne's Sarah Cracknell.

July 19
- The Manics play the Latitude Festival, billed below Noel Gallagher's High Flying Birds on the final day. The band will play a handful of festivals across the summer, including Japan's Fujirock.

September 12
- The final Manics show of the year takes place, playing second down the bill from headliners Elbow at London's On Blackheath festival.

September 30
- James interviews Paul McCartney about his 1983 album *Pipes of Peace* for *DIY* magazine.

November 9
- Perhaps inevitably *manics.co.uk* announces a 20th anniversary tour of *Everything Must Go*, including shows at London's Royal Albert Hall and Swansea's Liberty Stadium.

November 22
- James and Sean, along with 49 others, embark on a trek through the mountains of Patagonia, following in the footsteps of Welsh settlers in the country 150 years before, undertaken on foot and carrying their own gear. The trip is a fundraiser for Welsh cancer charity Velindre. Between them James and Sean raise almost £30,000.

2016

March 8
- A limited edition 12″ repressing of 'A Design For Life' is announced for Record Store Day.

March 10
- As the *Everything Must Go* tour approaches, a deluxe re-issue of the album is announced for later in the year.

March 22
- Making good on a promise they made in 1999, the band record the official anthem for the Wales Football Team's Euro 2016 campaign. The Manics had originally planned to rework Frankie Valli's 'Can't Take My Eyes Off You', which they had covered for the b-side of 'Australia', 20 years earlier. Unfortunately permission to use the track was refused, forcing the trio to write an original song with a similar feel.

April 13
- James and Nicky contribute a song to Patrick Jones' new play *Before I Leave*.

April 18
- The *Everything Must Go* tour kicks off in Tallinn, Estonia. The band will play in Finland, Sweden, Denmark, The Netherlands, Belgium and Spain before heading back to the UK.

May 13
- *Together Stronger (C'mon Wales)* (Sony)
  Tracklisting
  1. 'Together Stronger (C'mon Wales)'
  2. 'A Design For Life (David Wrench Remix)'
  Formats:
  CD/download/Streaming
- The UK leg of the *Everything Must Go* tour begins in Liverpool.

May 20
- The *Everything Must Go* 20th Anniversary reissue hits stores. The box includes the remastered album on CD and vinyl, a comprehensive set of b-sides, demos and sessions, the *Everything Live* Nynex show on both DVD and CD and *Freed From Memory*, a new documentary on the making of the album by Kieran Evans.

May 28
- Swansea's Liberty Stadium hosts the *Everything Must Go* tour, with support from Super Furry Animals. The show has an added buzz due to Wales' continued success in Euro 2016. The band perform 'Together Stronger (C'mon Wales)' for the first time.

June 10
- The Manics contribute a cover of Fiction Factory's 'Feels Like Heaven' to *Radio 2 Presents The Sound of the Eighties Volume 2*. The song has featured heavily in recent setlists.
- 'Together Stronger (C'mon Wales)' goes to number one in the physical singles chart, technically giving the band their third UK chart topper ... if CDs and records alone are counted. Unfortunately, due to the dominance of streaming and downloads, the single doesn't actually chart in the general top 100.

July 6
- Wales exit Euro 2016 in the semi-finals, losing 2–0 to eventual champions Portugal.

July 8
- A short Manics set features as part of a homecoming celebration for the Wales team, held at Cardiff City Stadium.

July 9
- The band play the Eden Project in Cornwall. Future collaborator The Anchoress, AKA Welsh singer/songwriter/producer Catherine Anne Davies, who is supporting at the show, fulfills a lifelong ambition by dueting on 'Little Baby Nothing'.

July 11
- With the Manics unable to renew their lease on Faster Studios, which will be demolished at the end of the year to make way for housing, the band are granted permission by the local council to convert a cottage near Newport into a new studio space, which they will name Door To The River Studios. The building is purchased with a mortgage held jointly by the three members.

October 19
- Kieran Evans' latest collaboration with the Manics, *Be Pure – Be Vigilante – Behave*, featuring footage from the *Holy Bible* tour shot documentary-style, premieres in Cardiff.

November 8/9
- The final shows of the *Everything Must Go* tour take place in Tokyo and Osaka, Japan.

November/December
- James, Sean and Nicky pause working on new music to move out of Faster Studios and get the new Door To The River space fit for purpose.

2017

January
- A short run of festivals and outdoor headline shows are announced for the summer, which James describes as intended to 'blow the cobwebs out'.

February 27
- James tells *NME* that the band hasn't 'played a note' together since November.

March 10
- James Dean Bradfield's score to *The Chamber*, a claustrophobic submarine thriller, filmed entirely in Wales, is released.

March 21
- 'Your Love Alone Is Not Enough' is re-released on limited edition 12″ for Record Store Day.

April 15
- Kieran Evans' latest Manics film, *Escape From History*, is broadcast on Sky Arts. An expansion of his *Freed From Memory*, which had been included in the *Everything Must Go* box-set, it tells the story of the band's journey from *The Holy Bible* to *Everything Must Go*'s success.

May 12
- *Send Away The Tigers* gets the tenth anniversary treatment, re-released in a hardback book format (matching each Manics album since *Postcards From A Young Man*) with bonus discs of demos, b-sides and extra tracks like 'The Ghost of Christmas' and 'Umbrella'. Strangely, the two-disc vinyl set enshrines the scrappy demos in wax rather than the b-sides and bonuses. For reasons best known to the band, 'Underdogs' is booted from the album proper and replaced with 'Welcome To The Dead Zone', a bonus track from the 'Your Love Alone Is Not Enough' single.

June
- Work is completed on Door To The River Studios near Newport, the new home of Manic Street Preachers.

June 22
- The Manics return to live action as part of the Bristol Sounds Festival, kicking off a comparatively light summer of less mainstream festivals and gigs, like the Llangollen International Eisteddfod, Chris Evans annual charity event; CarFest, Spain's MadCool Festival, Ireland's Indiependence, a headline show in Newcastle's Time Square and England's Bingley Music Live. Between shows they will continue work on their twelfth album at Door To The River.

June 30
- *You Love Us: Manic Street Preachers 1991–2001*, a book of photographs of the Manics by former *Melody Maker* photographer Tom Sheehan, is published by Flood Gallery Publishing.

July 7
- Art rock band Public Service Broadcasting release their third album, *Every Valley*, a concept record about the decline of the Welsh coal mining industry. James lends vocals and guitar to one song, 'Turn No More'.

July 8
- Nicky misses the band's show at Madrid's MadCool festival due to 'serious family illness'. Long-serving Manics tech Richard Beak stands in. Nicky is back on stage for the following day's show, the Llangollen International Eisteddfod.

August 24
- Public Service Broadcasting release 'Turn No More' as a single, James appears in the video.

September
- Sean raises nearly £20,000 for Welsh cancer charity Velindre by trecking through Peru.

October 6
- James, alongside Richard Hawley, plays three acoustic shows in three venues in a single night as part of Sheffield's Three Ring Circus event.

October 18
- The Manics play a headline show at London's Roundhouse with support from Sleaford Mods as part of the *Q* Awards. The Anchoress, who has

been working with the band in the studio, once again joins for 'Little Baby Nothing'. Earlier in the evening they are presented with Q's 'Inspiration Award' by Michael Sheen.

October 19
- Nicky tells the *NME* that he is unsure if the band will release another album, saying their last two records had 'sapped them of their creative juices', adding that they may rally and 'chuck something out' in the coming weeks. He also tells *BBC News* that 'it's really frightening, I just can't see one coming out at the moment'.

November 17
- The band announce details of their 12th album, *Resistance Is Futile*, due on April 6. Copies had been circulating amongst a handful of trusted writers and fans for weeks prior to Nicky's post-awards interview. A spring tour with The Coral is also announced. The album is promoted with a short film by Kieran Evans, who will shoot all of the video material and promos for the album cycle. A new single, 'International Blue' is scheduled for December.

December 8
- *International Blue* (Sony/Columbia)
  Tracklisting
  1. 'International Blue'
  2. 'International Blue (The Bluer Skies Version)'*
  3. 'Holding Patterns'**
  *Digital download only, **7" only.
  Formats:
  Digital download, streaming, 7" vinyl. At the time of writing (May 2021) 'International Blue' is the last Manic Street Preachers single to receive a physical release.

2018

January 8
- Nicky tells *NME* that, to the surprise of absolutely no-one, the band intend to celebrate the 20th anniversary of *This Is My Truth, Tell Me Yours* later in the year by playing the record all the way through at some shows.

January 9
- Kieran Evans' video for 'International Blue' is released.

February 2
- James and Nicky sit in for Iggy Pop on his BBC 6Music radio show. They play songs by The Fall (twice), Wolf Alice, Skids, Ryan Adams, Abba, David Bowie, John Cale, Rush, Wire and Lana Del Ray amongst others.

February 16
- A second track from *Resistance Is Futile*, 'Distant Colours' is made available on digital platforms. It is only the third Manics single to feature lyrics by James Dean Bradfield, following 2001's 'Ocean Spray' and 2013's 'Anthem For A Lost Cause'.

February 21
- Kieran Evans' video for 'Distant Colours' drops.

March 6
- It's announced that the Manics (plus support, The Anchoress) are among the bands hand-picked by The Cure's Robert Smith to play the 2018 Meltdown Festival at London's Royal Festival Hall. The gig will take place on June 19.

March 9
- Another new song, 'Dylan & Caitlin', a duet with The Anchoress, is made available on digital platforms.

April
- *Resistance Is Futile* gets a clutch of great notices from the press (four stars from *Q*, *The Independent*, *NME*, *Music OMH*, *Rolling Stone* and *Mojo*) though *The Guardian* stalls at three stars. For only the second time in 15 years there are no reviews saying it is their best album 'since *Everything Must Go*'.

April 6
- A fourth song is lifted from the album, 'Liverpool Revisited', a tribute to the 'Justice For The Victims Of Hillsborough' campaign, written in its entirety (including guitar solo) by Nicky Wire.

April 13
- *Resistance Is Futile* (Sony/Columbia)
  Tracklisting:
  1. 'People Give In'
  2. 'International Blue'
  3. 'Distant Colours'
  4. 'Vivian'

 5. 'Dylan & Caitlin'
 6. 'Liverpool Revisited'
 7. 'Sequels of Forgotten Wars'
 8. 'Hold Me Like A Heaven'
 9. 'In Eternity'
10. 'Broken Algorithms'
11. 'A Song For The Sadness'
12. 'The Left Behind (demi)'*
13. 'Concrete Fields'*
14. 'A Soundtrack to Complete Withdrawal'*
*Bonus disc only
Formats:
CD, deluxe 2-CD set with demo disc, 12″ vinyl

Resistance Is Futile

By Laura K Williams

'Something of value to add to the world'

Since the release of 'Generation Terrorists' in 1992, Manic Street Preachers have released an album roughly every one-to-three years; so when there seemed to be no hint of another record in the pipeline in the period following 2014's *Futurology*, rumours began to circulate that maybe, just maybe, it was finally the end of the line. The band was clearly tired and experiencing some significant life changes. They were all approaching their 50th birthdays, with James admitting they were patently aware that they were now closer to the end than the beginning.[32]

Nicky confessed to not knowing if the band had another record in them, admitting they were in a very 'funny place'. It sent an immediate wave of panic through the Manics' community. Personally, Nicky was having an incredibly difficult time; watching his mum, Irene's, health deteriorate after she was diagnosed with terminal leukemia. He lost her just months after the release of *Resistance Is Futile*. It's something James had been through before, losing his own mum to cancer in 1999 shortly after the release of *This Is My Truth, Tell Me Yours*. It's what inspired the song 'Ocean Spray'.

Faster Studios, the 'clubhouse' which had offered them space away from the hustle and bustle of family life, was bulldozed to make way for flats, in what James referred to as 'the ceaseless march of progress'. The studio had been an integral part of the band's life for a decade; half of their albums – *Lifeblood, Send Away the Tigers, Journal for Plague Lovers, Postcards of a Young Man, Rewind the Film* and *Futurology* – had been worked on there. As much as it was a place to work, it was also a place to connect – to chat, unwind and evolve. From listening to records, drinking tea and watching Countdown (true story) and endless sports, to trying to make sense of the huge societal and political changes occurring outside those walls. After a little deliberation,

---

32. It's worth noting here, that if the Manics stay together as long as the Rolling Stones, then James would be dead wrong about this: 2014 would not even be half-way through their career. - MB

the trio decided to buy their own place and found themselves with a joint mortgage on a studio on the outskirts of Newport (prompting James to joke that they weren't 'Noel Gallagher rich'.) The new studio, named 'Door to The River' after one of their earlier songs (and by virtue of the fact it overlooks the River Usk), offered some much-needed stability for the band at a very tumultuous time.

The wider world was rapidly changing. The UK spent the years that followed *Futurology* in the midst of Brexit hysteria, with the Conservative Party instigating a referendum in 2016 to decide on the country's membership of the EU. The result was very close indeed: almost fifty-two per cent voted to leave and just over forty-eight percent to remain. The country was divided, and it showed. Years of Tory austerity had taken its toll on the working class, with the unemployed, the underemployed and vulnerable groups like disabled people hardest hit. People were angry and frustrated, and they wanted change, change which many believed would come if they cut ties with the EU. The Manics were angry too, but like many musicians they saw the value of a united Europe – if only for the peace it had afforded the continent since World War II. The Leave campaign had been based largely on a single, simple message: 'Take Back Control'. Surrounding that message was a lot of misinformation, most famously the promise of '£350 million extra for the NHS every week', emblazoned on the side of the official campaign bus. The Remain campaign, meanwhile, was more convoluted and failed to address either a growing lack of trust in politicians or widespread concerns over immigration. The bitter arguments that ensued, particularly online, created an ever-growing gulf between the two sides – insults replaced respectful discussion and blocking and muting replaced persuasion and open-minded exploration.

Just months after the UK electorate responded to this simple message, the US electorate did similar; returning the celebrity billionaire Donald Trump as its 45th President under the campaign slogan: 'Make America Great Again'. Like in the UK, immigration was a hot topic with promises of tighter border controls and the idea of sticking it to the 'political elite' – a group into which Trump's opponent, Hillary Clinton, was painted. Both campaigns – Vote Leave and Trump's election campaign – relied heavily on the Internet and, particularly, social media, as a way of disseminating and reiterating messages, getting support and shutting down any counter arguments. They harnessed the power of personal data and social algorithms to secure votes, using tactics ranging from speaking directly to people on Twitter, to targeted ad campaigns, to reinforce existing opinions and outright misinformation. It's something the Manics went on to explore in their songwriting with 'Broken Algorithms'.

As the division increased and the process of leaving the EU played out, so did the in-fighting on each side – especially within the two main political parties in the UK. Both the Tories and Labour were home to a mixed bag of ardent leave voters and militant remainers; even the party leaders were not personally aligned with the majority of their voters. It was messy, mirroring the wider picture among the UK electorate.

'You've got the left attacking itself,' James told *NME*, 'Labour voters attacking each other, Tory voters attacking each other, Ken Clarke attacking Theresa May and then not even knowing if May's heart is really in Brexit. It really is just so intractable, it's unbelievable – every way you look at it.' Their disillusionment with politics only served to heighten the existential crisis of growing older in a world they recognised less and less.

After years of wearing their socialist credentials on their sleeves, knowing what they stood for and who to vote for to help deliver that, they found themselves politically homeless. Nicky described himself as a 'man without a fucking political creed' and lamented the 'Cold War age' he grew up in, where it was easy to know what you stood for or against. 'We've seen so many ideologies fail in our lifetime,' Nicky told *The Quietus*, 'Socialism, Thatcherism, neo-liberalism, coalitions – everything has, at some point, failed. It's really hard to believe in anything definite.' James agreed, telling *Louder Than War* that 'it's getting harder to know what my vote is standing for these days. I want people to work for my vote, to be held accountable for my vote. I'm fucked off with people like Labour not actually listening to people who live outside of cities. I'm fucked off at the Tories pretending they listen to people who live in towns. I'm sick of both of them.'

These feelings ran deep. They were born out of witnessing the decline of their homeland, watching the Valleys get left behind – decades passing with huge socio-political problems and no real investment following the devastating closure of the mines and obliteration of industry in South Wales, condemning entire communities to inter-generational poverty in the process. Nicky confessed to understanding why people in Wales voted leave, though neither he nor Sean voted that way themselves (James maintains his vote is 'between him and the ballot box').

'Sometimes when you think you've got investment from the EU it would amount to some fucking street art,' said James, who heads into the Valleys from his Cardiff home every week to visit both his dad and Nicky's brother Patrick. It was no accident that James's vocals featured on one of the tracks on Public Service Broadcasting's 2017 album *Every Valley*, a concept album exploring the decline of industry and its impact - with a particular focus on coal mining in South Wales. The song paints a poignant, yet tragic picture of the heartbreaking decline that they've witnessed across the Valleys since Thatcher left her mark in the 1980s.

Like many of their Valleys peers, the Manics come from a long line of Labour-voters; and like many of their Valleys peers, they too feel pushed to the peripheries, seeking other options as they feel abandoned by the party supposed to stand up for the working classes. 'For somebody that comes from a very staunchly Labour family', said James 'it's getting harder for me to make my choice at the ballot box these days. Safe to say my vote's never gonna go to the Tories, it's never gonna go to UKIP, but it's getting hard for me to follow my traditional choice.'

The Manics' conscious uncoupling with Labour started in earnest with the Iraq war in 2003 and was solidified with the bank bailouts around the 2008 financial crash. After the release of *Futurology*, the band were already talking about their disenchantment with what they saw as London-centric politics – both James and Nicky were living back in Wales, and Sean was just across the border in Bristol. There's always been a disconnect between London and the regions and it usually comes through in the north/south divide narrative, but the divide is very real for people in Wales and the West Country too.

Even a clear move to the left in the leadership of the Labour Party, in the shape of then-leader Jeremy Corbyn, couldn't win back their loyalty, or assure their vote. Labour was broadly split across two camps – the more left-wing Corbyn arm and the centrists drawn to the party during the New Labour era, operating under the Progress banner. Corbyn was an old-skool socialist veteran MP (representing Islington North in London since 1983 – three years before the embryonic Manics started playing together). He had managed to do what his two predecessors had failed to; capture the youth vote – despite himself pushing 70. A former trade union rep, Corbyn was that rare thing in successful political figures: an activist who was also an elected representative. He'd been involved in the Campaign for Nuclear Disarmament and the Anti-Apartheid movement in the 1980s, and was a vocal opponent of the Iraq war. His track record as an activist appealed to the idealism of a new generation of Labour supporters – especially the Momentum movement, formed to get him elected – and led to him achieving an almost cult-like status among younger voters.

Corbyn was likened to the late Tony Benn – not least because of the Euroscepticsm they both shared, and broad location on the political spectrum (left wing socialists). The Manics have been longtime fans of Benn, who they called the 'ultimate left-wing icon'. We witnessed Nicky fan-boying over him during a 2010 meeting of minds hosted by Manics' biographer Simon Price for *The Quietus*. During the interview, Nicky probed Benn about the current state of politics. It coincided with the end of a 13-year Labour Government and the beginning of another long reign for the Tories. Nicky asked Benn how he retained faith in humanity, to which the pipe-smoking stalwart replied; 'All progress is made by the fire of anger against injustice and the fire of hope you can build a better world, and if you abandon your resistance to injustice and the hope that you can change things then you become part of the system that oppresses people.' Nicky nodded in fervent agreement, but within a few years – around the same time as Benn's death in 2014 – this view appeared to be up for discussion and that hope waning. Corbyn offered hope of a different kind of politics to the 300,000 Labour Party members and affiliates who voted for him as leader. He wasn't the slick, media-savvy politician that we'd grown accustomed to since Tony Blair's landslide election in 1997, he said what he thought – even if it wasn't necessarily politically expedient – and he was an unashamed socialist, the perfect antidote to Tory individualism.

It would be easy to assume that Corbyn would be right up the Manics' socialist street, considering their love of Aneurin 'Nye' Bevan (Welsh MP) and Benn (Bristol MP – the city where Sean lives). But therein may lie a geographical clue to their reluctance to support Corbyn. Indeed, Nicky dubbed the new Labour leader a 'middle class, London-centric version' of the classic Labour politician he grew up with. James was on the same page. Despite living in London for many years himself, he says he never felt like a 'Londoner' and the hiraeth – a deep sense of longing – to return home to Wales never died, eventually leading him back to the mountains. Once a Valley boy ...

'I'm not one of those people that goes on about the liberal elite,' he told *The Guardian*, 'but I don't think he [Corbyn] understands what makes the working classes tick outside of London.' He cited an example of an ex-miner who had asked Corbyn: 'What do you expect us to do, Mr Corbyn, make fucking love spoons out of hemp?' – a headline that was picked up by *The Sun* newspaper and used as another attack on the Labour leader. When Corbyn fell from grace, a year after the release of *Resistance Is Futile*, many of his supporters blamed the media for what they saw as a targeted campaign. It is against the turbulent backdrop of Brexit, Trump and the relentless and bitter aftermath of this tribal division that the Manics released their 13th album: a remarkably youthful sounding record full of soaring anthems, probing lyrics and more than a passing resemblance – musically at least – to their 1990s material.

Condensed down, the album took just five or six weeks to complete, though that time was spread over a couple of years, resulting in the biggest gap between albums in the band's history. The first three songs came to life in Faster Studios, with the remainder of the album finished a year later at the new Door to the River (it taking six months to find a place to buy, followed by another six months prepping it for use). Still, when the trio finally got down to work things went relatively well. 'We arrived with some really sketchy demos,' James told *Long Live Vinyl*, 'and it went surprisingly well. In fact, one song just came out of the box, and fuck me it reminds me of being twenty-years old again. It is relentless in the sense that it's charging towards something, something hopeful.' He was referring to standout single, 'International Blue'. Eventually the album would produce a whopping six singles – 'International Blue', 'Distant Colours', 'Dylan & Caitlin', 'Liverpool Revisited', 'Hold Me Like A Heaven' and 'People Give In' – the most from any one Manics record since *Generation Terrorists*. But where the singles from their debut album were a big deal, today's streaming and shuffle culture has robbed the format of some of its impact. These weren't singles in the old-fashioned sense, in fact only 'International Blue' got a physical release at all, coming out on 7″ vinyl (and topping the vinyl singles charts). The rest were 'focus tracks', pulled out of the album-proper and intended for radio play or Spotify playlists. Things just didn't work in the same way anymore. 'A lot of our older songs shock me in how easy it was to have a clearer vision of life,' said James, 'and, in contrast, how ill-defined everything is now; how abstract life has become.'

'International Blue' is the most immediate of the crop – mid-paced and anthemic track with a singalong chorus and in a clear lineage of classic Manics jukebox singles ('A Design For Life', 'You Stole The Sun From My Heart', 'Your Love Alone Is Not Enough', 'It's Not War (Just the End of Love)'). The lyrics were never intended to be a Manic Street Preachers song, but were instead written as a kind of extended Haiku by Nicky, following an anniversary trip to Nice in the South of France. While there, he went to visit the Yves Klein museum and was captivated by the 'International Blue' colour, a pigment designed by Klein himself, in one of the paintings. When James was bugging him for lyrics for the new album, he nonchalantly handed over this poem, and out popped this indie pop belter.

Just as Nicky will step up to the mic on one song for his now-traditional lead vocal duties (here in the form of 'The Left Behind'), so James tries to sneak at least one lyric onto every album (both traditions harking back to

Know Your Enemy with 'Wattsville Blues' and 'Ocean Spray' respectively). He is under no illusion that it's usually pretty obvious which song is his when compared to chief lyricist Nicky's offerings[33]. Here, it comes in the shape of 'Distant Colours', a gorgeous, dense track which delves into Bradfield's disenchantment with the Labour Party – from the hope and promise of a better future delivered by Bevan and co's setting up of the Welfare State and the NHS, to the aftermath of years of austerity with more and more communities left behind, as the Valleys have been. James laments, '*I no longer know my left from my right*'. 'I find it very hard to choose at the moment,' he explained.' The echo chamber on both sides is filled with animosity and fake news and there's no way you can make the right or the left discernable from each other on that level.'

The Manics' stance on the Labour Party is indicative of the wider picture in Wales. In the 2019 election, following the release of *Resistance Is Futile*, Labour lost six seats in the country while the Tories picked up seven: a huge blow for a party which had enjoyed big wins in the past; safe seats creating a red wall in the West. That's not something anyone would have foreseen until the Brexit referendum captured the attention of people who had previously shown very little interest in politics. Many voters said that Brexit was the defining issue. It was simple: they'd voted to leave the European Union and the Tories were promising to deliver on that. Labour's policy was shakier, containing the possibility of further referendums and even a reversal of the vote. For those voters the issue was a black and white one. For the pro-European Manics, it was a much harder decision. *Resistance Is Futile* delves deep into this inner turmoil.

'In terms of politics, there's a lot that links in with that phrase ['Resistance Is Futile'],' says James, 'whether it being not knowing which party to vote for anymore, not knowing what side to take, not knowing what news to believe. All these things are quite strange for us. We come from an age where you define yourself by your targets and your enemies and it's harder to be that now. Nick gave me some amazing lyrics which absolutely sum up that political conclusion.'

Nicky studied politics at Swansea University, which helped shape his lyric writing – alongside a plethora of cultural resources from books and films to history and current affairs. Every Manics album is an education, you learn untold stories from across the globe, unpick political theories and

---

33. He should be less modest – When Manics biographer and known-authority Simon Price reviewed Futurology for The Quietus he showered Wire with praise for his lyrics on 'Next Jet To Leave Moscow', a song actually penned by Bradfield. -MB

find literary references throughout. *Resistance Is Futile* is no different. There are persistent themes which clearly capture the attention of the chief lyricist, rearing their head on more than one album – from poets to photographers of note to the Hillsborough disaster.

Following the success of the numerous duets on 2013's *Rewind The Film* and 2014's *Futurology,* the band were keen to continue using guest singers. On *Resistance* it's the turn of The Anchoress (aka Catherine Anne Davies), dueting with James on 'Dylan and Caitlin.' The song tells the story of Welsh poet Dylan Thomas and his rollercoaster relationship with wife, Caitlin. Davies also crops up providing backing vocals on 'Vivian', which tells the inspirational yet somewhat tragic story of US street photographer Vivian Maier who, like many good artists, only gathered recognition after her death when tens of thousands of negatives were uncovered in her Chicago apartment. It's not the first time the Manics have shared the story of a photographer, with 1996's 'Kevin Carter' focusing on the Pulitzer Prize-winning photojournalist who could not live with the horrors he'd seen and took his own life.

'Liverpool Revisited' is a sequel of sorts to 1998's 'S.Y.M.M', written about the 1989 Hillsborough disaster, where 96 people lost their lives in a horrific crush at Hillsborough Stadium in Sheffield during an FA Cup match between Liverpool and Nottingham Forest. 'S.Y.M.M' had focused on unanswered questions, 'Liverpool Revisited' moves the story on. There had been huge progress for the families of the victims with a full inquiry between the two Manics releases; inquests re-opened, public apologies made and charges brought. The song was written in Liverpool, very much as an ode to those families affected and the strength of conviction of those who the authorities and the media tried to suppress for so long. Nicky's lyrics would not be out of place on *The Holy Bible* in terms of gravity.

Inspired by a Philip Larkin poem, 'Hold Me Like A Heaven' talks of tattered manifestos, another nod to the Manics' disdain for the two main political parties. It's the last lyric Nicky wrote for this record and wraps it up nicely, acting – as is often the case with the last song written for a Manics album – as a summary for the themes explored. Musically, it's up there with 'International Blue' – the whoah-oh-oh crescendo ensuring the song's rent-free residence in your head for days.

The Manics' back catalogue is littered with political references; from song titles like 'Socialist Serenade', 'Democracy Coma' and 'The Love of Richard Nixon' to lyrical references to Margaret Thatcher, Neil Kinnock and Winston Churchill. Then there's the visit to Cuba to meet Fidel Castro and the small statue of Nye Bevan found in their recording studio. However, though they've not shied away from the subject, they've never been as *preachy* about politics as you might think. Wire thinks the idea of the band as a splenetic bastion of leftist propaganda has been overplayed over the years. 'There are some weird preconceptions of us, because our politics have always been socialist,' Nicky told *The Independent*, 'But there's been a massive amount of existentialism, and, dare I say it, fun, involved in that. Because the Situationists are as big an influence on us as Nye Bevan.'

It's true that the in-your-face dogma of *Generation Terrorists*, that revolutionary '*fuck queen and country*' attitude, has dissipated somewhat over the years, but listen to James during interviews around the time of *Resistance Is Futile*'s release and it's clearly still there, albeit taking a less brash shape. It's not just James, either. The usually quiet and composed Sean found his way onto Twitter and hit the ground running; sharing a mix of posts about the band, about his fundraising efforts and about politics. A clear 'remainer', Sean shared regular posts pulling apart the Brexit arguments – retweeting the likes of Gina Miller, who launched a legal challenge against Brexit, Tony Blair's former right-hand man Alastair Campbell and Labour MPs Angela Rayner, Rachel Reeves and David Lammy.

James himself – who's usually quite strict about what he will and won't talk about with journalists – has started speaking up about politics more as he's got older, marking a shift in the dynamic of the band. It appears he's very much leading the charge when it comes to sharing dissatisfaction with the current state of political discourse in the country. You won't find him on Twitter though, as he says he has no desire to talk to people he doesn't know about such issues. He confirmed that the band talks about it a fair bit. Both real-life politics and about the 'Liberal wet dream' that was *The West Wing*.

Created by Aaron Sorkin, who wrote every line of dialogue before departing from the show after its fourth season, *The West Wing* was a seven-season show from the early 2000s which took a romanticised look at American politics, a world away from the real-life situations of 2018. It featured a noble, flawed but compassionate President Jed Bartlett (played by Martin Sheen) working in the White House with a team of progressive, competent staff – equally flawed but with real integrity. It's the benchmark by which compassionate left-leaning people would want their country to be run. It is, of course, entirely fictional.

The West Wing crops up again when talking about the artwork for *Resistance Is Futile*. It wouldn't be a Manics album without something provocative to draw you in; as Manics artwork goes, this is up there with the Jenny Savile watercolours on the front of 1994's *The Holy Bible*. The search for a cover image usually involves Nicky taking an expedition through digital archives, photography books and art pamphlets – which is exactly how he arrived at this compelling image, one of a series of photos taken in the 19th century by pioneering Austrian photographer Baron Franz von Stillfried-Ratenicz, of what is believed to be Japan's last true Samurai. 'We love the double edged nature of the image,' said James. 'Knowing that the photo has captured something which is in its death throes but with that stubborn resistance. He's refusing to look in the camera. It's utterly poignant.' James went on to say it reminded him of the final shot from *The West Wing*, when outgoing President Jed Bartlett is taking off in Airforce One, leaving the White House to President Elect Matt Santos. He's looking through the window, into the distance, with a similar expression.

This feeling is present throughout the album too, from the title and artwork through the lyrics of each song. That resignation that some things are lost to the annals of time, never to be seen again. That includes the black and white nature of politics. In the past, if you were working class, you voted Labour. Especially if you were working class and from Wales. That simpler time has gone.

The defeatism of the title, *Resistance Is Futile*, combined with the inclusion of songs such as 'People Give In' point towards a degree of resignation that you cannot change the world – a far cry from the ambition and defiance they used to exhibit – with James chanting: *'Break down / Move on / Stay strong'*. Nicky told *Wales Online* that 'People Give In' was about urging people to be more empathetic towards each other. 'I can't believe we're taking that stance.' he said, 'We were the band that polarised everything. Now the polarisation is way too much for us even. We're living in a completely different time to the one we grew up in.'

Resistance Is Futile is far from a nostalgic sojourn to relive their youth, as although it does capture some of that energy, it's drenched in the cynical wisdom of a band that has stood the test of time – while their musical peers disbanded or moved from music-making into production, writing or teaching, the Manic Street Preachers continued to find the inspiration and the determination to keep creating music which speaks to people. *Resistance Is Futile* showed that the band still had something to say, something of value to add to the world – even though they themselves were feeling lost and disillusioned with everything, from technology and music to politics.

Musically, it doesn't feel as downcast as some of the language used throughout. Drenched in melody, it wears its rock influences on its sleeve. Think Bruce Springsteen and War On Drugs (regular records on the

Teac player in the studio); those big, anthemic, soaring sounds are evident throughout, with James confessing he fell in love with the middle eight during the making of the album – a musical tool to give the listener time and space within songs to pause and reflect. Middle eights aside, here we have big guitars, loud riffs and rousing choruses which don't always appeal to 'middle class and upper middle class journalists' (his words). He said: 'Well, fuck it, sometimes I like playing the guitar, sounding it out and saying follow us, fuckin; move. I'm not suspicious of that MO of music. It's got to be a good mix of everything. You can't have an arched eyebrow all the time, just let it go.' James' stubborn fears were unfounded: critics and fans alike responded well to the album, which like many of its predecessors (*Everything Must Go, Know Your Enemy, Send Away The Tigers, Futurology*) charted at number two – making it one of the most successful Manics albums, at least in terms of chart positions; much to the pleasure and slight surprise of the band.

James, Nicky and Sean are well-versed in working to create cohesive music - lyrics and sounds which, when brought together as an album, tell a story, encourage conversation and inspire minds, both young and old, and that's exactly what they've achieved here. There is an overall feeling of resignation to 'Resistance Is Futile' but if you look between the lines, you'll find that sense of defiance visible in the face of the last Samurai on the album cover.

This piece contains interviews done by the author and reproduced with permission.

Part Fifteen

2018–2021

2018 (continued)

April 14
• The first Manics show of the year takes place, an acoustic in store event at London's Rough Trade East records.

April 16
• *Resistance Is Futile* is album of the day on BBC 6 Music.

April 20
• *Resistance Is Futile* becomes the sixth Manic Street Preachers album to go straight into the UK charts at number two, but be doomed to go no higher.
• Nicky tells *NME* that he and his brother are writing a radio comedy.

April 23
• The *Resistance Is Futile* arena tour, the biggest the band have played in some years, kicks off in Newcastle.

May 4
• Catherine Anne Davies duets with the band at Wembley arena on three songs, 'Dylan & Caitlin', 'Little Baby Nothing' and 'Your Love Alone Is Not Enough' prompting Nicky to describe her 'our Tammi Terrell'.
• *Hold Me Like A Heaven* (Sony)
  Tracklisting:
  1. 'Hold Me Like A Heaven'
  2. 'Hold Me Like A Heaven (Warm Digits remix)'
  3. 'Hold Me Like A Heaven (Public Service Broadcasting remix)'
  Formats:
  Digital download, streaming

May 25
• The band begin a run of big summer shows, starting with BBC Radio's Biggest Weekend in Belfast, before heading to Germany to open for Guns N' Roses at three stadium gigs and a festival in Finland. Nicky is absent from the shows due to the death of his mother, Irene. Richard Beak fills bass duties.

June 19
• Nicky is once again back in the fold for the band's slot at Robert Smith's Meltdown, held at the Royal Festival Hall in London. They cover The Cure's 'Inbetween Days' (and a snatch of 'A Forest'). Opening act The Anchoress is once again present for duties on 'Little Baby Nothing' and 'Dylan & Caitlin'.

June 24
- The 2018 summer season begins at the Isle of Wight Festival. The band will play 10 festivals in six countries across the next few months.

July 27
- 'People Give In' is lifted as the final single from *Resistance Is Futile*, with a video by Kieran Evans. Technically the album has yielded as many singles (six) as *Generation Terrorists*, though with largely no b-sides or physical releases it's arguable only 'International Blue' (which got a vinyl release with an actual b-side) and 'Hold Me Like A Heaven' (which had a digital package with remixes) truly count as singles.

September 14
- An exhibition of Nicky Wire's polaroids and paintings opens at the Tenby Arts Centre.

October 22
- A 20th anniversary tour of *This Is My Truth, Tell Me Yours* is announced for May 2019.

December 7
- The inevitable 20th anniversary edition of *This Is My Truth, Tell Me Yours* is released, featuring demos, rehearsal tracks, remixes and b-sides as well as the remastered album on CD and vinyl. As with *Send Away The Tigers* the band take the opportunity to rewrite their past – 'Prologue To History' replaces 'Nobody Loved You' on the album proper, with the latter relegated to the bonus material.

2019

January 17
- The Manics' YouTube channel premiers a new Kieran Evans/Manics collaboration, *Truth and Memory*, a document of the *This Is My Truth* era composed entirely from footage filmed at the time.

January 20
- Nicky Wire celebrates his 50th birthday.

March 14
- A new book, *Withdrawn Traces: Searching For The Truth About Richey Manic*, by Sara Hawys Roberts, is published with the blessing of the Edwards family. Richey's sister, Rachel, provides a foreword. It presents

new evidence and theories around Richey's state of mind at the time of his disappearance.

May 12
- The *This Is My Truth, Tell Me Yours* UK tour kicks off in Dublin, it will run for 14 dates including two-night stands at Manchester's Ritz and London's Shepherds Bush Empire.

June 15
- The tour is interrupted by support slots at five huge stadium shows opening for Bon Jovi. It goes better than it did in 1993. The band cover Guns N' Roses 'Sweet Child O'Mine' at all five gigs.

June 29
- The final UK date of the *This Is My Truth* tour takes place, a huge sell-out show at Cardiff Castle.

August 5
- *4Real*, a biopic about Richey by filmmaker Lindy Heymann is announced. The band release a statement saying they have no comment on the film.

August 17
- The band headline the Hardwick Live Festival in Country Durham. It will be their last British show for almost two years.

September 26/27
- The *This Is My Truth* tour gets one last hurrah with two shows in Japan where, by staggering coincidence, the Rugby World Cup is being held.

November 1
- Kieran Evans' film, *Be Pure - Be Vigilant - Behave*, documenting 2014's *The Holy Bible* tour, gets a ten-date tour of its own, playing in arthouse and independent cinemas across the country.

2020

January 31
- A fresh call is made for information about Richey Edwards' whereabouts by the charity Missing People, on the eve of the 25th anniversary of his disappearance. The statement, by the charity's publicity coordinator Kate Graham, said 'Richard, if you are reading this, please call or text us on our free phone number, 116 000. It's confidential and we can't trace your call.

We just want to provide you with the support you need and help you to be safe. The helpline is here to support people who are missing or thinking of going missing and their loved ones who are left behind.' At the time of writing there is still no new information.

March 14
- James plays the closest thing 2020 will have to a Manic Street Preachers gig: an acoustic set at a fundraiser for the charity Valley Aid, held in Porth.

March 21
- Nicky tells *NME* that the Manics' next album has an 'expansive' sound, and that one of the songs will be called 'Orwellian'. The band anticipate a summer 2021 release.

Spring
- The COVID-19 pandemic sweeps across the world, cancelling a busy year for the Manics which was set to include massive stadium shows with The Killers and Green Day and several festivals, including Glastonbury.

April 8
- The band announce two shows at Cardiff Motorpoint Arena for December which will be free to NHS staff.

June 12
- *Gold Against The Soul*, for years the neglected child of the Manics reissue programme, finally gets the deluxe treatment. The handsome set features the remastered album on CD and vinyl plus the usual bonus disc of demos, b-sides and remixes, and a 120-page hardback book of photos taken by Mitch Ikeda, annotated by Nicky.

June 18
- A new Kieran Evans film, *Pieces of Sleep*, is shown on the band's YouTube channel. The film follows the band's 1993 tour of Japan using camcorder footage captured at the time, framed around a fictionalised Japanese fan's account.

June 26
- Details of a new James Dean Bradfield solo record emerge. *Even In Exile* is a concept album based around the life of Chilean activist Victor Jara, and has lyrics written by Patrick Jones. Two songs, 'There'll Come A War' and 'Seeking The Room With Three Windows' provide the vanguard.

July 1
- Steve Lamacq premieres James' single 'The Boy From The Plantation' on his 6 Music show.

August 5
- A three-part-podcast series, *Inspired By Jara*, hosted by James, is launched; delving into the life and influence of Victor Jara. The first episode features perennial Bradders favourites, Simple Minds.

August 14
- James Dean Bradfield's second solo album, *Even In Exile*, is released.

August 17
- James hints that Nicky has also been working on solo material.

October 14
- The Cardiff NHS shows are postponed until July 2021 after a fresh wave of COVID-19 cases are unleashed across the UK. The second wave also halts work on the new Manics album, which had been progressing at one of the band's favourite studios, Rockfield in Monmouthshire.

October 27
- James tells Radio X that the Manics are still writing toward their next album.

November 3
- The Anchoress unveils 'Show Your Face', the first song from her second album, featuring (quite unmistakably) James Dean Bradfield on guitar.

December 17
- The Manics release a new recording of 1991's 'Spectators Of Suicide', originally the b-side to 'You Love Us', featuring the folk singer and former Pipette, Gwenno Saunders. English and Welsh language versions are available from Heavenly Records' Bandcamp page.

2021

January 2
- News breaks that Steve Brown, the producer of *Generation Terrorists*, has died following 'a short illness relating to a fall'. Nicky pays tribute on Twitter, saying 'So very sad to hear of the passing of Steve Brown we had so much fun working with him-he taught us so much – so many memories and stories – 'Motorcycle Emptiness' was his masterpiece with us, but he produced many more – love and thoughts with his family and friends'.

January 10
- Nicky shares a list of prospective song titles for the forthcoming 14th Manic Street Preachers album: 'The Secret He Had Missed', 'Blank Entry Diary', 'Afterending', 'Diapause', 'Don't Let The Nights Divide Us', 'Happy Bored Alone', 'Orwellian', 'Still Snowing In Sapporo' and 'Quest For Ancient Colour'.

March 9
- The Anchoress releases the video for 'The Exchange', a duet with James Dean Bradfield taken from her forthcoming album *The Art of Losing*, itself released on March 12.

April 16
- James updates *Mojo* on the new album, likening it to 'The Clash playing Abba', confirming that much of it was recorded at Rockfield in 2020 and that it will include a duet with Mark Lanegan.

May 5
- Nicky posts a video of himself skipping to Twitter and Instagram. 'Thanks again for all your patience', he says, 'hope to have some Manics news soon'.

TO BE CONTINUED …

Epilogue

AfterEnding/Walking Through
the Apocalypse

This book was written during a pandemic that pretty much halted the world for much of 2020 and 2021. I don't know when you're reading it – It could still be 2021 for you, or it could be five years in the future. You could have found this for fifty pence at the back of a second-hand bookshop in 2051 … assuming you still have books. And shops. And money. For all I know, you could well be using a barter system following the great water wars of the 2030s. The point is that context is everything – something I hope you've picked up from this collection of essays, each with a different angle, a different perspective, a different *context*. Any of these writers, myself included, could have written their essay about any of these albums and because of their context, it would have been completely different.

I don't know the context *The Ultra Vivid Lament* will acquire in years to come. It could be one of those records that is beloved on release and then fades from memory, or one of those rare albums that, like Nicky Wire himself, has inexplicably long legs. It could be the final Manics album or the start of a whole new phase. History has a habit of recontextualising the Manic Street Preachers. Right now, however, it's an album inexorably associated with the COVID-19 pandemic, a theme Nicky – at least, I'm assuming it's Nicky – visits on the closing track, 'Afterending', with its talk of pointless clapping and fumbled government responses. For many of us the fourteenth Manics album will always be the soundtrack to the confused back-end of a global health emergency; a time of restrictions, vaccinations, lockdown, grim statistics, government briefings, dystopian scenes of queues outside hastily erected temporary test centres, cancelled events, closed shops and horribly sparse funerals. Deaths. Though a beautifully melodic and expansive record, thematically *The Ultra Vivid Lament* is about existing in a society at odds, in which nothing is quite working, where politics have become simplified to the point of meaningless and the world is twisted in upon itself. Intentionally or not, it syncs incredibly well with the existential dread and isolation of the previous year. Nicky addresses the perfection of the past (the gorgeous, sad memoir 'Snowing In Sapporo') to contrast a world where he doesn't 'know what I believe in any more' (at the time of writing we don't know who wrote what on this album, but if James Dean Bradfield came up with a belief system that 'involves misery and keeping still' I will hand in my Manics Fan badge). It feels like the Britain of 2021 to me: baffled, angry, sad, sighing.

The first song we heard from the album, 'Orwellian', has been knocking around since before the pandemic, mentioned by Nicky in an *NME* interview in that brief portion of 2020 not blighted by plague, which makes its key hook about walking someone 'through the apocalypse' prescient rather than merely 'a bit on-the-nose'. There's a lot to unpack in 'Orwellian': burning books, misrepresentations, the smashing together of woke culture, progressive politics and post-truth media; but in the summer of 2021 it's that line, 'walking through the apocalypse', that jumps out. See? *Context.*

This particularly dreary apocalypse actually timed itself rather well for the Manics. Promotional duties for *Resistance Is Futile* finished, the band had spent 2019 playing anniversary shows to mark 20 years of *This Is My Truth, Tell Me Yours,* alongside some big stadium supports with Bon Jovi and the odd festival. The 2020 live diary was looking fairly busy, but it was all paying-the-bills stuff; supports with The Killers and Green Day and a few festivals, including a no-doubt glorious return to Glastonbury to headline the Park Stage. Mostly though, 2020 was intended as a low-key year, dedicated to writing and recording, with more time off than on. James had a solo record planned, *Even In Exile,* co-written with Nicky's brother and long-time Manics collaborator Patrick Jones. There were even faint whispers of a Nicky Wire solo album which, alas, never materialised.

Had COVID-19 struck in 2018, pitched into a full tilt promo cycle and world tour, things may well have been much harder. Even so, the Manics were still affected: All live shows were pulled as the pandemic closed-down cities across the world. James and Patrick's excellent *Even In Exile* came and went, promoted via podcasts and Zoom calls rather than touring and telly. A deluxe re-issue of *Gold Against The Soul* (something fans had clamoured for for years) was the band's only substantial release of the year, and was largely unpromoted by the trio. The closest thing to new material was a re-recording of 'Spectators Of Suicide', quietly released on Bandcamp to mark a Heavenly Records anniversary. The Manics announced a pair of shows in Cardiff for later in the year, with free tickets given to NHS workers to thank them for the trauma they had endured, but that proved optimistic: the pandemic stretched on, and the gigs were rescheduled (twice). At the time of writing they still haven't happened, and have been folded into the band's upcoming tour cycle.

What the pandemic gave back, however, was time. Nicky has said that the band were the best rehearsed they have ever been before recording, working everything up at their own Door To The River studios near Newport, before transferring to Rockfield to work with go-to Manics knob-twiddler Dave Eringa. The extra attention shows. There's a gorgeous depth and polish to *The Ultra Vivid Lament*, it sounds *expensive*, expansive, textured. Musically there's a lineage here that began with *This Is My Truth* – alienated, sparse sounds to reflect alienated, sparse moods, meeting a European widescreen electronica that started to emerge with *Futurology* and *Resistance Is Futile*, here rendered more focussed, denser. As usual with Manics albums there's a tagline (*Lifeblood* was 'elegiac pop', *Send Away The Tigers* was 'Guns N' Roses covering 'All You Need Is Love'', while *Postcards From A Young Man* got saddled with 'heavy metal Tamla Motown'). The results are rarely in line with the prediction. This time around we were told that the sound would be 'The Clash covering Abba', a phrase that unusually comes from James rather than Nicky, and, as it turns out – even more unusually – is entirely bang on. Bradfield, for pretty much the first time, wrote a lot of what became *The Ultra Vivid Lament* on piano rather than guitar, and though his keys playing is a little rudimentary, his melodic instincts are bulletproof. Filtered through a different instrument, these songs genuinely feel like a different Manic Street Preachers: Melodically fluid, with a bright and layered production, James' piano lines ring out like bells, especially on 'The Secret He Had Missed' with it's 'Dancing Queen'-aping descending riff. The Piano-grounding gives the album the robustness of classic pop. 'Don't Let The Night Divide Us' (which I suspect is a James Dean Bradfield lyric, but I have absolutely nothing to base that on but gut feeling) and 'Into The Waves of Love' meld melancholy and optimism in a way that, sonically at least, brings to mind Frankie Valley and the Four Seasons, 'Complicated Illusions' is one of those great, sad Manics ballads that would have been handled any number of ways in the band's history, but here sounds like The Faces produced by Phil Spector. The Abba influence is most obvious on a final pair of songs: The sparkling arpeggios of 'Happy Bored Alone', (which joins 'Sex, Power, Love and Money', 'Little Baby Nothing' and 'Faster' in the pantheon of Manic-Manifesto lyrics), and 'Afterending', the chorus of which somehow manages to nod to 'The Winner Takes It All' without sounding anything like 'The Winner Takes It All'. The Manics have been all sorts of things over the last thirty years: Bratty punk upstarts, novelty revivalists, hard-rock wannabes, post-punk existentialists, Britrock everymen, indie elder statesmen, Eurosynth retro-futurists ... like all the best classic British bands[1] reinvention is built into their very DNA. It's why they've lasted so long. That and the sheer, bloody-minded stubbornness. *The Ultra Vivid Lament* is a fluid evolution from the *Resistance Is Futile* era, that recasts the trio as pop classicists. The strange circumstances of 2020 and early 2021 gave that aesthetic the polish and depth it needed. We're left with one of the most self-contained, self-aware and satisfying Manic Street Preachers albums in quite some time; a record with a distinct and pleasing sonic identity, that though lyrically is tinted with sighing resignation (essentially, Nicky Wire's brand since 1998), is something of an audio duvet: comforting, softening, welcoming.

And honestly, we've needed that. The last, what, eighteen months, have been *so* weird. So uncomfortable. So tainted with anger and illness and death. So completely unprecedented. So ridiculously fucking *existential*, and exhausting that such a musical comfort blanket is welcome. Not that the lyrics themselves are anything like so cosy. As I said; it's a record about bafflement, alienation and anger. But then that's true of most Manics albums, and there's still comfort to be found in all of them.

Back in 2014 a music critic I know got an early listen to *Futurology*, I asked him what it was like. 'Oh, ya know,' he said, waving the question away, all matter-of-fact, 'the Manics have made their album again'. And while that might seem like a strange comment of *Futurology*, a high-watermark that pushed the band into new territory (something that particular writer focused on his review, incidentally), I knew exactly what he meant. There's a fundamental, unshifting Manic-Street-Preachersness that infects all of their albums, that creates a through-line between records as contradictory as *Generation Terrorists* and *Rewind The Film*. And as much as that essence is equal parts bile, melancholy and despair, it's also very comforting. *The Ultra Vivid Lament* is another Manic Street Preachers album at a time when I ... we ... you, desperately needed another Manic Street Preachers album. Thank fuck.

As I said at the top, I cannot predict the way the future will view *The Ultra Vivid Lament*. Some albums change with time. In 1995 the music press fell over themselves to declare Blur's *The Great Escape* to be genius and Oasis' *What's The Story (Morning Glory)* to be an average, meat-and-

---

1 With the possible exception of Status Quo, whose name proves once and for all the power of nominative determinism.

potatoes plodder. Within a year that same press had quietly swapped those two evaluations and hoped no-one would notice. We could be talking about this one as folly in five years time. I don't know. What I *can* tell you, is that it's the Manic Street Preachers album I needed right now.

What can the future hold for the Manics? Providing we make it out of this strange medical quagmire of a year? Prediction is a risky business. No-one reviewing *Gold Against The Soul* would have reasonably predicted the three albums that would follow it. The band have made a career out of right-angle turns. Personally, I don't think this will be the last Manic Street Preachers album. They've been at this for so long now, I don't think they know who or what they are, if not The Manics. I added a footnote to one of the essays in this book that pointed out that if MSP's career was mapped onto that of the Rolling Stones, *we're not even halfway through*. They'll keep on being one of our great heritage acts. Keep on smashing out 'Motorcycle Emptiness' and 'Motown Junk' at festivals as if they were 25 again. Every once in a while they'll surprise us with another special record, a complete statement that music critics who grew up on 90s *NME* will slaver over and unpack. They'll likely follow that up with another 'shot at mass communication' that will get half as much attention. We're probably due one of their scratchy, uncompromising punk albums next, or another *Send Away The Tigers*-style widdley-widdley rock n' roll feast. Or maybe it'll be solo albums, or completely electronic bangers, or a covers record. Maybe Richey comes back and gifts them a new testament. Maybe they hang up their stageware and play golf and are never heard from again. Me? I think we've got the Manics forever. We need them, and they need us, and while there's an audience there'll be a band, and while there's a band there'll be new music, and it'll all be rich and valuable in one way or another. I'll just wait and see. They can do whatever they want. They've earned it.

Marc Burrows, July 1, 2021

Bibliography and Resources

Books:
Shutkever, Paula – *Manic Street Preachers: A Design For Living,* Virgin Books, *1996*
Price, Simon – *Everything (A Book About Manic Street Preachers),* Virgin Books, *1998*
Gillen, Kieron, Jamie McKelvie: *Phonogram vol 1: Rue Britannia,* Image Comics, 2007
Power, Martin – *Nailed To History: The Story of Manic Street Preachers, Omnibus Press, 2010*
Wire, Nicky – *The Death of the Polaroid – A Manics Family Album,* Faber & Faber, 2011
Cummins, Kevin – *Assassinated Beauty: Photographs of Manic Street Preachers,* Faber & Faber, 2014
Sounes, Howard – *Amy, 27: Amy Winehouse and the 27 Club,* Hodder Paperbacks, 2014
Jones, Rhian E, Lues, Daniel, Wodtke, Larissa – *Triptych: Three Studies of the Manic Street Preachers' The Holy Bible* Repeater Books, 2017
Chaney, Sarah – *Psyche On The Skin*: A history of self harm, reaktion books, 2017
Ewens, Hannah – *FANGIRLS: Scenes from Modern Music Culture,* Quadrille Publishing, 2019
Evans, Dave – *33⅓: The Holy Bible,* Bloomsbury, 2019

Selected Discography (albums and EPs) - excludes digital only EPs
Manic Street Preachers
• *New Art Riot EP,* Damaged Goods, 1990
• *Generation Terrorists,* Columbia, 1992
• *Gold Against The Soul,* Columbia, 1993
• *Life Becoming a Landslide EP,* Columbia, 1994
• *The Holy Bible,* Epic, 1994
• *Everything Must Go,* Epic, 19945
• *This Is My Truth, Tell Me Yours,* Epic, 1998
• *Know Your Enemy,* Epic, 2001
• *Forever Delayed: The Best of Manic Street Preachers,* Epic, 2002
• *Lipstick Traces (A Secret History of Manic Street Preachers),* Epic, 2003
• *Lifeblood,* Epic, 2004
• *The Holy Bible: 10th Anniversary Reissue,* Epic, 2004
• *Gold Save The Manics EP,* Epic, 2005
• *Send Away The Tigers,* Columbia, 2006
• *Everything Must Go: 10th Anniversary Reissue,* Epic, 2006
• *Journal For Plague Lovers,* Columbia, 2008
• *Postcards From A Young Man,* Columbia, 2010
• *National Treasures – The complete Singles,* Columbia, 2011
• *Generation Terrorists : 20th Anniversary Collector's Edition,* Columbia, 2012
• *Rewind The Film,* Columbia, 2013
• *Futurology,* Columbia, 2014
• *The Holy Bible 20,* Epic, 2014
• *Everything Must Go 20,* Epic, 2016
• *Send Away The Tigers: 10 Year Collector's Edition,* Columbia, 2017
• *Resistance Is Futile,* Columbia, 2018

- *This Is My Truth, Tell Me Yours: 20 Year Collector's Edition*, Epic, 2018
- *Gold Against The Soul: Deluxe Remastered Edition*, Columbia, 2020

James Dean Bradfield
- *The Great Western*, Columbia, 2006
- *The Chamber* (soundtrack), Music On Vinyl, 2017
- *Even In Exile*, MontyRay, 2020

Nicky Wire
- *I Killed The Zeitgeist*, Red Ink, 2006

Television, documentaries and films
- *Snub TV*, BBC Two, 1991
- *Def II TV*, BBC Two, 1992
- *Top of the Pops*, BBC1, 1992–2006
- *Channel 4 at Glastonbury*, Channel 4, 1994
- *Butt ... Naked*, Channel 4, 1994
- *Missing At Christmas*, ITV, 1995
- *Later ... With Jools Holland*, BBC Two, 1996–2018
- *The Vanishing of Richey Manic*, Channel 4, 1996
- *Manic Street Preachers: Everything (Live)*, home video, Epic, 1997
- *Close Up: From Here To There*, BBC Two, 1998
- *Glastonbury 1999*, BBC One, BBC Two, 1999
- *2000 Today*, BBC Two, 1999/2000
- *Manic Street Preachers: Leaving the 20th Century*, home video, Epic, 2000
- *James Dean Bradfield: All Back To Mine*, Channel 4, 2000
- *Our Manics In Havana*, Channel 4, 2001
- *Manic Street Preachers: Louder Than War*, home video, Epic, 2001
- *Forever Delayed: The Best of Manic Street Preachers*, home video, Epic, 2002
- *CD:UK*, ITV, 2002–2006
- *Glastonbury 2003*, BBC One, BBC Two, BBC Three, 2003
- *Planet Rock Profiles*, VH1, 2003
- *My Life In Music: James Dean Bradfield*, 2006
- *Glastonbury 2007*, BBC Two, 2007
- *One Last Shot At Mass Communication*, Channel 4, 2010
- *Strictly Come Dancing*, BBC One, 2010
- *Manic Street Preachers: Homecoming*, BBC Radio 2, 2011
- *Manics: Back To Blackwood*, BBC Wales, 2011
- *Culture, Alienation, Boredom and Despair*, Evans, Kieran and Turner, Robin, 2012
- *Hyde Park Live*, BBC iPlayer, 2013
- *British and Irish Lions Raw*, 2013
- *Glastonbury 2014*, BBC iPlayer, BBC Two, 2014
- *The Late Late Show with James Cordon*, CBS, 2014
- *Richey Edwards – No Thoughts To Forget*, YouTube, 2014
- *When Pop Ruled My Life*, BBC Four, 2015
- *Music For Misfits: The Story of Indie*, BBC Four, 2015
- *Cardiff Castle Live*, BBC Wales/BBC iPlayer, 2015
- *The Story of Wales at Euro 2016*, BBC Radio Wales, 2016
- *Manic Street Preachers: Escape From History*, Evans, Kieran, Sky Arts, 2016
- *The Biggest Weekend*, BBC iPlayer, BBC 6Music, 2018
- *Truth and Memory*, Evans, Kirean, 2019
- *BePureBeVigilanteBehave*, Evans, Kieran, 2019
- *Pieces Of Sleep*, Evans, Keiran, 2020

Notable podcasts and radio appearances
Mark Goodier's Evening Session (first radio appearance), BBC Radio 1, 1991
Sleeping With The NME, BBC Radio 5, 1991
Live At Milton Keynes Bowl, September, 1992
In Concert, Manic Street Preachers, BBC Radio 1, 1997
Manic Street Preachers Live at Manchester NYNEX Arena, BBC Radio 1, 1997
This Is My Truth Tell Me Yours, BBC Radio Wales, 1998
A Design For Life, BBC Radio 2, 2002
Front Row, BBC Radio 4, 2003
Guardian Music, May 2009,
Swansong: The Holy Bible, BBC Radio 4 Xtra, Oct 2012
The Making Of Everything Must Go, Phantom 105.2, 2010
James Dean Bradfield's Freak Show, BBC 6Music, 2013
Guardian Music, September 2013,
Mastertapes: Manic Street Preachers, BBC Radio 4, 2014
Classic Albums, This Day In Music Radio, 2016
Mark Goodyear's Classic Album Playback, Absolute Radio, 2018
The John Robb Tapes – Manic Street Preachers, June 2019
Who Killed The Radio Star? The Strange Disappearance of Richey Edwards, Jul 2019
Phil Taggart's Slacker Podcast, September 2019
The Adam Buxton Podcast – Nicky Wire, November 2019
Do You Love Us (A Podcast About Manic Street Preachers), Jan 2020–Mar 2021
HELP! The Story of the War Child Album, September 2020
Manic Street Speakers, Nov 2020–
Inspired By Jara, (Four episodes) 2020
Pictures of Lily, May 2021

Periodicals and websites

3voor12	*BBC 6 Music*
78s	*BBC America*
A Music Blog, Yea?	*BBC Culture*
ABC.es	*BBC Music*
Acoustic Magazine	*BBC Music Blog*
Adelaide Advertiser	*BBC News*
Adelaide Sunday Mail	*BBC Online*
Aftonbladet	*BBC Wales*
Albumism	*BBC Wales News*
Algemeen Dagblad	*BBC Wales Online*
AlienatedZine	*Beat*
Alternative Ulster Magazine	*Beat Magazine*
Amazon.co.uk	*Belfast News Letter*
Amiga Power	*Belfast Newsletter*
AOL Music	*Belfast Telegraph*
Arena	*Bergensavisen*
Attitude	*Berliner Zeitung*
Avisa Nordland	*BEST*
b92.net	*BIG Lottery Fund Magazine Wales*
Backbeat	*Billboard*
Bang	*Billboard.com*
Bangkok Post	*Birmingham Evening Mail*
bangshowbiz.com	*Birmingham Mail*
BARKS	*Birmingham Post*
Bath Chronicle	*Black Velvet*

Black Velvet Magazine
Boston Herald
Bournemouth Daily Echo
Brisbane Courier Mail
Britpop
Brum
Burrn!
Buzz
Buzz (Japan)
BZ Berlin
C.O.R.E.
Caerphilly Campaign
Caerphilly Observer
Cake
Campus Galicia
campus–web.de
Carlisle News & Star
CD Journal
CD Now
Channel NewsAsia
Chart
Check This Out!
Chester
Chicago Sun Times
Chicago Sun-Times
Ciculo Mixup
Clash Music
Classic Rock Germany
Classic Rock Magazine
Club International
CNN.com
Coffee And TV
Colorado Springs Independent
Consumable
Cookie Scene
Creative Loafing
Crossbeat
Cutting Edge
Dagbladet
Dagsavisen
Daily Express
Daily Mail
Daily Mirror
Daily Mirror Northern Ireland
Daily Record
Daily Star
Daily Telegraph
Dazed
dBMagazine
Deadline
Deia
Delano
Deposito Sonoro

Destination Pop
Devil In The Woods Magazine
Digging A Hole
Digital Spy
DIY Magazine
Doll
Dolphin Music
Dotmusic
Drowned In Sound
DRUGSTORᴲ CULTURE
Dziennik
Dzika Banda
E.P. Magazine
Eastern Daily Press
Edinburgh Evening News
Efe Eme
El Asombrario & Co.
El Nuevo Herald
Entertainment Focus
Entertainment Weekly
Eska Rock
Esquire
Excellent Online
Exeter Express and Echo
Expressen
Eye Magazine
Faceless Millions
Fachblatt Muiskmagazin
Faremusica
Faro De Vigo
FHM
FHM Russia
Filter
Flamman
Flipside
Fort Apache
ForeverDelayed.co.uk
FRONT
Fufkin.com
Full Moon
Fusion Musique
GAFFA
GamesMaster
Gay Times
Gazette
gazettelive.com
Getintothis
Gigwise
Gitarist
Gitarre & Bass
Glasgow Evening Times
Glo
Goal

God Is In The TV
Golden Plec
Golf Punk
Golwg
GQ
Grazia
Guitarist
Guitarist Magazine
Guitarre & Bass
Halifax Courier
Hall Or Nothing
Ham & High
Hamilton Spectator
Hard Force Magazine
Helsingin Sanomat
Herald Scotland
Hereford Times
Het Parool
High Life
hip online
HISS!G MUSIKKMAGASIN
Hit CD
HMV
HMV.com
Hobart Mercury
Hospodářské Noviny
Hot Press
Hotspur Magazine
Hottracks
Huck Magazine
Huffington Post
Hull Daily Mail
i-D
Icon El Pais
iDNES
iDNES.cz
Ilta-Sanomat
Iltalehti
Impact
Impress Magazine
In Dublin
Incendiary Magazine
Independent On Sunday
Independent.ie
Indiecator
INROCK
International.Wales
Intro.de
ireallylovemusic.co.uk
Ireland On-Line
Irish Evening Herald
Irish Examiner
Irish Herald

Irish Independent
Irish Mail On Sunday
Irish Press
ITV News
JAM!
Jetzt
Juice
Julie Fahrenheit
Juventud Rebelde
Kerrang
Kölner Stadt-Anzeiger
La Tercera
La Verdad
Landsorganisationen i Sverige
laut.de
Le Courrier
Leicester Mercury
Lime Lizard
Lithium
Live XS
Liverpool Daily Echo
Liverpool Daily Post
Liverpool etc
Loaded
Long Live Vinyl
Loud & Quiet
Louder
Louder Than War
Louder Than War Magazine
Love It Loud
Magic!
Mail On Sunday
Making Music
Manchester Evening News
Manchester Metro News
Mariskal Rock
Maximum RockNRoll
mbl.is
Melbourne Herald Sun
Melody Maker
Metal CD
Metal Forces
Metal Hammer
Metal Shock
Metro
MOJO
MOJO Collections
Mondo Sonoro
MondoSonoro
Monmouthshire Free Press
Morgunblaðið
Morning Star
Motor.de

MTV Asia
MTV/Yahoo UK
Muse
Music Life
Music Week
Musician
musicMAG.pl
Musicmaker
Musikexpress
Muzika.hr
Muzyka z Głośnika
Myspace
Native Monster
Nettavisen
New Statesman
New York Metro
New York Observer
New York Post
New Zealand Herald
Newcastle Chronicle
Newcastle Courier
Newcastle Sunday Sun
News Of The World
Nieuwe Revu
NME
NME Blog
NME Student Guide
NME.com
Noise Of The Nineties
Noisey
Nottingham Evening Post
Novinky.cz
NRC Handelsblad
Observer Sunday
Official Charts
OKEJ
Onet
Onet Muzyka
Oor
Orange.co.uk
Overkillspoonman Blog
Página/12
Paint It Red
Pause & Play
Peterborough Evening Telegraph
Petőfi
Pitchfork
Plan B Magazine
Planet Sound
Player
Playlouder.com
Pobechuk
Pop Culture Press

POPCONNECTION
POPGEAR
PopMatters
Prensa Latina
Prog
PSN Europe
Público
Pulse!
PureVolume
Putte I Parken Magazine
Q Magazine
Q Online
Rada7
Rage
RAW
Ray Gun
RCD Magazine
Reading/Leeds Festival Official Programme
Real Groove
Record Collector
Record Mirror
RedHanded Magazine
Reforma
Regioactive.de
Reverb Magazine
Rhythm
Riff Raff
RiffYou
RIP
Rip It Up
RipItUp
rock & pop
Rock De Lux
Rock Hard
Rock Power
Rock Sound
Rock World
Rockaxis
Rockerilla
Rockin'on
Rolling Stone Germany
Rolling Stone Indonesia
RTÉ Ten
Rumore
Ruta 66
Sächsische Zeitung
San Francisco Examiner
Scotland On Sunday
Scottish Herald
Scottish Mail
Seanzine
Sega Power
Select

Selector
ShortList
Siren
Sky
Sky Sports
SLAM
Smash Hits
Snoozer
Socialism Magazine
SonntagsZeitung
Soot Magazine
Sorted MagAZine
Sound On Sound
Soundi
Sounds
South Wales Argus
South Wales Echo
South Wales Evening Post
Spex
Spiegel Online
Spin
Spinner Music
Spiral Scratch
St Petersburg Times
St. Paul Pioneer Press
Start Up
State News
State.ie
Stay Sonic
Stereogum
Stern
Student-Direct.co.uk
students.ch
Subway Magazin
Süddeutsche Zeitung
Suite101
Sunday Business Post
Sunday Herald Sun
Sunday Independent
Sunday Mail
Sunday Mirror
Sunday Morning Herald
Sunday Star-Times
Svenska Yle
Sydney Daily Telegraph
Sydney Morning Herald
Sydney Sun Herald
Sydney Sunday Telegraph
Synkooppi
Taz Popblog
Tempo
Tenby Observer
Teraz Rock

The Advertiser
The Age
The Album Chart Show
The Auckland Sunday News
The Base
The Big Issue
The Buffalo News
The Courier Mail
The Daily Mirror
The Daily Note
The Daily Record
The Dubliner
The Evening Standard
The Event Guide
The Face
The Flint Journal
The Georgia Straight
The Guardian
The GW Hatchet
The Herald
The Huffington Post
The i Paper
The Illustrated Ape
The Independent
The Independent On Sunday
The Indiependent
The Inverness Courier
The Irish News
The Irish Times
The Japan Times
The Kerryman
The Line Of Best Fit
The List
The London Free Press
The Los Angeles Times
The Moscow Times
The Musician Journal
The Nation
The National
The New European
The New Zealand Herald
The News Of The World
The Observer
The Press Of Atlantic City
The Quarterly
The Quietus
The Ringer
The Scotsman
The Skinny
The Star Malaysia
The Star Online
The Stool Pigeon
The Straits Times

The Sun
The Sunday Herald
The Sunday Mirror
The Sunday Times
The Sydney Morning Herald
The Telegraph
The Times
The Toronto Star
The Troglodyte
The West Australian
The Western Mail
The Word
The Yorkshire Post
The Zine
thegap
Time Out
Time Out Dubai
Time Out Hong Kong
TJECK
Toggenburger Tagblatt
Tonedeaf.com.au
tonspion
tonyvisconti.com
Top Of The Pops
Toronto Star
Toronto Sun
Total Guitar
Trouw
Tuba.pl
Týdeník Respek
Ultimate Guitar
Unclesally*s
Under The Radar

Vanyaland
Venue
VIBE-NET
VirginMega.com
Visit Wales
Volume
Vozpópuli
Vulture Hound
Wales Arts Review
Wales On Sunday
Wales Online
We Are Cult
Welsh Bands Weekly
WELT
Welt Am Sonntag
West Briton
Western Daily Press
Western Mail
Western Telegraph
Westfälische Nachrichten
whatsonhighlands
Wirtualna Polska
worldpop
Written In Music
manics.co.uk
manicstreetpreachers.com
nickyssecretsociety.com
X-Press Magazine
X-Ray
Yahoo
YleX
Yorkshire Evening Post

Fanzines

A Fanzine Called White Lemonade
Aspire For Life
Back To Nowhere
Beat The Street
Carpe Diem
Catharsis
Caught In The Crossfire
Delirium On Helium
Food, Lust And Guitars
Iconoclastic Glitter
Insane

Last Exit
Molotov Cocktails
My Little Empire
Scathe
Soliloquy
Teenage Kicks
Terrible Beauty
Tortured Rebellion
Us Against You
Velocet